Choosing *Him*
All Over Again

"God writes the best love stories—and Juana's is one of the best! When Juana was trying to write her love story, she failed miserably. But when she turned it over to God, He did the impossible."

—SHEILA WRAY GREGOIRE
Inspirational Speaker, blogger at ToLoveHonorAndVacuum.com

"Juana is a lovely and godly woman who speaks from her heart, personally and honestly to her audience. She glorifies God with her honesty and candidness, and draws her listeners in with Truth and Grace from the Spirit who lives in her. I highly recommend her to you!"

—VALERIE ELLIOT SHEPARD
Author of *Pilipinto's Happiness,* daughter of Jim and Elisabeth Elliot

"*Choosing Him* is a transparent testimony of the power of God to change lives and marriages. Juana so beautifully weaves her story of brokenness as she unravels the mystery of God's way in marriage. God used Juana's search to find herself—to find Him! And now, she is sharing all the wisdom she learned on her journey with us! I believe marriages will be saved and changed for God's glory with the message of this book."

—COURTNEY JOSEPH
Author of the book *Women Living Well* and blogger at
WomenLivingWell.org

"A clear message that conveys the love of Christ through insightful, biblical wisdom."

—SALLIE HITE McDANIEL
author of *Jesus is My Thesis*

"Juana Mikels leads us through an incredible message of hope. There is no marriage that's beyond the scope of God's redeeming power. With a blend of wisdom and warmth, *Choosing Him All Over Again* reminds us that marriage is worth fighting for."

—DARLENE SCHACHT
Author of *Messy Beautiful Love: Hope and Redemption for Real-Life Marriages*

"Dumping her husband for the 'good life,' Juana Mikels decided she could create a much better life on her own, so she took off . . . heading the wrong way down a one-way street. Then Juana crashed . . . right into Jesus and His plan for her life. Finally, after so much 'me-ism,' she came face to face with Jesus and His Word. When she gave her life to Him, her parallel path with Him began. She, without realizing it, started what would become an intense love relationship with her Lord and Savior. She kept up her pace with Jesus, and miracles began on the other path. This book is a life changer. Juana's story is for every woman: single or married!"

—NANCY COBB
Author of *The Politically Incorrect Wife* and *How to Get Your Husband to Listen to You*

"Juana is real, she is honest, and she constantly points you back to the only One who brings hope, joy, and peace—Jesus Christ. You will leave with a deeper understanding that God's plan is always best and He brings beauty out of our brokenness."

—LEANNE BURDA
Writer, Blogger, Speaker, Women's Ministry

ENDORSEMENTS CONTINUED ON PAGE 380 . . .

Choosing *Him* All Over Again

A Story of Romance & Redemption

JUANA MIKELS

AMBASSADOR INTERNATIONAL
GREENVILLE, SOUTH CAROLINA & BELFAST, NORTHERN IRELAND

www.ambassador-international.com

Choosing Him All Over Again
A Story of Romance and Redemption

© 2015 by Juana Mikels
All rights reserved
Hardcover ISBN: 978-1-64960-269-5
Paperback ISBN: 978-1-62020-291-3
eISBN: 978-1-62020-395-8

Cover Design and Page Layout by Hannah Nichols
eBook Conversion by Anna Raats
Author Photograph by Ray Barbour

AMBASSADOR INTERNATIONAL
Emerald House Group, Inc.
411 University Ridge, Suite B14
Greenville, SC 29601
United States
www.ambassador-international.com

AMBASSADOR BOOKS
The Mount
2 Woodstock Link
Belfast, BT6 8DD
Northern Ireland, United Kingdom
www.ambassadormedia.co.uk

The colophon is a trademark of Ambassador, a Christian publishing company.

For my husband, Terry,
with whom I have the family
I could never have imagined

CONTENTS

FOREWORD

MY REFLECTIONS REGARDING THE
TESTIMONY GOD HAS GIVEN TO JUANA

I have known Juana Mikels for nearly ten years and have
seen her grow in the Lord and in her willingness to be taught
by any of those godly women who have been with her through
thick and thin.

On one of my radio programs some years ago, I spoke about
the need for women to keep house. I received some flack from
those programs—who wants to keep house in this day and age?
Isn't it more fun to be out and about, getting a job, making money,
etc., rather than being a quiet and gentle spirit, busy at home (as
the scripture clearly states). Juana wrote to me about one of her
husband's pet peeves. Juana has long black hair, and when her
husband came into the bathroom he often found it on the floor.
She regarded that as such a small thing—why on earth would he
be disgusted by it? What should she do? Of course the answer
was very simple—sweep your hair off the floor and put it in the
wastebasket. Too much trouble? Do it for the Lord Jesus, if you
think you ought not to have done it for your husband!

Juana was willing to receive suggestions from me, even though I often felt that they were none of my business. She is a woman who thinks for herself and thinks through things. Juana had the family memorize James 1:2—"consider it pure joy . . . whenever you face trials of many kinds, because you know that the testing of your faith develops perseverance." Surely that has been a special watchword for each one of that very special family. Juana surprised me recently when she told me we had written thirty-five letters to each other! Thank you, dear Juana, for your willingness to be vulnerable, to be corrected (as I sometimes, alas, do!) and to be mentored. And to God be all the glory!

Juana is clearly a woman who is serious about her walk with Christ. She has a sweet message for the stay-at-home mothers and wives who want to learn to love their husbands. She has a marvelous testimony, and I wish all those whose marriages are in trouble could know her story. I was amazed and amused, in the laughter and in the seriousness. She indeed has a testimony which will encourage and strengthen others. She has a platform that I do not have. People always say to me, "But you're Elisabeth Elliot and you grew up a Christian with so many advantages."

Juana has a story to tell of mending a broken marriage that must be told, and she certainly has been willing to bare her soul. Sock it to 'em, Juana! Gently, of course!

Elisabeth Elliot
Magnolia, Massachusetts
January 23, 2002

AUTHOR'S NOTE

I am indebted to Elisabeth Elliot for mentoring me, visiting me, and writing me. Over the years, Elisabeth wrote me thirty-five letters, which I treasure. Yes, old-fashioned typed notes and letters. She also urged me to write the book you are holding—suggesting the title—after she had invited me to speak on her program in 1996 to share the story you are about to read. Nearly twelve years to the day after we left that recording studio, I sat down at my laptop and began typing out my story. The events chronicled in this book occurred before I met dear Elisabeth; I have, however, included spiritual applications due to her later influence and from the imprint made upon my soul by Christian thinkers and heroes she introduced me to, figuratively speaking. Their combined wisdom will forever be part of my spiritual heritage, alongside other admirable people God used. (But I must save some surprises!)

Elisabeth wrote the preceding reflection for this specific work in advance a decade ago because, sadly, she was already beginning the onset of dementia, and I knew it would be years before I could get this book written. "For we are God's handiwork, created in Christ Jesus to do good works, which God prepared in advance for us to do" (Ephesians 2:10). Since Elisabeth has lost her ability to get out her thoughts via voice or typewriter, I am all the more grateful to have her godly wisdom stored in my letters, journals— and better yet—in my heart and mind. In more recent days, as Elisabeth and her husband, Lars Gren, have stayed in our home and I in theirs, I have been honored to serve the dear woman who taught me what it means to serve Christ by giving up my right to myself and serving others—namely my husband.

As I write to you today, I am in a hotel room in New York City where I am completing this manuscript to send to my publisher tomorrow. Elisabeth's daughter and my friend, Valerie Shepard, just phoned and prayed with me for the completion of this work. She told me I was in good company, for her mother wrote her first book, *Through Gates of Splendor,* in six weeks from an apartment in New York City. I love that. What's more, tomorrow is my thirty-third wedding anniversary. To that, I'll say with Elisabeth, "And to God be all the glory!"

Juana Mikels
New York City
April 3, 2014

PREFACE

A few summers ago, I had the pleasure of meeting love-story writer Nicholas Sparks. He told the women who were gathered that afternoon in Atlantic Beach, North Carolina, how happily people waited in line at book signings for his first happy-ending love story. His second love story had an unpopular ending, and his readers stood with crossed arms and furrowed brows as they stood waiting in line for an autograph. When asked, "Why did you end the second book like you did?" Nicholas, who gains inspirational material from his family's lives replied, "Because that's the *way it happened.*"

I've written *Choosing Him All Over Again* the way I did, ending and all, because that's the way it happened—to me. My story is a story of romance and redemption, with twists and turns that will leave you thinking at different points that you have it all figured out, only to find out that you don't. By reading the whole story, you'll be able to see how God mysteriously works over the course of our lives.

No one likes to relive bad memories. There is something heart-wrenching and emotionally draining about recalling a difficult time in your life—especially a difficult time in your marriage. Who naturally *wants* to write a book recounting how you left your spouse? Wouldn't it be a lot easier to remain anonymous and not have to think about it? Why did I write a book about keeping your husband through adversity in a world that offers throwaway ease and swift, popular no-fault divorce so people can forget their marriages?

The answer can be found in one word: *REMEMBER*. Did you know there are over 150 occurrences of the word *remember* in the Bible? The word in Hebrew, *zâkar*, means "to remember, to bring to mind, to keep, to record a memorial, a record."

The Hebrew children were commanded by God through Joshua to take twelve stones from the center of the Jordan River when God miraculously delivered them from their enemies so that when their children asked, "What do these stones mean?" their parents could tell them that the stones were to remind them of how God faithfully rescued them.

By remembering, they could impress upon their children the unfailing character of God—fulfilling God's command to tell the next generation about the Lord. (How fitting that as I wrote the draft on this very portion, it was Memorial Day in the United States!)

What God impressed upon my heart can be best summed up in Moses' words spoken to the Israelites thousands of years ago, soon after he received the Ten Commandments: "Remember today that your children were not the ones who saw and experienced the discipline of the Lord your God: his majesty, his mighty hand, his outstretched arm . . . the things he did . . . It was not your children who saw what he did for you. But it was with your own eyes that saw all these great things the Lord has done" (Deuteronomy 11: 2–3a. 5,7).

How can my children remember what they have not seen? They must be told.

Maybe you are like I was, afraid of reviewing the past. Don't be! We have nothing to be afraid of when God brings our past to mind. Your memory is your friend, because God can take your past and your "might have beens" and use them in the future for good in your life (and in the lives of others). What better place to apply this truth than in our less-than-perfect marriages? Consider what Oswald Chambers said: "Let memory have its way . . . God will turn the 'might have been' into a wonderful culture for the future."

Maybe you have a pretty good marriage some days, but others aren't as good, and you want to read our story and be reminded of how you fell in love with your husband, and to be aware of any warning signs that work against your marriage.

Perhaps your marriage is on shaky ground, and you need to know that there is hope.

Maybe you are a Christian but your spouse is not, and you need encouragement to hang in there from someone who has been where you are.

Maybe you are not yet married, but you want to gain biblical advice for preparation for marriage.

Perhaps you know someone who is separated, and you want to know how you can help them.

Maybe you, like me, did not come from a home where the Bible was taught, and you want hope that you too, can lay a foundation for a Christian home despite your past. And finally, you may have left your spouse or your spouse is leaving you, and you were given this book as a resource to reconsider your actions or try to understand your spouse's decision. You won't find tips and techniques to restore your marriage as you would in a traditional counseling-based marriage book. But you will hear how we handled our separation, the consequences of it, and how we were able to come back together despite the strong emotions and actions surrounding my decision to leave my husband, and the voices of those saying we needed to divorce.

I interviewed over forty people for the book, all of whom had been either separated or divorced at one time. I have used a few incidents from their stories for your benefit.

I had you in mind, dear reader, as I recounted our story on paper, because I wanted to be able to offer our story as encouragement to those who are currently in a battle for their marriage. Keeping a solid, stable marriage takes a lot of work even on the best days!

I hope to offer encouragement to you if you are married to a nonbeliever. I became a Christian seven years before my husband became a believer. In the years that have intervened since many of the events I'll share with you took place, I have been given slight glimpses into God's purposes for the trials I have faced. You see, we have now been married 33 years!

I've added scriptural content that has helped me to see God at work in my life, although at the time of the experience I did not know these truths. This book is divided into three parts: *The Old Life, The New Life, and The Life of Faith and Marriage.* Parts one and two are the narrative of my story intermixed with faith lessons, while part three goes deeper into the Christian faith and includes nine areas I focused on during my separation and reconciliation, as well as eleven checkpoints for refreshing any marriage.

At the back of the book, I have included two appendices containing prayers I pray for my husband that you can also pray, and a note to Christian women married to unbelievers, or married to Christian men who are not acting as believers should.

∽

There are two biblical principles that have been themes in my life and are threaded throughout my story. Thank you to Hannah Whitall Smith, a Christian writer from the 1800s, who best summarized these principles for me. I feel like Hannah and I would have shared a great friendship had we lived in the same century!

The first principle is "man's part is to trust, and God's part is to work."[1] The second principle is to receive everything in your life as if it has come directly from God's hand.[2]

When I began this manuscript, I had a huge hurdle to overcome. You see, I was awful at writing in school. I didn't like writing, and never really learned how to do it; I was a numbers girl. Perhaps a conversation I had in my heart with God best explains my trepidation about writing:

Lord, I feel so strange publishing my story. Are you sure you have the right woman?

The Lord seemed to whisper His thoughts to my heart. His gentle voice lets us know something is right and true in spite of our natural inclinations to run in the opposite direction.

That gentle voice seemed to say to me:

"That is not your concern. Your part is to trust and obey Me. Leave the results of your obedience to Me—that is My business, not yours. You write, and I will do the spiritual work.

"Tell everyone when you first learned of Me, when you first fell in love with Me—after I reached down to you and loved you first.

"Tell the difference I've made in your life.

"Tell how you did the trusting part, and how I did the work.

"I will help you. You will not be put to shame.

"Tell the story I gave you to tell."

So I wrote our story.

I want to share my past with you because it will help fill in the rest of my story, and perhaps yours too. Maybe you, like me, didn't come from a solid Christian background. Maybe you did, but you have made a decision to stop loving your husband or have decided to leave him emotionally in your heart. My story is for you, in the hopes that you will see yourself and your situation as hopeful—not hopeless. It is my prayer that you will be encouraged and able to love your husband and to *choose* him again. It is my delight to share my history with you because my story is a story of God's grace. You see, my new friend—it's really *His story.*

My hope is that you will see yourself somewhere in my story or in the lives of those I interviewed, and that through this you will find encouragement. I have been praying for you. Will you pray with me now, before you begin reading?

Lord, I am willing to receive what you send, to lack what you withhold, to relinquish what you take, to suffer what You inflict, to do what you command, to be what you require.

—Anonymous

I'm delighted that you've chosen to join me, so grab a cup of tea or coffee and get settled in your favorite cozy chair. I've already invited the Holy Spirit to join us.

Juana Mikels
Raleigh, North Carolina
May 2014

PART ONE
THE OLD LIFE

This is the worst disease. People have . . . no time for each other, no time to enjoy each other. . . . The solution is to spread love everywhere you go, first of all in your own home. Give love . . . to your wife or husband.

—MOTHER TERESA

CHAPTER ONE

SOMETHING'S MISSING

I VIVIDLY REMEMBER WRITING THE note that October night. It stands out in my mind as if it were written with a permanent marker. It was a defining moment, a pivotal decision. It felt like an awakening.

With a growing intensity, I decided that I wanted out of my marriage. This was why, while on a recent business trip, I had moved my college ring over to my left hand. I did not yet have the nerve to take off my wedding and engagement rings, but moving my black onyx Meredith College ring on top of my wedding rings reflected the uncertainty that was in my heart about being married to Terry. The winsome personalities of the corporate sales instructors I had just met fascinated me. I thought they seemed much more like the type of man I should have married. This confirmed to me what had already been taking place in my heart and mind.

It would be years before I would be able to discern the difference between surface-level charm and deep strength of character. Little did I know then, but my husband would have easily won out over those instructors based on his underlying strength of character—if I had only possessed some kind of crystal ball or X-ray vision that would have enabled me to perceive it. I would later pay dearly for the misguided path I was about to choose.

But on the flight home from that business trip, all I could think was that I should have married a man like one of those outgoing instructors. They seemed so naturally lighthearted and humorous. *Was a fun-loving nature the missing component in our marriage?* I wondered. *Certainly these men are not as attractive as my husband, but I bet they're the type of person who would understand me. That's the type of person I should have married. Did I jump the gun by getting married too soon? Did I make a mistake?*

"Would you like something to drink?" The flight attendant interrupted my thoughts.

"No, no thank you," I replied. I looked out the window with my mind spinning out of control. *Had I married the wrong person? Should I have married someone like Mr. Jones, our bald-headed neighbor who, when I was growing up, seemed so jovial and played badminton with us? But wait. Hadn't I learned that even Mr. and Mrs. Jones had divorced in later years? Are there people out there really living the dream of being madly in love with the person they married? Would the chain of brokenness that had begun in past generations of my family continue in my life too? Would I be added to that line of broken relationships? Oh, why does life have to be so complicated?*

I was new to my national account sales position and had much to learn, so I was quiet and like a sponge in the training class. I was in a field dominated by men and nearly everyone was a good ten years older than me, but my colleagues from our Fortune 500 corporation genuinely included me right from the start. We continued our conversations over our meals together, and more than once I found myself comparing these men to Terry.

If only I had known about the true love that lies at the center of the mystery of marriage.

When I was a little girl, I dreamed of the man who would someday be my husband. I remember often standing in front of the bathroom mirror. I would look at my reflection and be filled with wonder thinking that somewhere in the world was a boy who would one day be my husband. My husband! Yes, I would think about him and wait for him! He would pick me over everyone else and love me out of all the girls in the world! Where was he? I loved to imagine him. Everything felt warm and good when I thought about him.

But now, as I sat on that plane, all I could do was compare Terry to other men. I was not at all familiar with what the Bible had to say about marriage because I was not taught the Bible in our home, nor do I remember anyone ever sharing a specific scripture with me for practical application. I had never read the scripture that says: "*When they measure themselves by themselves and compare themselves with themselves, they are not wise.*"³ Nor did I know that comparing Terry to other men would only lead to discontentment.

I felt the ticking of the time bomb in my heart and felt sure that once I made the right decision I would *feel* content. But I couldn't have been further from the truth.

❧

What did I know about what was wise and what wasn't a wise choice? I didn't have a clue about real wisdom or where to get it. I had never heard that the Bible says, "The fear of the Lord is the beginning of wisdom."⁴ Unfortunately, with no foundation, I was flying solo, with absolutely no source of understanding about my life other than my own misguided emotions and my own very limited perspective. I had no control tower to guide my clouded decision-making.

So on that October night, nearly two decades after fantasizing about my Prince Charming and how we would love each other madly forever, I allowed my mind to muse without restraint, entertaining thoughts of being appreciated by someone other than my husband. Since I was a newcomer to the sales group, I had cautiously kept my distance from these men, but now that I was going home my mind was spinning. For the last year and a half of our three-year marriage, I had tried to tell Terry that something was missing. Something in me knew that I was at a crossroads.

Away from home and in my mind, I created a scenario in which I was free to date. How effortlessly I had laughed in class during that week. How naturally my sense of humor seemed to match that of the instructors. They had made the dry material so engaging and fun. Was this what our marriage was missing—the fun and emotional intimacy I had always wanted my whole life?

But the week of fun was over; I would be home in less than an hour. I distinctly remember the thoughts I had on that airplane: *I feel so strange. I don't want to go home.* The pilot announced that we were making our descent into the Raleigh-Durham airport.

Saturday mornings were the worst for me. Terry and I would be busy all week in our sales positions with Burroughs and Xerox, but then Saturday would arrive. The sun would be shining, and Terry would be preparing to wash his car and get ready to go play golf, and I would be idle and sad.

But then Monday would come again and I would get busy at work all week, and I would bounce back. But then Saturday would return . . . I would be idle again . . . and so sad. So the balloons and note my husband had left for me to welcome me home that Friday evening were a stark contrast to what I was feeling. They meant nothing to me. *It's all too late. I don't feel anything for him anymore. I feel restless and empty as I have felt for so long now.* I wanted to go back to the bubble of the training center, a world where I was meeting new people who all seemed so positive and like me. It seemed like a new world was opening up to me.

> If it's a marriage problem, then it's an "us" problem, not a "you" or "me" problem. —Mitch Temple

But now, the time bomb felt like it was about to explode with anxiety regarding the future. So many unanswered questions had seemed to flow through my head when I was on the airplane. *How can I be married to someone for sixty years with no assurance that I married the right person? This is no way to live. I have been trying to tell him for nearly two years that something is missing in our marriage. I don't think I even love him! How could I, if I feel this way? He must not be the one for me. We should have just been friends.*

My mind was racing. The questions about my future persisted like a nagging toothache, and I had to find what was missing from my life. Life was too short to miss my destiny! What was missing must be love, I thought. Doesn't everyone dream of finding and knowing true love?

I knew that something was missing, but what? Romance? Candles? Admiration? Respect? Passion? *What could it be that had departed?* I wondered to myself. *Or, if it could depart, was it ever really there in the first place? If our love was real, shouldn't we have been able to sustain it?*

These questions plagued my mind, but I had no answers. I only had misconceptions—misconceptions about what love really was. I was searching for a love that delivered continual, unfading romance. I wanted to sustain the spontaneity and newness from when Terry and I first met. If only I had known about the true love at the center of the mystery of marriage. Sacrificial love seeks the good of the other person rooted in yet another Person I had not yet met.

How was I to know that in my heart I was chasing after an image of a love that did not exist? I was about to forfeit the fragile, immature love that we shared by breaking my vows. I had no idea that our unstable love comprised the potential for a deeper, lasting love if rooted in a foundation that we knew nothing of at that time.

The night I returned home from my business trip, I was drifting away like a leaf in a fast-moving current. I had already decided that I wanted out of my marriage.

I had no idea that what had brought us together in the first place could hold us together—and that there was something supernatural behind the scenes that was much bigger than all my emotions and fears. It was something outside of myself that I could not have produced or controlled anymore than I could have chosen to be born. There was a living God who wanted me to know Him, and He wanted to use the closest of human relationships, my marriage, so that I would know Him. When I had tried to tell Terry that something was missing from our marriage, he had said it was my problem. So what was I to do? Oh, how oblivious we both were. Listen to what Mitch Temple, former pastor and counselor specializing in marriage and family crisis for over twenty years says: "Don't approach the issue of getting help with the [attitude of] 'you need help, I don't' routine. Realize that you both have a problem. If it's a marriage problem, it's an 'us' problem versus a 'you' or 'me' problem."[5] Today, Terry totally agrees with Mitch.

All I knew at the time, though, was that something was wrong: terribly wrong. What could it be? Terry and I had no idea that my discovery that "something was missing" would take us to places we didn't want to go. We were both so young and foolish.

CHAPTER TWO

THE NOTE

THE BALLOONS MY HUSBAND HAD put out to greet me that Friday afternoon contrasted with my sullen bleakness, and I was also not thrilled to learn that we had dinner plans with some friends. My restless mind was in no condition to make small talk, and I may have even tried to get out of it. But we went.

We jumped in the car and quickly met another couple for dinner in North Raleigh at a popular, upscale Mexican restaurant. Throughout the meal, I couldn't help but notice that this couple picked on one another and showed no appreciation for each other.

While both of them were very attractive on the outside, their rudeness to one another was unbecoming, and it added to my inward disillusionment in my own marriage. I picked at my food, but I couldn't eat. My restless thoughts spoiled my appetite. *I can't stand the way they treat one another. Is this where we are headed, too? Is anyone out there head-over-heels in love with their spouse?*

I can't remember if Terry and I talked later that night about my feeling that something was missing in our marriage. We may have come home and talked about how I was bothered by how that couple had treated one another. Terry was leaving the following morning for a trip, and I stuffed all that I was feeling into a corner of my heart. I only remember reaching a turning point in my mind regarding my own marriage, which I kept from Terry for the moment.

I didn't want to think of the vows I had taken with my husband to love him until death parted us. I wanted to put that away from my mind.

What new, unwritten vow was I now wanting to live by? My new vow that reflected my current state of mind would have been something like, "I promise to love you until I think someone else better comes along, and then this vow becomes null and void, as I will stop loving you to redirect my love to someone else." No one would ever dream of saying that at the altar, yet that is *exactly* what I was doing.

But, hadn't I always considered myself a positive, persevering individual? Wouldn't bailing out be giving up? No, not if I put a spin on it. I could look at the bright side. I didn't have to look far: it was staring me right between the eyes. Looking back, I know now that I was simply looking for anything to justify the actions I was about to take. I wanted to do what I wanted to do, and I didn't want anyone to stop me.

There were three factors driving me. First, we didn't have any children. That was a good thing, I thought, as children would only complicate matters further, and I was determined to get my life straightened out before children were brought into the situation. I was so glad that I was going to move on with my life before I became a mother, even if it meant divorce!

The second factor was that I was still young. Since I had married at twenty-two, I still had time to start again at a relatively young age. While nearly all my friends were married already, I knew there had to be another man out there for me, somewhere! I just needed to be available, and the sooner the better. *I never thought I would get divorced,* I told myself, *but if I'm going to, I need to make this move while I'm still young. Who wants to live a long life full of regrets?*

There was one more persuasive motivation that clinched it for me. I had lots of practice trying to make peace for other people, especially peace between my parents and peace between my sister and my parents. *After all,* I convinced myself, *shouldn't I focus on finding peace in my own life for once? Wasn't it finally my turn?*

Looking back now, what I didn't know then was that I was buying into a subtle but deadly lie. The lie came in the form of a thought—a noble-sounding thought at first glance, but I now see it for what it was: evil to the core. *It can't be helped,* I reasoned. *I always think of other people, but it is time I think of myself for once!*

If we get our own way, we nurse a hideous idol called self. But if we give up our own way, we get God.
—Janet Erskin Stewart

Seeing my thoughts in print all these years later makes me laugh. *Always* think of other people? Think of myself for *once*? Who was I kidding? I ate what I wanted, worked where I wanted, lived where I wanted, dressed like I wanted, drove where I wanted, parked where I wanted; and the list could go on and on. Yet I said with a straight face that I *always thought about other people,* but *now* it was time for me.

So why did I always want the best parking spot I could get and not like it when someone pulled into a spot I had my eye on "first?"

At twenty-six years of age, I followed in our Grandmother Eve's footsteps as I listened to Satan's voice of deception disguised as a worthy thought: *"Juana, it's your turn. You deserve to find peace. After all, you have been the peacemaker in your birth family for so long. Now it is time to think of yourself. You've paid your dues. You deserve this. You need to be happy. You have to think of yourself now—what's best for you."*

Eve was the first woman of mankind, bless her heart. "Following in her footsteps" means to follow her negative example. Sin entered the human race through Adam and Eve's disobedience, and, like a virus attacking a computer, it has filtered down through the human race ever since.

Oh! What a foolish woman I was! For me not to know what God's Word had to say about how to live life was to give an open door to wickedness—wickedness packaged as "thinking what's best for *me,*" which I then tried to rationalize and defend! I didn't know that I was embarking on a downward spiral and heading for a tragic life of self-centeredness.

I knew nothing of the correlation between self-sacrifice and fulfillment. Between morals and destiny. Between suffering and glory.[6]

And what sane, healthy person would choose suffering in her life?

I didn't know that I was standing at a crossroads and needed to be rescued from my own self and from wasting my life on my selfish ways. I was entirely self-absorbed. Janet Erskin Stewart writes, "If we get our own way, we nurse a hideous idol called self.

But if we give up our own way, we get God." But you see, I didn't care about my wickedness then—in a way, I was rather enjoying it (or I thought I was). I was desperate to follow my feelings of restlessness and anxiousness and did not know there was help available to influence me to choose a better way by a sheer act of my will over my feelings (and, mysteriously, even that would have been by the grace of God).

Suffice it to say, when Frank Sinatra used to sing, "I did it my way," it was not good advice to follow. Scripture says, "There is a way that seems right to a man, but in the end, it leads to death."[7] I like the way Eugene Peterson's contemporary paraphrase in *The Message* Bible words it:

There's a way of life that looks harmless enough;

Look again—it leads straight to hell.

Sure, those people appear to be having a good time,

But all that laughter will end in heartbreak.

So that's where I was that unforgettable weekend, only I didn't know it. To say that it is dangerous to live your life unaware of God's instruction would be an understatement—it's a matter of life and death! But what did I know of godly wisdom, when I had never read the manual that tells us how to live "on earth as it is in heaven"? How do you know you're about to make the wrong decision, when it doesn't cross your mind to consult with the One who made you and created marriage to be the place where real work and commitment take place?

Not only did I not know what the Bible said was the way to heaven, but I had no idea what it said about how to live here on Planet Earth. Maybe I could have told you one or two of the Ten Commandments, the Noah and the ark story, and a few other Bible stories, but that would have been the sum total of my Bible knowledge. I didn't know then that God wanted to make a tangible, practical difference in my life. Worse yet, I didn't even know that I didn't know, and I surely didn't know that it had anything important to do with my life.

The only thing I did know was that I had to do something about the desperation and anxiety I felt inside. How pleased Satan must have been that I did not know the scriptures—especially verses such as, "Cast all your anxiety on Him because He cares for you."[8] How could I have grown up going to church and missed the central theme of the Bible: that God loves me. He's crazy about me (and you)!

But I had no passion for the things God cares about. He wants me to care about the things He cares about. He wants to take everything that concerns me and carry it for me. He provided a way to do that . . . but I was completely in the dark. I was trying to make life decisions in my own puny strength, with my own limited knowledge, and from just my own sinful perspective— living life totally independent of the One who made me.

My enemy, whom the Bible compares to a roaring lion "looking for someone to devour,"[9] delighted as I basked in searching for self-gratification, self-awareness, self-satisfaction, self-pity, and self, self, self. . . . It all now makes me so sick I could throw up.

Besides, it was only halftime, so to speak! Who cares what the score is at halftime? It's meaningless; it's how you finish that matters. But first, let's go back to that crossroads where I stood that memorable weekend in 1984.

Worse yet, I didn't even know that I didn't know!

The morning after our dinner at the Mexican restaurant, Terry left to meet a friend to watch an automobile race in Charlotte, North Carolina, about three hours away. He had never been to the Charlotte Motor Speedway. He wasn't the only one doing something they had never done before. While he was gone, I made up my mind—I was moving out.

I had just had my twenty-sixth birthday and was certain of one thing: our marriage of three and one-half years was over. I called a girlfriend who lived alone that I did not see very often. I told her that Terry and I were separating, and asked if I could come stay with her for a while. She was in disbelief, and she said something about having thought that we were the "ideal couple." But she said immediately that I could come.

I grabbed the clothes I would need to last for a couple of weeks. I told no one else, not my mother, not any of my friends. I knew they would all be shocked, but worse, they might try to get me to change my mind, and I didn't want to hear it. I didn't want anyone rocking my future world and interfering with my plans and the one person who was the most important person in my life: me.

As I packed, I felt a sense of relief. Finally, no more Saturday morning discussions ending with me crying and talking about how I did not want us to end up divorced. It was time to start fresh. My thoughts echoed in my mind: *I can be free. I can just leave. I feel so relieved to be finally doing something about this!*

∽

Looking back, I have no doubt that my soul's enemy was plotting my spiritual death, hoping once and for all to keep me on his side. The age-old evil disguised in an attractive package, scheming to bring me down. How alive and real our enemy is! How often we simply give in to his voice because we do not recognize its source. Imagine with me for a moment our enemy's tactics. The demons probably would converse something like this for my eternal soul:

"Yes! She's falling for my trap perfectly. I'll just keep whispering to her that true freedom and happiness will come from her promoting herself and keep her thinking she will attain it when she finds someone else to marry. I must convince her that the perfect soul mate is sure to bring her satisfaction.

I'll pour in thoughts of the importance of being loved, of being served, . . . of being understood.

And for the love of Satan, I've got to make sure she stays busy. She can even go to church meetings, in fact, the more the better, yes, . . . anything to keep her from giving her time to think, for that could be fatal. I don't even mind if she is in a Bible study, as long as she doesn't really study; in fact,

I will suggest three or four. . . . Yes, I'll send some spiritual indigestion—as soon as she hears one message it will be time for another one. . . . She won't even be able to keep up with them all and so they will just exasperate her. She can hear as many sermons as she likes, as long as she doesn't do anything about what she hears. I'll keep her busy reading about prayer—as long as she doesn't pray.

If, after a couple more marriages, she starts thinking that there must be more to life, I'll do my best to influence her to wander unaware a few years thinking that living with a man with no commitment in marriage will do the trick. That is bound to tie her restlessness and anxiousness down for a few more years.

I'll just have to make sure she doesn't read the Bible: that weapon in her hand could ruin everything! I don't mind her decorating her bookshelves with Bibles—so long as they stay there. I'll use entertainment. Television and computers alone should be enough to keep her from reading her Bible.

Anything to prevent her from getting on her knees. "Whatever their bodies do affects their souls. It is funny how mortals always picture us as putting things into their minds: in reality our best work is done by keeping things out."[10]

How can I promote getting rid of all suffering in her life; that's my job right now. Now's my chance . . . let me just whisper, "Write the note; write the note."[11]

❦

All I had left to do was write a note. The note would serve as a stake in the ground for me. It would create a line that I wanted to cross so I could move forward.

I brought my suitcase downstairs. I stood for a moment in the kitchen and looked at the new peach and aqua wallpaper that I had selected only a few short weeks earlier. Somehow, I felt the urge to say goodbye to my house; leaving it was like leaving a part of myself. Standing in the kitchen of the new 2,200-square-foot home we had completed just five weeks earlier, that still smelled of fresh wood and paint, I penned a note for Terry and left it on the desk in the kitchen. The note I wrote that October night in 1984 went something like this:

> *Dear Terry,*
>
> *I have decided to move out and am staying with a girlfriend. I cannot be married any longer with all the uncertainty that I feel. I am sorry that our marriage did not work out. You don't need to try to contact me. I'll be in touch in a couple weeks to get the rest of my things. I do hope the best for you.*
>
> *Juana*

My husband arrived home late the next night to a dark house. He found the note, and I was gone. I had Terry's full attention now, but I did not want it. I *had* wanted his undivided attention for the last two years of our marriage, trying to let him know that something was wrong. The first year had been so new and fun, like playing house. It was the second year when my dissatisfaction rose when the newness had worn off. When I approached him on Saturday mornings, his response had been the same: "Juana, you have a problem. I'm not the one upset—you are. You need to get some counseling."

On that October night, though, it really didn't matter, because our relationship was now over. You see, I was not playing a game. I was through talking—no more pouring my heart out in tears before Terry left to go wash his MG and play golf on Saturday mornings. The case was closed. End of marriage.

It was as if I had jumped into a beautiful sailboat— unknowingly heading for Niagara Falls.

Terry tried to contact me immediately, but it took time for him to track me down, since I had chosen to stay with an old friend with whom I had not been in contact in recent months. When he finally reached me by phone, he was desperate and begged me to let him come over to talk. But I did not want to see him. I continued to justify my actions, announcing to Terry, "Now it's time to think about me!"

At first I told Terry that it wasn't a good idea for him to come see me. I later gave in only because I truly felt sorry for him. When Terry came over, he seemed desperate, and his eyes filled with tears as he recounted the events of the last several days. He told me he was devastated, that the night he had come home to our dark house and discovered the note and was unable to reach me, he had lain on the driveway at our house and looked up at the stars and sobbed. He told me he could not sleep or eat.

When he came over, he brought a picture of himself that I had surprised him with in our first year of marriage. It was a black and white picture of Terry in the second grade, sporting a huge smile—and I had written across the top of the paper in red ink, "Introducing my precious husband!" Terry was hoping, I'm sure, that seeing this picture would spark a change in my heart and attitude. He wanted me to have the photo, and I took it. I contemplated throwing it away, as I was doing with him, but strangely enough, I kept it.

It was a surreal experience as I listened to Terry: it was as if he were someone I had known and cared for long before, but someone to whom I wanted no present attachment. Part of me wanted to hug him and to tell him that everything would be all right. It was heart-wrenching to see the man I had known so well for seven years, the man I had promised to love and cherish, suffer so greatly.

And I was the one who was the source of his present pain! But there was a war raging inside me over what I would allow myself to feel and do. I had cried nearly every Saturday morning for over a year, and I was fed up with crying. I was not going back to that empty life where he would wash his car and go and have a happy life playing golf with the sun shining, and I would be at home crying, not really knowing why, wondering if I had married the wrong person.

Finally, my heart made a calculated, split-second decision, and I chose to be cold toward Terry as I watched him—totally wounded and vulnerable. I sensed that I was already forcing myself to completely disengage myself from him. Part of me did not want to give him false hope, and part of me might even have been glad (in a sinful way) that now it was *his* turn to hurt. I cannot say I thought the latter for sure, because I honestly do not remember. But as I write this now, I ashamedly would not be surprised if it were true.

I did feel bad for Terry, but I had decided that it was simply too late. I don't remember hugging him or offering any words of comfort when he came to see me. *Why had he not responded in the past when it had been just as important? Why did he respond so quickly and earnestly only now when our relationship had reached a crisis?*

No, I did not want this marriage any longer. It was time to turn the page on this chapter in my life, for I had places to go and people to meet! I was going full speed ahead in a new direction. The problem was, I was going full blast in the wrong direction. It was as if I had jumped into a beautiful sailboat—unknowingly heading toward Niagara Falls. I had made a complete U-turn, and there was no turning back; . . . or so I thought.

All these years later, how I wish there had been huge signs on the roadway of my life. Signs that said,

"DO NOT ENTER!"

"TURN AROUND!"

"HUGE COSTS AHEAD"

"NIAGARA FALLS AHEAD!"

Those signs could have saved a lot of heartache. But, perhaps at that time I wasn't ready to read the signs had they even been there, because I was totally committed in the wrong direction. I think it far more likely that I would have just plowed carelessly ahead on life's road.

CHAPTER THREE

A LOOK FURTHER BACK

WHEN WE MARRY, WE BRING our past with us. Some call that past "baggage." Me? Let's just say I traveled with a whole trunkful. That trunk is filled with laughter and good times, but it also contains a lot of tears, because although my parents were married to each other for twenty-four years (until my father's death), both of them had been married previously and so had experienced the trauma of divorce.

Growing up, I was blessed with a father who I believe loved me very much, but I don't think he knew how to tell me this. I remember once when I so badly wanted to tell my father that I loved him, and in my ten-year-old mind, I was resolved to tell him. I mustered up all the nerve I could, and tapped on the door to his room.

He was reading in bed with the bedside lamp on, right beside his silver ashtray filled with cigarette butts. (I always loved the way those cigarette butts smelled—probably because they reminded me of my Daddy. I used to pretend I was smoking them!) I said, "I came to hug you goodnight." I leaned over and hugged him and he hugged me, and my mind was raging, saying, "Tell him, tell him, tell him; now, now, now!"

In that brief moment I softly whispered, "I love you, Daddy." I don't remember what he said; he may have said he loved me too. I like to think that he did. All I remember is, I had done it! I had broken the ice! I knew that I had done the hard, but right thing— the thing I longed to do, and I was so happy and relieved at the same time. I don't remember telling him again, or his ever telling me, but I am thankful for that memory.

Why is it that some families can't or don't say, "I love you"?

Why did my birth family not say it?

Did their parents and grandparents not say it either?

What was so hard about it?

I honestly don't understand.

Perhaps my father was never told by his parents that they loved him. I don't know. His father died when he was only thirteen. I met my grandmother on my father's side only once, because she lived so far away. My mother's parents lived in a foreign country. My father died when I was a junior in college. Perhaps, a few short years later, after I married, my search for the security that was missing in my father's love exacerbated the restlessness inside me. How wonderful that I was soon going to come face to face with my Heavenly Father's love.

But I'm getting ahead of myself. I want to tell you about my mother.

My mother had her own struggles. Raised in Spain and Mexico, she had married the love of her life when she was only seventeen. By the time she was in her early twenties, they had three small children. Sadly, after he moved alone from their homeland in Mexico to the United States to finish his medical residency, her husband left her for another woman.[12]

After divorcing my mother, her husband took their two young sons to live with him and his new wife. My mother was left with no recourse; she had no power to change his decision. She didn't realize that she would not see her sons again on a regular basis.

My mother began her new life in Richmond, Virginia, with her young daughter, Susanna. She also remarried. She married a tall, dark, and handsome American named John Ruble, who later became my biological father.

Fifty years after Mama's divorce, in the spring of 2005, Mama was widowed, and I helped her move out of her house of forty-six years in Richmond. She was relocating closer to my sister, Susanna, and me in North Carolina. While packing her belongings, I found a worn, burgundy leather pocketbook in her attic stuffed with all those letters from her sons—letters now yellowed with age. Overwhelmed at the thought of leaving the security of her familiar home and surroundings, Mama was not able to process things normally, and she told me to just throw everything out. Without telling her, I saved the letters.

As I was writing this book, I decided to get out those letters written to Mama, which I have stored for nine years now in a memento drawer where I keep my children's special baby clothes and other keepsakes. Mama had read them to me as a little girl. Tears unexpectedly streamed down my face as I looked through the years of letters. How could I be filled with such strong emotions at just the sight of these letters?

My heart burst for what could have been, as questions raced through my mind.

I was crying for all the years lost—for two young boys who had to grow up hundreds of miles away from their mother. I was crying for my sister, Susanna, who suddenly no longer lived with her two brothers. Seeing the boys' young handwriting, in Spanish on homemade color-penciled cards and notebook paper, now faded, pierced my heart. Christmas cards, Mother's Day cards, New Year's notes to "Mamacita"—a term of endearment in Spanish for "Little Mama."

Perhaps because I have two sons of my own, I cannot imagine what life was like for the three of them: Mama and her sons. What happened to their young, little hearts as days turned into weeks, which turned into years without them seeing their mother? Did their hearts harden? Did aunts and uncles include them? What was life like with their new American stepmother? Did she read stories to them? Did she tuck them in bed each night and kiss them good night? Did she tell them she loved them? Did their father tell them he loved them? Were they able to be happy, carefree children enjoying their childhoods? Were they often sad without knowing why?

As I continued scanning those old letters, I observed that their handwriting transformed from large, juvenile lettering to the manly penmanship of young men. Through their letters, I could almost hear their voices deepening with each passing year. And always closing each letter with "your son who loves you," or "your son who will never forget you." Did they know that Mama, too, was suffering, over a thousand miles away?

To this day, Mama still dreams about her young sons, and they are always wearing the cowboy outfits that my father gave them when he was dating Mama; they are frozen in time in her dreams. They are always nine and seven years of age, their ages at that traumatic time in all their lives when the boys were separated from Mama to live with their birth father, at his insistence.

When Mama was in her sixties, I made her a new photo album with photos she had not seen in years that chronicled her life, including her young boys. I became inspired after finding a roll of undeveloped film that, unbeknownst to me at the time of my discovery, was over forty years old. It had pictures from the last Christmas Mama had shared with her sons, in 1954, when my father was dating my mother. In the photos taken in Richmond, he had given Mama's three children special gifts—the cowboy outfits I mentioned above—that the boys would eventually take with them on their sudden move back to Mexico with their father. (Unknown to anyone at the time, that move was to be in less than one year.)

While I was making this photo album, I had a newborn baby and two other small children, so making the album was a labor of love that I did in the wee hours of the morning while my young family slept. I needed to concentrate on the pictures, to place them in order and to mount them with special corner mounts on each photo. When Mama unwrapped the box and then opened the album to the first page, her countenance dropped and she suddenly closed the book. It stirred up such deep-seated emotions that she could not speak as she began to weep.

At first, I was so disappointed as she closed the book. I had worked so hard on her special gift. Then it hit me. Divorce leaves so many wounds in its path. Even though it had been over fifty years since many of the pictures were taken, Mama instantaneously was transported emotionally to an area of deep pain. I had totally missed it. Now that I was a mother myself with two little boys of my own, I was beginning to understand my mother as I never had before.

My half-brothers struggled with a difficult relationship with their father; I don't know much about the relationship with their stepmother. I do know that there has been much anger, hurt, and unresolved conflict. One son married and divorced, the other never married. Broken marriages can leave broken children who are left to pick up the broken pieces.

My heart aches for all of them. Divorce leaves a trail of shattered, broken lives, and the heartache and consequences affect the generations that follow. I know this is why God says, "*I hate divorce.*"[13] Tears are flowing down my face for them, as I think of all that they missed because of divorce. Years that can never be recaptured—they are gone forever. Now I understand why one of my half-brothers, at nearly sixty years of age, cried in Mama's arms as he said repeatedly, "You should not have let us go!" I also know that deep heart wounds cannot be healed without love and forgiveness, and an acceptance of the past. The past is gone; we only have today. This present moment is what we are given.

But let us remember that we serve a God of hope! We read in Romans 8:28 that "God works all things out for the good for them that love God and are called according to His purpose." He did not say that all things *are* good, but that He works out all things *for* good, for those who love Him. He will use the good and the bad to work out all things for the Christian for what is best in their life. And one of those things includes our past.

> Deep heart wounds cannot be healed without love, forgiveness, and an acceptance of the past.

I want to get on with my story, but first, let us remember that God truly is a merciful, loving God! He punishes "the children for the sins of the fathers to the third and fourth generation of those who hate me, *but showing love to a thousand generations of those who love me and keep my commandments*"[14] (italics mine—JM). He demonstrates love to a thousand generations of those who love Him, instead of exercising consequences to two or three generations of those who do not acknowledge Him. Now that is a loving God! It is my deepest desire for the next generation beginning with me (*and you!*) and including my children (*and yours!*) to learn from the past, to walk closely with Christ, and to go on to have godly families of our own. One shining family for Christ is a light on a hill to a world that is unraveling.

Someone once said, "Those who do not know the past are condemned to repeat it." I was about to be a casualty to divorce in my own marriage at twenty-six years of age, and so repeat the cycle of dysfunction and brokenness I had inherited from my parents.

We live in a fallen world, yet God can accomplish His purposes no matter what has happened in our past.

I believe there comes a time, as part of maturing in life, to put the past behind us. We were not created to continually stumble over our past mistakes, but to learn from them. For those of us who call ourselves Christians, we have God's direction in His Word. "One thing I do: Forgetting what is behind, and straining toward what is ahead, I press on toward the goal to win the prize for which God has called me heavenward in Christ Jesus."[15]

Even though I don't know the details of your circumstances and we have probably never met, dear reader, this is my hope for you, too. Oh, that we would "throw off everything that hinders and the sin that so easily entangles."[16] The writer of this passage tells us to throw off our self-centered desires.

Self-pity is satanic. It is from the pit of hell. By "throwing off" resentment, bitterness, and self-pity, we are freed to be like Christ! Is the Christian life hard? No. It is impossible! And for some of you it is impossible to let go of the past, but *Christ wants to do it through you.*

> God will use everything in our life—the bad and the good—to shape us into the image of Christ.

He did it for me, and He will do it for you. Give Him your pain and your sorrow if that is all you have to give, and He will take it. I like to physically make a cup with my hands, and I extend my arms upwards toward heaven saying, "Lord, take this!" If all you have to give Him is pain, hurt, indifference, reluctance, coldness, or anything else—give it to Him.

Then trust Him and do the next thing He gives you to do. He will work it all out in the end. In the next chapter, I will tell you how He did it for me. For when I was in my mid-twenties, my life changed forever.

I am so thankful that we Christians serve a God who is sovereign over our mistakes, and that He can bring good out of anything. Because I would not be here had my mom's first marriage not disintegrated.

∽

In my interviews for this book with couples who experienced troubled marriages, several of the children of divorce were young when the divorce occurred. They now are in their teens, but they still have unresolved issues about why their parents split up. In several cases, the wounded partner has not told the children of the former spouse's unfaithfulness, as they want the children to learn on their own what they need to know. As these children are getting older, they have clearly begun looking for answers, for nearly all children, deep inside, want their parents to be together.

Another common thread that I detected in the interviews concerned the heartaches in marriage that are associated with substance abuse. This was probably the most common problem that I discovered, and nearly all these marriages ended in divorce.

One woman told me how she returned home one day only to discover that the power company had turned off the electricity due to lack of payment. Her husband was spending every penny they had to support his substance abuse habit, but he refused to own up to the truth. She wanted to do all she could to keep her young family together, but her husband's continual lies and deception eventually led to the disintegration of their marriage.

Another woman I interviewed (I'll call her Donna) has struggled with her husband's alcoholism their entire married life. An outwardly gorgeous woman, Donna married the love of her life while she was still in her teens. He was not a womanizer, but alcohol and a traveling job proved to be all the temptation he needed to become unfaithful. When she discovered her husband's unfaithfulness and substance abuse, Donna became severely depressed. Once a wonderful, conscientious mother, Donna could hardly get out of bed. At one point, she and her husband separated for three years.

Eventually, Donna became a believer and became immersed in the Word. She has grown tremendously in the Lord and in not enabling her husband's self-destructive (and family-destructive) choices. His substance abuse began over thirty years ago, but she says they now have a good marriage; she just doesn't talk with him when he chooses to drink. At the time of this writing, they are about to celebrate their fiftieth wedding anniversary.

I did not have to go far to see the effects of alcohol on a family. My own father struggled with alcoholism. Fortunately, my father wasn't mean or abusive when he had been drinking; he simply withdrew. Sadly, he would sit alone in the den listening to his jazz albums, remembering days of yesteryear. He would have months where he didn't drink, but then he would pick it back up again on Saturday nights. If conflict ensued, my parents would both retreat alone for the evening to opposite ends of our ranch-style house. I can only imagine that it was lonesome for them both.

Even in marriage, there will be times of loneliness.

But the Bible tells us it is not good for man to be alone: "cut off" from other people, as it were. We read in Genesis that we are made in the "image of God." We are designed to be in the likeness of our Creator, growing in the image of the character of the living God! God, the Creator of the Universe, who loves us and sent His son to die on the cross for us that we may have a personal relationship with Him through Christ (more on that later), cares deeply about personal relationships. He created us as social beings. He cares about personal relationships, and we are made in His image, hence, personal relationships should be important to us. They are to be our top priority, second only to our personal relationship with God.

What is the closest personal relationship among human beings here on earth? The husband-wife relationship. So much so, that the Bible says the "two become one" when united in holy matrimony. "For this reason a man shall leave his father and his mother, and be joined to his wife; and they shall become one flesh."[17] The Bible tells us of a unique problem that man had, before God created marriage:

> God said, "It's not good for the Man to be alone; I'll make him a helper, a companion." So God formed from the dirt of the ground all the animals of the field and all the birds of the air. He brought them to the Man to see what he would name them. Whatever the Man called each living creature, that was its name. The Man named the cattle, named the birds of the air, named the wild animals; but he didn't find a suitable companion.[18]

The old adage says a dog is man's best friend, but this thinking is not biblical. As much as we might adore our pets, something was missing among that vast array of creatures that made up the first man's community. What does the Bible say this missing element was? *Suitable companionship.* He was alone. But God knew it wasn't good that Adam had no companion with whom he could fully identify and share life with. Let's see what God's remedy was for this man.

God put the Man into a deep sleep. As he slept he removed one of his ribs and replaced it with flesh. God then used the rib that he had taken from the Man to make Woman and presented her to the Man.

The Man said,

"Finally! Bone of my bone, flesh of my flesh!

Name her Woman, for she was made from Man."

Therefore a man leaves his father and mother and embraces his wife.[19]

Loneliness can manifest in many settings. You can be in a crowd of hundreds and yet experience loneliness. The Psalmist tells us that God "sets the lonely in families" (Psalm 68:6). A Christian family is intended by God to be a place of acceptance and love.

Yes, disagreements are unavoidable. Two people will not agree on everything. But our homes need to be characterized by an atmosphere of peace, support, encouragement, and love. Christian author Gladys Hunt defines a home as "a safe place, a place where one is free from attack, a place where one experiences secure relationships and affirmation. It is a place where people share and understand each other. Its relationships are nurturing.

The people in it do not need to be perfect; instead they need to be honest, loving, supportive, recognizing a common humanity that makes us all vulnerable."

But where bad habits have been allowed to run without restraint, even Christian families can miss the soothing balm the Lord intended a well-functioning family unit to be. Don't underestimate the power of a bad habit, no matter how small the practice may seem at first. A small leak in a dam, left unchecked, can lead to ruin!

Perhaps you are physically in the same house with your husband, but you've fallen into the bad habit of retreating to separate rooms to watch your own favorite TV programs, at the cost of increased loneliness in your marriage. In our modern society with all its diversions, we can even be in the same room with people and be lonely. With all the laptops, tablets, cell phones, and earphones constantly calling for attention, you can be sitting right beside your husband and experience loneliness. It can become so commonplace that you are actually indifferent to loneliness.

It is also easy in our electronic society to fall into bad habits that allow the tool to manage us, instead of us managing the tool. Do you send text messages while your husband is speaking to you? I admit that I have done this. With God's help, though, I am going to stop this rude practice. My actions need to back up my belief that my husband is the most important person on the planet to me; I have failed horribly at this by texting while he has been speaking to me. Our actions need to back up what we believe. When we text message while our husbands are speaking to us, we are telling them, *"the person I am talking to is more important than you."*

We need to unplug in order to share quality companionship time with our spouse. Centuries ago, Thomas à Kempis said, "Overcome habit by habit." This rule still applies today: we must replace bad habits with the good.

But you may ask, "What if my husband doesn't want to share companionship with me?"

In marriage, there will be loneliness. Why do we make the assumption that any person can meet all our needs? This is a completely unreasonable expectation. Oh, how I wish I had known this truth as a young bride! "Marriage teaches us that even the most intimate human companionship cannot satisfy the deepest places of the heart. Our hearts are lonely till they rest in Him who made us for Himself."[20]

With Jesus, we can know His companionship all the time, even in our loneliness. "For we do not have a high priest who is unable to empathize with our weaknesses."[21] He, too, suffered loneliness; He walked a lonesome path that no one else in all of human history ever has nor ever will.

As I write this, winter is melting into Spring, and Easter will be here soon. Before that very first Easter, Jesus experienced the full weight of carrying all our sin and sorrows. I love the song "Via Dolorosa," which literally means "the way of suffering," and is the route over which Christ was led to His crucifixion.[22] Listening to "Via Dolorosa" helps me to ponder Jesus's suffering; He carried our sorrows, suffered, and died, even though He was innocent of any sin.

You may want to stop reading this book and take time to simply meditate on what Jesus did for you. We live in a Good Friday world, but as Christians we are Easter people whom God wants to live abundant, victorious lives in the midst of suffering. As you think of Him willingly going down this ultimate lonesome road, think also how this now-risen, living Jesus who chose to bear and identify with our pain, "heals the broken in spirit and binds up their wounds."[23]

∽

Maybe you grew up in a family that had its share of sorrows. No family can escape suffering of some type—wanting what you don't have or having what you don't want. We all will suffer in some way.

The Bible tells us that there are two kinds of suffering. We will experience suffering from doing things our own way, or we will experience suffering from doing things God's way; either way, we will experience suffering. Suffering is unavoidable. The question is, are we suffering because we are choosing our own selfish ways independent of God, or are we suffering, with an utter dependence upon God, for doing what is right and good? "Who is going to harm you if you are eager to do good? But even if you should suffer for what is right, you are blessed. . . . It is better, if it is God's will, to suffer for doing good than for doing evil."[24]

Mama told me that nearly everyone in her large extended family in Mexico talked loudly and at the same time. I'm sure the decibels in the room got quite high. As I look back now—sadly—when my father drank, my mother naturally became upset. It became a source of much loud arguing, yelling, and slamming of doors. I remember when the first man landed on the moon, my sister and I watched the landing from our neighbor's house, huddled around their black and white television in the wee hours in our pajamas, because my parents were having a loud argument.

To this day, I am slow to learn that arguing does not bring about the righteous life that God desires for us. (See James 1:20 on anger.) Even as I am typing this, I have on my desk a 3x5 card as a daily reminder to myself with the following handwritten words:

> Don't have anything to do with foolish and stupid arguments, because you know they produce quarrels. And the Lord's servant must not be quarrelsome but must be kind to everyone, able to teach, not resentful.[25]

Oh, how easy it is for a husband and wife to quarrel! After the apostle Peter specifically addressed the roles of Christian wives and husbands, he directed everyone to live in harmony with one another. "Live in harmony with one another . . . be sympathetic, love . . . compassionate . . . humble . . . don't repay evil with evil or insult with insult, but with blessing . . . keep tongue from evil and do good . . . seek peace."[26] (We'll discuss these gender roles later in chapter seventeen, "Reflections on Marriage.")

After witnessing disharmony and strife between my parents stemming from my father's drinking and my mother's poor handling of it, I was determined to be a peacemaker. But to continually play the role of peacemaker in a family takes a toll on a young child: children are not designed to carry the burden for the family! I could never let my guard down, because I always had to be strong for everyone else. This would later affect me as an adult, as my birth family would still default to the roles we played in childhood. (It was years later before I realized my mother's inner turmoil from having to move to a different country and so not being able to raise her sons. So she too, had unresolved heartaches.)

It makes sense to me now that, when I first met Terry, I almost looked to him as a child looks toward a father. I think I wanted him to fulfill that role. He may have even treated me as a child, but I don't think I even minded in the beginning of our relationship and in our early marriage.

But after a while, I didn't want a father. I wanted a husband. I wanted someone to listen to me and share life's decisions. All the while, my birth family was still looking to me as the one never needing anything or being vulnerable, for I was the one who had always tried to hold everyone else together.

I'm not making excuses for my later actions, it's just a fact that I got tired of being the peacemaker, and in some way it may have contributed to the unraveling in my life in my early twenties. The Bible calls us to be peacemakers, and it is a very good character trait to have. But there are seasons in life, and childhood is not the time to feel obligated to shoulder the burden of holding a family together.

Because of all this stress, I unknowingly was like a rubber band just waiting to pop. I'm not a supporter of the victim mentality that our present-day culture coddles, and I am not saying that I'm off the hook for shirking my adult responsibilities because of childhood patterns. I just think that everything in our lives contributes to the people we become.

There comes a time to put childish ways behind us and to move forward, if we are to grow as adults. I'm not saying that we should live in denial of life's problems and the results of sin, but we need to take responsibility for ourselves if we are to grow in maturity and move forward. We can ask: What can *I learn* from this? What is God *teaching me* through this?

The Bible says, "When I was a child, I talked like a child, I thought like a child, I reasoned like a child. When I became a man, I put childish ways behind me."[27] When I was younger, though, I knew very little about God's wisdom. We did not pray as a family about life's joys and challenges. While we went to church, I did not see or possess any connection between what I heard on Sunday morning and the rest of the week.

Our past does not have to be a ball and chain, but rather something that God uses to shape and mold us into the people we are today. Scripture tells us that "God works all things together for good for them that love God,"[28] and He will use everything in your life—the bad and the good—to shape us into the image of Christ.

I believe that God wants to use the scars, sadness, and disappointments in life to shape us into the people He wants us to be. He also wants to use any brokenness in our lives to comfort others with the same comfort that we have received.[29] I want my children to know of their heritage and to learn from it. Now I'd like to tell you just how and when I met a very warm and handsome young man named Terry Mikels.

CHAPTER FOUR

MEETING MR. RIGHT

I CAN REMEMBER OPENING THE mailbox one day during my senior year of high school and seeing the envelope addressed to me. The upper left hand corner held the return address for the University of Virginia. My heart nearly skipped a beat, as I knew I was about to find out if I had been admitted! As I walked down our sidewalk, I eagerly tore open the letter. *"Your name has been placed on a waiting list,"* is all I remember reading. My heart sank.

I should have known that a thin envelope meant that I did not receive the "Welcome to the University of Virginia" packet. I had so wanted to go to school in nearby Charlottesville—such a beautiful, prestigious school, founded by Thomas Jefferson. I had heard about UVA since the fourth grade, when we studied the history of Virginia. Where I come from—Richmond, Virginia— going to see Monticello, Jefferson's personal residence, and visiting the university was part of every fifth grader's experience.

Fortunately I had also applied to Meredith College, a small liberal arts college for women located in Raleigh, North Carolina, as a back-up plan. I had one of the latest birthdays in my class, so I was always the youngest, rounding a birthday at the end of every September. That's why I was only seventeen when I left for college. I decided I would go to Meredith for two years, and reapply to Virginia as a transfer student.

What I didn't know, as I disappointingly held that waiting list letter, was that God reveals His will by the closing and opening of doors. I didn't know that His refusals are His greatest mercies. I had never heard that "our disappointments are God's appointments." I had no assurance that there was a personal God who cared about the important decisions in my life, who wanted a personal relationship with me. I thought it was all up to me to do everything right.

A friend's father, who was a politician, had offered to write a referral letter for me for the University of Virginia, but I had not wanted that. Prideful, I wanted to get in on my own merit. Had I made a mistake? It was too late now; I hadn't gotten in. Since I didn't read the Bible, I didn't know the scripture that says, "What He opens no one can shut, and what He shuts no one can open."[30] I had no idea that God was about to set a plan in motion to bring me to two people who would change my life. One being the man I would later marry, and the other being the Lord Jesus Christ Himself.

Meredith College is a small women's college of twelve hundred students. I chose not to live on the hall with all the other Richmond girls, since I wanted to meet new people. I wasn't worried about attending an all-female college because North Carolina State University was located about one mile away from the college, and the University of North Carolina at Chapel Hill was only about thirty minutes away. Each enrolled over twenty thousand students, so I knew there would be plenty of guys not too far away. I could enjoy hanging out with the girls and still know that somewhere near there were a lot of guys.

I was so excited to meet so many girls from all over North Carolina. We would sit in each other's rooms in our pajamas and talk, and in no time it was as if I had known them my whole life! Many of the girls started meeting people and going out at night to parties from the first day, but I was in no rush. In fact, I didn't leave the campus for a week, as there was so much to talk about with the new girls I was meeting. To this day over thirty years later, we all have remained friends.

My Meredith College friends share a close, lifelong bond, and we all support one another in the joys and sufferings of life. Each September, we plan a beach reunion weekend. We know that the close relationships we all share with one another are very special, and we attribute it to living together on the same hall in college. Our beach conversations have spanned child-rearing, dating, college orientations, planning weddings of children now in the group, hair color, aging gracefully versus using Botox, and more recently . . . hot flashes. We kid that when men get together they play golf and sweat . . . we just sit and talk. Some people say it is cheaper than psychotherapy, though!

I've known many of my college friends just one week longer than my husband, since I met Terry the first night I went to a college fraternity party. I was with Laura Page from Meredith, and we had just entered the Pi Kappa Alpha fraternity house at North Carolina State University. (Everyone just calls it "State.") There were open parties going on in nearly every fraternity house. We met a couple who were very friendly, and they kept saying they wanted to get us dates for the upcoming State football game. The room was lively and packed, with the sounds of Marvin Gay, Harold Melvin and the Bluenotes, and Billy Stewart filling the air. We smiled, laughed, and conversed with that couple for a while, when Laura confided in me that she missed her boyfriend (who went to college in Virginia), so she was ready to head back to Meredith. We were about to leave, when, across the noisy, crowded room, I noticed a nice-looking guy. *I want to meet him!* I thought to myself.

So we chatted a few more minutes with the friendly couple, when they suddenly told me they had someone they wanted me to meet. I'm not sure why they picked me; maybe it was because Laura had told them she already had a boyfriend. It turned out the guy they wanted to introduce me to was the same guy I had noticed across the room. And he looked even better up close! His beautiful hazel eyes were stunning with his dark hair. When he turned to the side, his profile showed more of his soft, feathery hair that I could now see held slight bits of gray, evenly dispersed. This was Terry Mikels.

The couple introduced us and then walked off, leaving Terry and me standing there alone. "You're beautiful," he said. Those were the first words he ever spoke to me! I was taken aback. No one had ever said anything like that to me before! *Was this a dream? Was this really happening?* I just smiled and said, "It's nice to meet you." The fairy tale began here with a very charming prince!

Terry asked if there was anything he could get me, and I said yes, that I very much wanted a Coke. I knew that would tell him something about me, and I thought he might as well know it right off the bat. If he wasn't interested in me because I didn't drink alcohol, then I definitely would not be interested in him either.

He left to get the drink. But he didn't come back, and it seemed that more than enough time had transpired for him to get me a Coke and return. I began to wonder if he was going to return. *Oh, I hope he does*, I thought. Suddenly I saw him coming through the crowd with the Coke. *He hasn't forgotten me!* He handed me the drink, saying, "You know who to ask if you need anything else." I was all geared up to talk with him more, . . . but he handed me the Coke and walked away! (I found out years later that he was trying to keep two conversations going: one with me in one room, and one with another girl in another room!)

I must have won over "the other woman," either that or maybe she was busy, because Terry ended up asking me to go to the football game with him, and then the next game, and then the next game, and then the next game . . . for four years. In fact, I never had another date in college after I met Terry that first night.

I liked Terry right from the start. He had a naturalness about him that told me he was the real deal. He never tried to impress me with any big talk, but quite the opposite. Once, when I told him about the little house I grew up in, we got out a sheet of paper and drew each other's simple houses! They were in two different states, but they looked so similar.

At this time in Terry's fraternity, the brothers made fun of a guy if he had fallen for a girl. Terry humbled himself, though, and was not afraid to let anyone know that he enjoyed spending time with me. There was a lake on the grounds of my school, and even though we had only known one another for a few days, Terry came over so we could feed the ducks together. We snapped a picture that day; it was the first picture we were in together.

A van passed by with one of Terry's fraternity brothers in it, and the driver waved at us. I didn't think much about it. When Terry got back to his fraternity, though, about ten guys sang Terry a song about falling for a girl, and the last stanza repeated, "Quack, quack, quack," since they had spotted Terry committing the unmentionable act of feeding ducks with a girl! For several months afterwards, he could not walk in or out of his fraternity house without several guys breaking out singing that song, with its infamous "Quack, quack, quack" on the end.

Not long after we met, Terry said to me, "Have you ever met someone before and you liked everything about them? That's the way I feel about you!" No, that had never happened to me, nor had anyone ever said anything like this to me before, but I appreciated Terry's honesty. He made no attempt to play any kind of games concerning how he felt. I really liked how transparent he was. I really liked him, but for Terry it was love at first sight! A song by Dionne Warwick was popular when we were in school, and how we loved dancing to it!

> *Do you believe in love at first sight?*
> *Cause I believe that it happened tonight*
> *Saw you there and the feeling was right*
> *Now I believe in love at first sight.*[31]

Terry did make one tiny mistake. He went back and told a buddy how he had met me, and that he liked everything about me. That wouldn't have been so bad, but with his next statement Terry hung himself: he said he thought I had pretty hands. He never could live that one down. I liked that he was so unguarded, though, and that he had the courage to be himself. It was as if he had the innocence of a child, but the courage of a man!

I distinctly remember Terry calling me, soon after I had met him, to ask me to attend a chicken roast with him. His fraternity was having a party and was going to roast 150 chickens. Funny how I remember it was 150 chickens! Little did I know then that God cares about numbers and accuracy. He knows them all and has recorded many of them for us. Think of it, He counts the stars and the hairs on our head! We even know exactly how many fish the disciples caught when they followed Jesus's instructions! Only, I wasn't asking God for instruction at that time in my life. What an orderly and precise God Whom I knew very little about.

When I told Terry that I couldn't attend because I had a test the day after the party, he was not a happy camper. I wondered why he would get so upset at such a thing? I was so disappointed that I could not go with him, but the truth was, I had studied hard all my life! I always studied over a period of days for difficult tests, and there was no way I was going out the night before my first big college test. Making high grades was very important to me, even if it meant I had to give up something that I would like to do. My father was always so proud of my grades, and he told me so.

This was the beginning of many miscommunications that Terry and I would have. I knew he was angry, but I thought he was being unreasonable. Why couldn't he understand? I didn't like the tension that I was feeling on the phone. Sometime later, he told me why he was so agitated with me for turning him down. He thought I was playing hard to get, and he was disappointed and upset that I would try a stunt like that.

Until that point, he had thought I was "so sweet," and that our growing friendship was based on complete honesty. In fact, in those early days of our relationship, he never said goodbye without telling me, "You are the sweetest person I have ever met."

We made it past our first miscommunication and continued to see each other often. Terry was a year ahead of me in school, and was majoring in business administration and management. He had to take a calculus class, and after finding out that I liked math, I began tutoring him with his calculus homework. We would meet in a quiet area of the student center on my college campus, and he was very appreciative of my helping him. It gave us more time to talk and get to know one another, as we would get something from the snack bar afterward and just chat.

Terry drove a little mustard-colored MG convertible. He would put the top up for me, though, because I did not want my hair to blow after just working on it to get ready for our date! Terry had purchased this car with his own money, because he knew how to work on MGs. My father loved MGs. From my earliest memories as a young child, my father participated in car rallies through the Virginia Motor Sports Club, and he had lots of trophies to show for it. I had grown up with bug-eyed Austin-Healey Sprites and MGs, so I felt right at home in Terry's car.

I remember sitting in class one day during that first semester of my college experience. I would daydream about Terry's name, going over his name in my mind. *Terry Mikels. Terry Lee Mikels. Have I actually met an honest, caring, attractive guy who thinks about me when I am away from him like I do him? Who seems to genuinely care for me? Is this really happening to me, and not someone else?*

You see, no one had ever singled me out before as being special. I had dated several guys in high school, but we only went out a few times. There just wasn't much interest on either end. I was fine with that, because my priority was studying and babysitting, so I could make good grades and earn spending money. I sometimes let my date kiss me when we said good night, but it was always so awkward, and I dreaded it. I wish someone had told me that I didn't have to kiss them. Sometimes I would just race inside to escape the situation! I didn't know that I had a choice under those porch lights unless I made a fast exit into the house. I thought that I owed those boys a kiss, but now I realize that you don't owe anyone anything on a date, except a good time.

I'd like to take just a minute to speak to the singles. If you are reading this and you're single, then run, don't walk, to purchase two must-read books for singles by Elisabeth Elliot: *Passion and Purity* and *Quest for Love*. Our culture seems to have plenty of the passion part, but a shortage of the purity part. Elisabeth's mother taught her to keep boys at arm's length, and that she did, in spite of being deeply in love with a man she never knew she would even see again after her college graduation. What's more, they would be going to two different continents, or so she thought. In *Passion and Purity*, Elisabeth recounts her own personal love story with Jim Elliot, and her five-year wait on God to bring them together.

The roles for men and women have become so blurry nowadays that women will pursue a man like nobody's business; and men are capitulating from being the initiators. Let me just say it, so that no one is confused: the job of initiating goes to the man. Our job, ladies, is to be the receiver. You don't need to send a message to him that you're interested, either; if he's interested, he knows where to find you. Our job is to trust God and get busy doing the work He's given us to do: becoming the person He desires us to be.

Look how simply stated the procedure was in Elisabeth's home growing up:

1. Boy asks girl, not the reverse.
2. He has a definite plan for the evening.
3. She has her parents' permission to say yes. He dresses like a gentleman and behaves like a gentleman.
4. There is no physical contact at all.
5. He complies with the curfew rule.[32]

In *Quest for Love*, Elisabeth tells story after story of how God brought couples together in His way and in His timing, of those who tried to honor God in their love lives. I love the story of a man who was not a Christian when he first began to search for a wife. He tried the world's way, thinking he had to find her entirely on his own. After becoming a Christian, he slowly learned to trust that God would provide the wife of His choosing, so he resolved to do things God's way. (After one relapse, during a lonely period in his life, when he tried to do it the world's way again to "help

God out.") Finally, when he was thirty-two, God planted a very unlikely name in his ear: the name of a young woman who later clearly turned out to be God's choice for his wife. They married when he was thirty-three, and the man learned the invaluable spiritual lesson of trusting God's perfect timing over his own very fallible timing. No wonder God couldn't have presented him with his wife when the man first longed to be married, at age twenty-one: his wife-to-be was then only in the fourth grade! He had to wait twelve years—which once seemed an eternity when he didn't have God's perspective.

Elisabeth Elliot also cites the sad letters she received of many who did the very opposite and got heavily involved physically while dating, and the ensuing chaos that resulted with the "but we're just friends; no we're more than friends; now he just wants to be my friend" games that generally ended in heartbreak. She recounts stories of restraint, including one of a couple whose first kiss was at the marriage altar. Is physical restraint like that really possible? It is. When I met Terry, I told him that I didn't believe in premarital sex. He waited five years for me for our wedding night. Ladies, if your boyfriend won't wait until you are his wife, he is not the one for you. Remember, you get to write your own story.

Start with your assignment to read *Passion and Purity*. You will be inspired to read of two people who were fully masculine and fully feminine in every sense, issuing total restraint until God's green light came. You can do it too.

I recently heard one of our former pastors, Dave Owen, tell the story of how he tried to kiss his wife for the first time when they were both single and riding a ski lift together. She deduced in record time what he was up to, and she had to nerve to say, "You aren't getting ready to kiss me, are you?" I wish I had known that I could have said that!

⟨∾⟩

Terry comes from a stable family. His parents have now been married over fifty years, and he has lots of uncles, aunts, and cousins. They are a close family, and Terry feels like his cousins are more like brothers. Most of his family live near one another, and they get together regularly for birthdays and holidays. Everyone has a great time, gets along great, and there is no arguing. I am so glad for my children that they have all that family just a couple of hours away, for I didn't grow up with any extended family—no uncles, no grandparents, no cousins.

Terry grew up with no one in his family attending church regularly. He had two of the sweetest grandmothers a person could have, but he doesn't remember them attending church regularly, either. His only memory of them going to church was for a funeral or a wedding. Terry's mother would occasionally take Terry, his brother, and his sister to church, but she would just drop them off.

Terry knew the basic teachings of Jesus, such as His birth at Christmas and His death and resurrection at Easter, but he really didn't know anything about what the Bible had to say. He got a small, red leather, King James Version of the Bible on his ninth birthday from his parents, and it still looks nearly as new today as it did then. Terry did not like reading when he was young, though; he really didn't enjoy reading until he was out of school. But even with his very limited Bible knowledge, Terry believes that from a young age he knew that he should give his heart to the Lord and become more like Christ, but he just never did.

As soon as he became old enough to drive, Terry quit going to church at all. Everyone else was staying home, so when he got an opportunity to stay home, he stayed home too. He just figured he would get his life right with Jesus later. When Terry left for North Carolina State to begin college, he continued to put Jesus on hold, and just hoped that he wouldn't die before he had the chance to get right with God.

Terry was different from anyone I had ever known. He was so free with his words to me. I was not so free with my words. I was beginning to care deeply for him as my first fall in college turned into winter, but I had a natural restraint: having someone whom I was attracted to show me all this attention was still so new for me.

Terry seemed to understand, and he was very patient with me. That drew me to him more. I was reluctant to call Terry my boyfriend, though, having never had a boyfriend. I didn't want to fall in love with the *idea of having a boyfriend.* I remember the first time I introduced Terry to someone as my boyfriend after having dated him over a year. I almost choked on my words! (I literally stuttered it out.) The whole time, Terry took it all in stride. Terry found college life to be not only a breeze, but also a dream come true. He loved living in the house with forty other guys. He would go on to become lifelong friends with many of them. He had worked hard playing football in high school because his hometown of High Point, North Carolina, was extremely sports-minded, even winning the state's 4-A championship. In addition, each summer, he worked a hard, hot, difficult, but well-paying job on an assembly line in a plant in High Point that made school buses that were shipped all over the country. After growing up watching college football from a television-side seat, and viewing all those students dressed up and cheering for their team on beautiful North Carolina autumn days, he was elated to be there in person. Terry believes that experiencing those fall college football games together while we were in college were the happiest days of his life.

❧

I never even considered transferring to the University of Virginia. It was no longer an option not only because I loved my Meredith College friends, but mainly because I wanted to be near Terry. We had so many fun experiences dating during our college years, too many to tell here.

All these years later, we enjoy so many memories that bring smiles to our faces because we share so much history together.

I was only seventeen when we met, and Terry was nineteen. Neither one of us knew a thing about how to communicate, other than boy meets girl. One memory stands out, though, that Terry would say was not so fun. In my junior year, Terry convinced me that there were more opportunities for employment if I majored in business, plus I had some other influences in my life steering me toward business that I will tell you about later. I decided to follow his advice but also to earn a double major in math, since I had already taken so many math courses. The only thing was,

I had always secretly wanted to sing in the music department because of my love for singing. My academic load didn't allow any time for this luxury, though.

I had gotten a taste of singing when I landed a job with a live shows group at King's Dominion Family Entertainment Center, just north of Richmond, the summer after I graduated from high school. I had always wanted to take another crack at singing before I graduated from college. When I saw the signs in my senior year calling for auditions for the fall musical production, I decided it was now or never. I was just hoping to get a spot in the chorus.

I practiced "The Trolley Song" for my audition every chance I got, until my entire hall of girls could sing it in their sleep. My good friend Ella tried out as a dancer in the same show. She said, "Well, since you're trying out to sing, I might as well audition to dance." (She had taken dance and ballet for years before college.) Well, I got in, but not in the chorus: I landed the role as the supporting actress, and had one solo! Ella got in as a dancer too, including a dance where she was featured, and we both were ecstatic!

I couldn't wait to tell Terry. He had not been crazy about the idea of my being in a play, though, and when I got a key part, he was even less enthusiastic. It was our first big disagreement that I can remember. He later told me that it was immaturity on his part, as he was feeling some jealous feelings about my getting attention from other people that did not include him.

But Terry realized his mistake and, to his credit, he shared what he was feeling with me and apologized for his behavior. He told me he hoped the play would be a great experience for me. He added, "Just make sure you don't have to kiss anybody in that play!" I replied, "Oh, don't worry about that! I am not the lead. I'm just the supporting actress. I'm sure there won't be any kiss to worry about."

We were going through a reading of the play, and I was reading opposite the supporting actor. (Women's colleges get male actors by advertising locally.) Suddenly, I did a double-take; beside "Connie," my character's name, I distinctly read, *"kisses so-and-so"* in italics. The gestures and directional actions were always written in italics. *This couldn't be!* I looked again. No doubt about it, Connie had a scene with a kiss.

It was just a peck, but to Terry—a kiss was a kiss! (Funny how my convictions are so different now; I wouldn't even take on a role now that included a kiss. It's not necessarily a sin for those who do, though—it's a conviction of mine, put on me by the Holy Spirit, that He may not require of someone else.)

I couldn't believe it: my character had a kiss! *Why did my character have to be the one with a kiss?* I dreaded the kiss scene, but even more—I dreaded telling Terry!

It did not go over well. It went against every fiber in his being! I wasn't even sure he was going to attend the play when it opened, but again to his credit, he humbled himself and came. I think he was glad when the play was finally over, and I think I was too, for that matter.

That spring of my senior year, girls were getting engaged in rather rapid succession (down South, we say girls for everybody who is age sixteen to ninety-six.) Suddenly you would hear the screams of excitement coming from down the hall, and you would know that someone else had just become engaged. The only other thing that stands out in my mind similar in excitement was Valentine's Day. The front hall of the school looked like a florist shop, as it was flooded with flower deliveries! I suppose it bothered some girls if they were not engaged by the time graduation came. Perhaps they thought that if they couldn't get a husband with over 12,000 men in town at NC State, not to mention another 12,000 or so at nearby UNC-Chapel Hill, their chances of getting engaged after graduating were greatly reduced, but I didn't feel that way at all. I didn't have "ring fever," and I did not want to be planning a wedding as I approached graduation. I wanted to work first and think about marriage later. And that is exactly what happened.

Terry had graduated from State the previous year, and he was already working as a sales representative out of Jacksonville, Florida. He traveled the state of Florida, and other than an uncle in Boynton Beach and his business contact, he knew no one in the entire state. At first, he had thought driving around Florida sounded fun and exciting, but after one year of driving all over the place he wanted the "North Carolina grass back under his feet," as he tells it.

Terry realized he was going a little stir-crazy when he was in the umpteenth hotel room on one particular night. He was watching a boxing match on television and decided to "shadow-box" all fourteen rounds "alongside" the fighters, complete with a towel around his neck to wipe off his sweat! When the final round was over, something must have clicked inside him, for he told me that he thought, *"I've gotta get back home. Normal people don't do this!"*

I had found out about an immediate job opening for a sales position in Raleigh, with Burroughs Corporation, and I had unknowingly interviewed on Terry's behalf, since he was in Florida. Burroughs offered me a job to begin right away, but I knew that Terry badly wanted to relocate back to Raleigh, so during the interview I explained that I still had six months of school left, but I knew someone who would be excellent who was available and wanted to relocate to Raleigh. Terry came up, interviewed, and got the position.

I didn't mention that Terry was my boyfriend, even though they were words I no longer had to choke out. I guess the district manager figured it out long after Terry was hired when I accompanied Terry to business dinners, and later as I sat in the stands watching Terry coach his manager's son in little league football.

CHAPTER FIVE

ME? A GENTLE AND QUIET SPIRIT?

IT WAS LATE AUGUST IN the summer of 1980; I had just graduated from college. I was twenty-one and delightedly working as a sales representative trainee for the Xerox Corporation. While other students had been basking in the sun during our junior and senior years, my type-A personality propelled me to "camp out" (figuratively speaking) at the career placement office. I began interviewing with potential employers for post-graduation. Xerox had not been one of the companies that visited our campus—I sought them out. I had met a teacher-turned-Xerox sales representative while working a summer job before my junior year, and I determined that was what I wanted to do when I graduated.

Initially, I faced rejection by them several times. The first rejection came in Richmond, Virginia, where I decided to begin the process. The attractive woman at the front desk was obviously the "queen bee" and would not let me speak to a soul there. She said they were not hiring. No matter, I decided; I would pursue

Xerox through their North Carolina office. I had two years until graduation, so I wasn't ready to be hired yet, anyway.

Then came rejection number two: after I had stopped by their North Carolina office, a letter arrived to say they would not be needing anyone in administration. Administration? I wanted sales! So right back to the typewriter I went to straighten that out. I had one or two more rejection letters from them, as I recall, before things started looking up. I finally underwent a lengthy interview process with Xerox in which they identified fifty candidates to invite in to interview for two sales positions.

About this time, my friends at school played a trick on me. I was in the middle of a deep sleep when my friend Bitsey ran in to tell me that the Xerox people were downstairs. I jumped up in a stupor to get dressed, when it hit me that it was past midnight. Bitsey got a good laugh out of it; with my face plastered with a dried, greenish mud-bath that I slept with, she said I looked like a zombie returning to the land of the living to get that job. I did follow up on my interview, and the hiring manager said in jest that I was "getting to be a little pest." My perseverance paid off, though; I was thrilled when I was selected as one of the two people who were hired for the openings! I started in sales with Xerox the day after graduation.

My territory included the picturesque mountain town of Boone, located in western North Carolina. I was young, self-assured, independent, and assertive, and my recent Xerox sales training had further fueled these personality traits. An incident that occurred one day—a sudden unexpected confrontation—humorously illustrates my fearlessness. I was in the parking lot of the Boone Holiday Inn, about to go in to the lobby to use the telephone (this was before cell phones). I grabbed some change, but left my wallet, purse, and keys spread out on the front passenger seat. Not bothering to lock the car, I slammed my driver's side door shut while glancing at the contents of my purse scattered loosely about. *I really shouldn't leave my purse and keys out like that,* I thought. Then, making a split-second decision to just leave everything as it was and to hurry back, I thought no more of it. After all, no one had ever stolen anything from me before. Bad call.

That day was the fourth anniversary of me meeting Terry, so to mark the memorable occasion I decided to give him a nice plant for his apartment. As I began dialing the number of a florist in Raleigh, the man using the phone next to me turned around and said, "Hi, Juana." There stood Ronnie, who also worked with Xerox. He had an excellent reputation both as a stellar salesperson and as a respected individual. Ronnie was a hardworking, great big guy, with a smile and demeanor like Gomer Pyle in the 1960s TV sitcom, "The Andy Griffith Show," and he came complete with Gomer's Southern accent. Someone once said of Ronnie, "He sells more Xerox equipment than there are businesses in Boone." I believe it. I later wondered how this man, with such a gentle personality, was so successful in sales—where you have to face rejection daily. Later, his manager unveiled the secret to me: "Ronnie is patiently persistent with people." To this day, when I think of persistence, I think of Ronnie. Something in me wanted to pursue that kind of excellence.

Ronnie and I chatted a bit between phone calls. I think he was genuinely glad for the conversation, because for years he had been the only Xerox sales rep in that part of the state. I finished my calls, said goodbye to Ronnie, and walked out of the hotel.

Suddenly remembering my wallet lying out in the open, I looked out in the parking lot and saw four men hovering around my car, two on each side. They looked like typical young, masculine, Appalachian mountain men, complete with beards and flannel shirts. But one of them was stuffing my wallet into his shirt . . . and they were about to steal my car! Deducing what was happening in record time, and with my high heels clicking and vintage gold add-a-bead necklace flying, I ran out to them, waving my hands and yelling, "Stop! Stop! Stop!" (I had bought that car with my hard-earned student babysitting money and was not about to let anyone drive off with it!)

Leaning breathless across the car to block it, I felt compelled to tell them one thing between my gasps for air: "If you put everything back, I will NOT call the police!" I repeated again: "If you just put everything back, I will NOT call the police!"

The men didn't move. They didn't budge. They didn't say a word. They just stood there.

Why aren't they saying something? I thought. *I can't believe that I have caught these thieves red-handed and they aren't saying anything! They need to own up to this! They need to say something! But they aren't even running away!*

Then one of the men interrupted my thoughts. Calmly and firmly he said, "Uh, lady, look at the license plate on this car."

I couldn't see the license plate because I was leaning so far forward on the trunk and my heart was beating 200 miles per hour from the adrenaline rush and my sprint in high heels across the parking lot. I was sure they could see my heart beating almost out of my chest. Leaving my hands on the car (as if I could keep them from running off with it!), I backed my body away so I could see the license plate. I stared at it. Slowly, puzzled, I said, "This is not my car; . . . this is not my car."

The men just stood there looking at me as if I were from another planet. No words, no smiles. . . . Just strange looks as they stared at me, intermixed with their eyes shifting to each other's faces and then back to me again.

I was so embarrassed that I didn't know what to say. The only words that came out of my mouth were, "It *looked* like my car."

Then, turning my head to the right, I scanned the parking lot. There was my car, about six cars down—right where I had left it. It was just sitting there. No one was stealing it. And now for the really bad news: my car was an Oldsmobile Cutlass Supreme; theirs was a Ford Mustang. But I'm afraid there's even more. My car was a rust-like color; theirs was purple. (And as far as I know I am not color blind, either before or since then!) The realization of the huge mistake I had made was even more embarrassing than mistakenly thinking they were going to steal my car.

What do you say next in a situation like that? As we all just stood there, mind-boggled, I said, "Uhh, well, I'm so sorry. I thought it was my car. Have a nice day."

I walked off toward my car, got in, and began to drive off, hoping that when I looked up the men would already be gone, but no such luck. It seemed as if everything was happening in slow motion, but with spectators watching me. Unfortunately, from where I was parked, there was only one way out of the parking lot.

I had to drive right past those men, making it impossible to escape their notice. Even worse than them continuing to stare at me, they would see what my car actually looked like! When I drove by, they were still standing there with dumbfounded expressions on their faces. I just gave them a sheepish wave and drove off.

Ronnie told me weeks later that he had come out of the hotel and witnessed the entire episode, and that he instinctively knew what was going on. He also maintains that he has told the story to every living soul who will listen. At the time, I had no idea that anyone had observed my impulsive attempt to control my circumstances, even including a fantasized robbery.

ᲜᲨ

About two months later, in September of 1980, on my twenty-second birthday, Terry and I became engaged. Before then, we had talked of marriage as "out there" for us, even though Terry had not formally popped the question. I shudder now when I think of how forward I was about our apparent engagement. I told him that he could talk to my mom about getting the ring that my dad had given my mom, since I knew my mom no longer wore it. I even told him how I would change the ring! As you can tell, I knew *nothing* about waiting and following! (Looking back at myself now, I am more shocked that I didn't just dial the number for him and tell him Mama was on the phone to discuss the ring!)

At least I didn't know that Terry did indeed take my suggestion. He called my mother behind the scenes and worked out getting the ring from her. We went to an upscale Polynesian restaurant for my birthday, and before the meal he gave me a birthday card with his handwritten words on the back saying, "Will you marry me?" I immediately told him, "Yes!" He had disguised the ring inside a perfume box. He had taken it to a jeweler to have the diamond lifted into a tiffany setting and reset into a gold ring. (Mama's ring was silver.) So at least I was *partly* surprised. One thing I knew: I wanted this man! I loved Terry and I was marrying him! This man had moved from my boyfriend to my fiancé. I could hardly believe that I was actually going to be a bride.

ᐧᐧ

By now you've probably easily deduced that I do not naturally possess what is referred to as a "gentle and quiet spirit."

The term "gentle and quiet spirit" is referred to in 1 Peter 3:4 as a positive description of women who put their trust and confidence in God. It is the cornerstone definition of biblical femininity and inner beauty of character, and the Bible adds that it is "of great worth in God's sight."

Your beauty should not come from outward adornment, such as elaborate hairstyles and the wearing of gold jewelry or fine clothes. Rather, it should be that of your inner self, the unfading beauty of a gentle and quiet spirit, which is of great worth in God's sight.

It is spoken of in the context of adornment, warning women to not let their beauty be based on the outside, but on the inside—a gentle and quiet spirit is something that God produces in the godly woman's character who trusts in Him. What did I know of that? All I knew about was Maybelline and other cosmetics for beauty. The gentle and quiet spirit was a way of life that I knew nothing about in my early twenties.

Elsewhere in the Bible we also read that, for the Christian woman, although outwardly the body is wasting away, inwardly her spirit is being renewed day by day as she earnestly seeks Christ.[33] Could this be the secret of the unfading beauty that Peter was speaking of? I think it was. Michelangelo understood a marvelous truth that reflects this spiritual application when he said, "the more the marble wears, the better the image grows." As a woman places her full confidence in God, as the years increase He can produce in her the inner beauty of a gentle and quiet spirit.

Juana Mikels, on the other hand, can too often allow quite an independent, driven spirit to dominate her. No doubt you also figured out that I easily jump to conclusions without knowing the truth, as I did that day in the parking lot in Boone. Both characteristics have gotten me (and still get me) in big trouble.

"Do you see a man who is hasty in his words? There is more hope for a fool than for him" (Proverbs 29:20, NAS). Jumping to conclusions is not a virtuous characteristic. If you're thinking that it's stupid, you're right. Just look what the Bible says about it: "What a shame—yes, how stupid!—to decide before knowing the facts!?" (Proverbs 18:13, Living Bible).

It is only God living through us that enables us to live a Christian life.

At that time in my life, though, I didn't even know that with God we can change: "For we are God's handiwork, created in Christ Jesus to do good works, which God prepared in advance for us to do" (Ephesians 2:10). Some translations say we are His "workmanship." Once we become Christians, we are actually totally remade, new creations, by the Master Designer. I thought that having an independent spirit was just the way I was wired, and that my destiny was to fulfill being "me." I would never have recognized my independent behavior as me always insisting on being in complete control.

I didn't know then the biblical principle that I mentioned in a previous chapter: that our part is to trust, and God's part is to work. There is much work to be done! Wrong attitudes need to be changed, evil habits need to be overcome, sins need to be conquered, minds need to be transformed—and as we trust Him, God accomplishes these results.[34] At that time in my life, though, I just made assumptions and reacted.

The biggest consequence that day in Boone—when I thought those young men were stealing my car—was bearing up under the awful embarrassment as I drove past the "thieves." All the pain of my stupidity was squeezed into a very awkward and humiliating five minutes of my life—but that was the end of the consequence! Contrarily, just five years later, at age twenty-six, on that fateful October night I told you about in chapter one, I would again jump to conclusions because of not knowing the truth. Only this second time, a five-minute decision was to have heart-wrenching consequences that would negatively affect every aspect of my life.

∞

When Terry and I became engaged, I was living with my good friend, Mary. One evening our phone rang and Mary answered it. Terry and I had just been talking about our upcoming honeymoon, discussing where we might like to go. We had ended our conversation talking about the possibility of going on a cruise. Mary hollered out, "Juana, phone . . . it's Terry!"

Remembering that we had just been talking about our possible cruise honeymoon, I put the receiver to my ear, and instead of saying, "Hello," I broke out in song. I sang the theme song from *The Love Boat*. At the time, *The Love Boat* was a popular television show that featured romantic adventures on a cruise ship. I had managed to sing my way all the way through two verses when the voice on the other end of the line abruptly said, "Carl Aley here." Carl was my sales manager at Xerox!

As Mary tells the story, she says that my face immediately changed from relaxed and smiling to a look of total shock. All she could hear me saying was, "Oh, yes sir. This is Juana. Your voice sounded like my fiancé's!" Well, Terry and I didn't end up going on a cruise, but I doubt my case of mistaken identity had anything to do with it.

Terry and I only met twice with my hometown minister before getting married. At the first meeting, he asked us to each individually write out our expectations in six areas: husband and wife roles, in-laws, economics, religion, sexual relations, and children. When we reconvened, there wasn't time in our session to receive guidance in these areas; he only had us do the exercise to emphasize the importance of communicating about these areas.

In other words, we did not get equipped for marriage and how to deal with the conflicts in marriage; we only met once to read what each other had written. J.R. Miller in his book *Home-Making* states that "if there were more wise and honest forethought with regard to marriage, there would be less after-thought of regret and repenting." Great care should be taken *before* entering into the marriage covenant.

A young female friend of mine who recently married told me that her church requires everyone they marry to take an entire course for marital preparation. I wholeheartedly agree that it should be required. She also told me that her church requires that couples living together must live separately and abstain from sexual relations until marriage. I totally agree, in order to preserve the distinction of biblical marriage.

While preparing this manuscript, I found the original reflections that Terry and I prepared for that second and last meeting with the minister on our expectations for marriage. It is almost humorous how immature we were, and how trite our writings were in each of the categories. I was shocked to read that I wrote that I wanted the Lord to be the center of our home, for when I was first married, I hardly ever remember even *thinking* about the Lord. I mostly just felt guilty that I seldom prayed or went to church.

I spoke of striving for a "Christian way of life," but I didn't know anything about a personal relationship with Christ. I did not know then that the Christian life was not hard, *it is impossible,* as we spoke about in an earlier chapter. I would find out a few years later that it is only God living through us through the person of Jesus Christ that enables us to live a Christian life.

Under "children" I had written that I wanted two children. That desire was to greatly change after I got right with God. Terry had written that he wanted one or two children, and that he didn't want to be fifty years old and have a child in junior high.

Sadly, we entered marriage with only a superficial understanding of each other, no real knowledge of the differences between men and women, nor what marriage was truly about. I spent most of the time preparing for our wedding and only about two hours preparing for our marriage. That was very foolish of me, as I was to learn. In spite of that, I do believe that every effort should be put into making the wedding day and ceremony as delightful as it can be. It is the beginning of the lifelong holy union, is witnessed by the closest of friends, and is to be cherished as a joyful, grateful, pleasant, sacred memory all the way until the spouses reach old age together! The day and time of our wedding was 2:00 in the afternoon, April 4, 1981, in Richmond, Virginia. I hold dear, happy memories of our wedding day.

We recently attended the wedding of two young committed Christians. Jamie and Callie truly desired that God be glorified on their wedding day and in their marriage. I knew it was going to be a memorable wedding when I received the invitation and learned that the ceremony would be held outdoors under the spreading oaks along the river. There was a scripture card enclosed with the invitation, engraved with the words of Isaiah 61:3: "For the Lord has planted them like strong and graceful oaks for his own glory." The wedding was gorgeous in every way, from the weather to the wedding gown to the calligraphy place cards to the outdoor setting under the oak trees by the glistening river. But it was a simple sentence the couple had framed on their photograph table, among old wedding photos of their parents and their grandparents, that really grabbed my attention. It read, *"I want a marriage more beautiful than my wedding."* Now that's the right perspective!

❧

As I looked into Terry's eyes right before it was my turn to say my vows, I noticed a tear fall from the corner of his eye. I was overwhelmed thinking of his tenderness in that special moment in our lives together. The minister said for me to repeat after him, "I, Juana, take you, Terry," but I could not speak a word, so the minister leaned in towards me. Still nothing would come out of my mouth, for fear that I would burst out crying after having seen that tear stream down Terry's face. At this point, Terry leaned in closer, waiting for me to speak. Finally, I was able to get the words out.

Immediately after the service was over, as we were alone outside holding hands to the chiming of the wedding bells, Terry asked me what had happened. I said, "I was doing just fine until I saw your tear!" With a bewildered look on his face, he said, "Tear? What tear? I was sweating!"

It was the first of many miscommunications in our marriage. While we have laughed many times over the "tear story," good communication in marriage is serious business, and continual miscommunication can lead to the disintegration of a marriage. (For more on communication in marriage, see the section "Communication is Critical" in chapter 17.)

Even for a woman who is very close to her husband, she cannot read his mind, nor can he read hers. "For who knows a person's thoughts except their own spirit within them? In the same way, no one knows the thoughts of God except the Spirit of God" (1 Corinthians 2:11).

Our miscommunication started early—at the altar!

CHAPTER SIX

A HOUSE BUILT ON SAND

WE HONEYMOONED IN SEA ISLAND, Georgia, before returning to Raleigh to live. Neither of us had ever before stayed in such an elegant place nor seen such a beautiful spread of food! We signed up to ride the horses on the beach because it sounded so romantic when we first read about it. Unfortunately, Terry's horse, named "Tonto," reared up on his hind legs when he saw a bee. He almost threw Terry off his back, and later nearly laid down in the surf with Terry still hanging on for dear life! So much for the romantic ride on the beach! Little did I know that marriage is like breaking in a young horse.

I cannot remember how I knew for so long that I wanted to save myself for marriage. Maybe it was something Mama and I had talked about as I sat beside her while she sewed. I only knew it was a gift that could only be given once, and it was to be valued. I thought that, after marriage, physical intimacy would just come naturally. Maybe that was why I could not understand why the minister had told us we would have to "work" at our marriage. I now know that in the area of physical intimacy, this is particularly true. It does take practice, work, energy, and time commitment like other areas of marriage. All of marriage is a work in progress.

It took me a number of years to realize that the wife has a hidden, God-given influence with her husband. It is from God and that makes it divine; we need to use our sexual attraction with our husbands for good in their lives, enjoying one another and protecting them from temptation.

Before we married, I had virginity before marriage as the goal, but was totally ignorant about the broader concept of purity. God is not just concerned with one act; He desires for us to give our complete sexual desires, mind and body, totally over to Him. He wants the marriage bed kept pure both before and after marriage.[35] He is not trying to stop us from having fun. He made us, and knows what is best for us!

We have no claim on one another's body until we are married. Scripture tells us that after marriage, "the wife's body does not belong to her alone but also to her husband. In the same way, the husband's body does not belong to him alone but also to his wife."[36] Because sex in the confines of marriage is from God, it is holy. It was His idea for a husband and wife! He created it, just as He created the sun, the moon, the stars, the flowers, and all the newborn babies. After marriage, sex is to be a vibrant, active part of our lives together.

Two Christian friends recently shared with me that it had been months since they had had physical intimacy with their husbands. One friend told me she just had no desire and felt unattractive and did not care that it had been months. But God wants us to do what is right *in spite of* how we feel. We are our choices, not our feelings. We don't have to follow our feelings!

A dear couple in our church credit the Lord with helping them with the normal struggles in their forty-five year marriage. When Winston and Jayne were traveling in their car toward their honeymoon destination, they asked one another what they thought God wanted for their marriage. What kind of home did He desire for them? What Christian values did they want to live by and establish in their home? They had both come from homes that did not pass on a spiritual heritage to them. Winston and Jayne, though, did pass on a spiritual heritage to their children and now their grown children also walk with the Lord.

Now Winston and Jayne want other couples to grow in the Lord in their marriages, so they began a married couples' date night at our church to help couples focus on their marriages and to learn God's design for marriage. I think the enemy keeps couples away from these great opportunities by planting a false idea: "We can't go to that! People may think we have problems!" We do have problems: all of us are sinners! Every married couple should get biblical marriage input whenever possible! Any marriage can benefit from it when the input is based on God's Word.

At our recent Couple's Date Night we watched a DVD on biblical marriage, taught by Jimmy Evans. Jimmy reminded the men to be more conversational in order to meet their wife's needs, while he reminded the women to be more sexual to meet their husband's needs. (Normally the husband desires sex more often than the wife, but Jimmy says that in 20% of marriages, the women are more sexual.) Jimmy told us wives that husbands prefer naked or lingerie—no flannel or canvas. Everyone laughed, but we knew it was true. Be willing to give your husband what he likes! Surprise him!

I think we Christian wives can really shine for Jesus here. After all, we have the life manual, the Bible, and we're told to consider one another's interest *ahead of our own*. Why not be the one to suggest sexual intimacy every one out of five or so times, because it will please your husband? He doesn't just want you to comply, he wants to know that you desire him. Text him when no one is home (or little ones are napping) that you are waiting for him upstairs with nothing on. Have a secret code for him only that means "Why not leave for a sexual rendezvous with me at home?" If he's been out of town for a few days, anticipate his arrival back home and be available and ready (for sexual intimacy) when he returns. He wants to know that you enjoy him. Pinch his bottom when he's getting dressed or when no one else is looking. Doing these little things lets him know that he still "has it"! He may not get the million dollar sale, but knowing that he has a wife at home who desires him and believes he is her awesome lover will do wonders for him. Think what that does for his confidence! He may just get the million dollar sale after knowing how desired he is by his wife.

Let someone else go to the Bible study social meeting; let someone else walk the dog (actually in my case I do this because it makes my husband happy); and let someone else work concessions for the game—because *only you* can be physically intimate with your husband! I'm not saying you shouldn't do those other things, but don't do them if you are helping everyone else at the expense of saving energy for your husband.

If you cannot be what you need to be in both places, by all means, be it at *home!* Remember, the need is never the call. It is not spiritual to go just because there is a need. The need is an opportunity. Our call is to do the will of the Father—just as Jesus did. Jesus said that just as God had sent Him, so He was sending us (see John 20:21).[37] Our loyalty must be to Jesus and what He asks us to do, not merely to what some other person asks us to do.

If you have let this area of your marriage go for a long time, wives, you might have to get radical—but even if you have to schedule time together, do it! Take the time to plan to be with your husband, so you will be ready and totally *there*. Jim Elliot, a young, deeply committed Christian and American missionary who was martyred for his faith (along with four other missionaries), said, "Wherever you are, be all there! Live to the hilt every situation you believe to be the will of God." Certainly, physical intimacy with our husband is the will of God. Do it do the hilt! Maybe you need to prepare for your husband by thinking about him while you are apart, or soaking in a bubble bath before he arrives home.

Some will need to ask themselves the hard questions. Is there a deeper problem? Are you angry about something? Do you need to get your heart right before God in making your spouse a priority? Have you allowed your priorities to get totally out of order? Are you overcommitted? Do you need to resign from your second Bible study when one at a time is enough? We need to be doers, not only hearers of the Word. (Oh dear, I fear I am treading on very thin ice here, and now have totally gone to meddling.)

> It is not can we have a Christian home, but will we establish a Christian home?

In his book *Walden,* Henry David Thoreau said that most men "lead lives of quiet desperation." That is a club I do not want membership in! I don't know about you, but I do not want to lead a life of quiet desperation behind closed doors by enduring poor physical intimacy out of duty. Don't allow physical intimacy to become nothing but an obligation as the years go by, allowing your lack of desire to turn into a disdain of sexual relations with your spouse.

The point is, make whatever changes you need to make to improve your physical intimacy together and make it as great as God designed it to be. It is never too late to begin again with your spouse! I am living proof of that, as you will see as you continue reading. Be willing to be the first one to change. If the problem lies in the relationship, it will take real work on the relationship. Keeping the romance burning will be worth the investment, though, so you don't end up with a lifelong membership in Thoreau's quiet desperation club.

God not only created sexual intimacy in marriage so we can cooperate with Him in creating children, but He intended it for our pleasure. Physical intimacy should be a regular, vital part of your lives together, just like eating and sleeping. From flirting and playing together to the two becoming one, it all honors God, because it was all His idea! Like two birds frolicking in the sky together, enjoying each other fully and romantically after marriage delights God and evokes His full blessing, declaring that it is *very good!*[38] Enjoy practicing, practicing, and practicing with the right heart attitude and watch it get better and better!

I hadn't planned on interjecting this "birds and bees" talk when I began writing out my story. After speaking with women I interviewed for the book, though, and finding out how far off priorities were among some Christian women, I couldn't not bring it up.

The best thing you can do if you are struggling is to get on your knees and surrender this area to the Lord. It may be that you need to confess to the Lord that you have disobeyed Him by not giving yourself wholeheartedly to your husband. The Bible is very clear on this, and you may want to re-read the scriptures I quoted earlier in this chapter. It's amazing how things can improve simply through praying about them. You may need to stop reading this book and get on your knees now.

If you are single and know you have blown it in this area, know that God can restore your purity. (He cannot restore your virginity, as that is a gift that can only be given one time.) You can start fresh with the Lord this very minute. Acknowledge to Him what you have done (He already knows, but He wants you to come to Him as His child) and ask for His forgiveness for not doing things His way in your love life. "Do not offer the parts of your body to sin, as instruments of wickedness, but rather offer yourselves to God, as those who have been brought from death to life; and offer the parts of your body to him as instruments of righteousness."[39] You have been called for God's purposes. Holiness is being "set apart," which is why you will live your life differently from this point forward. Trust God's timing for marriage and obey Him as you wait on Him. It will be worth the wait! God's will is different from what we imagine—but it is more glorious than we can imagine!

Be willing to be the first one to change.

If you just stopped and confessed where you have strayed from God's ways in your love life, you are covered fresh in Christ's purity! You need never doubt it! I told a young woman who wrote me who was living with her boyfriend: *repent, get your things, and get out.* Sadly, I don't think she moved out. She thinks he wants to marry her, but he has no need since he "has his cake": he has all the "goods" with none of the responsibilities or commitments. The reason she needs to move out is because living with a man you are not married to is contrary to God's Word. Sex was designed by God for marriage, and is not to be aroused until its time![40]

Thankfully, there are fabulous examples of many wives who have made sexual intimacy a top priority in their marriages. Sheila Wray Gregoire is a shining example. She has authored the book, *The Good Girl's Guide to Great Sex: And You Thought Bad Girls Have All The Fun,* which may give you a good jumpstart. Sheila also boldly talks about sex, marriage, and intimacy issues daily at her blog ToLoveHonorandVacuum.com. Linda Dillow and Dr. Juli Slattery have coauthored *Passion Pursuit: What Kind of Love Are You Making?,* which is a ten-week Bible study for women about sex. Who would have guessed, even a few years ago, that these titles would be available from Christian publishers?

The Christian classic *Intended for Pleasure,* by Ed Wheat, M.D., and his wife Gaye Wheat, gets down to the nitty-gritty as the ultimate Christian sex manual from the honeymoon to the sunset years; it includes solutions to sexual problems, birth control, having sex during pregnancy, and more.

We are blessed to live in a time when Christian authors discuss intimacy appropriately and from a godly perspective in order to help others in the body of Christ. Get help if you need it.

You can tell that I feel strongly about this issue. It's no use going around with a Bible and teaching a Bible study if you are not fully meeting your husband's needs or God's divine intent for marriage. First things first! There are three things you alone can do as his wife: pray for him as his wife, take showers with him, and share physical intimacy together regularly. No one else but you gets to do these things, so be your husband's wife fully, with God's complete blessing!

So often Christians jump on the bandwagon to complain about the too-open, permissive attitude of our culture, while forgetting that God wants us to BE IT at home! A godly woman has no sex before marriage, but LOTS of it afterward. Remember, sex was God's beautiful idea, not Hollywood's distorted one. Okay, enough said for now on that topic; back to the story.

In the early months of our marriage, I truly enjoyed being married. It was like playing house! Terry and I had bought a small home together, and we moved in as soon as we returned from our honeymoon. Most of our friends had also settled in Raleigh after college, and we frequently got together with them or had them over to our house to cook out.

I'll let Terry tell you what he thought of our early married life. Here are his words as he told them to a group of about two hundred people, several years after he had become a Christian.

Married life wasn't bad. I kind of enjoyed married life, because I spent as much time with my buddies as I did my wife. We went on golf trips to the beach all the time. We were playing golf every night until it got dark. My relationship with my wife was good in my eyes, but I certainly wasn't looking out for her needs, and I didn't truly appreciate my marriage. I was just looking for ways to make myself happy. I was full of self-centeredness.

All things considered, our life was good and pretty easy. We both had good jobs with Fortune 500 companies. Before long, we had the good news that Terry had won a sales incentive trip to Hawaii. We were so excited about going to Hawaii together, when we suddenly found out that I had won a sales incentive trip with Xerox to Puerto Rico. The two trips were scheduled three weeks apart, and we had so much fun on both of them. We had great jobs, owned our own home, had good cars, had college friends living nearby, and had an "All-American marriage." I was making more income than Terry, but we didn't really talk about it.

Going to church was something we seldom did as a married couple in Raleigh. To me, church was something that was reserved for back home in Richmond. I had church in the same category with getting my hair cut, since I still went back to Richmond every few months to go to a familiar hair stylist. It was a three-hour drive, but I could visit my mom, get a familiar haircut, and go to my home church.

I did visit a church once in Raleigh when we were first married. I had some visitors at the door one day when I was vacuuming. They invited us to come to their church, but we didn't go. Sometime later I was vacuuming again, and they again knocked at the door. I don't think I vacuumed that much, but sure enough, that's what I was doing when they came knocking again. This time I promised them that we would visit, because of their persistence. And I did visit, but alone. (I don't know why I went alone: maybe Terry was out of town.)

The service didn't seem that unusual until the preacher got up to speak. Then he began to yell at the top of his lungs. I am telling you, it was really loud; so loud that I could not concentrate one bit on what he was saying. I did not like it. Sometime later (I don't think I was vacuuming this time!) there was a knock at the door and some different people were inviting me to that same church.

"Oh, I visited your church." I told them.

"You did? What did you think?"

I wrestled in that moment with what to say, and finally I said, "The preacher really likes to talk loud, doesn't he?"

"Oh, yes!" they answered with enthusiasm. "Didn't you just love him?"

I have no idea what I said next; all I can say is, I had no desire to go back to church.

I grew up going to church, though. The church parking lot of Derbyshire Baptist Church was located right behind my house. My father had a gate put in our fence so we could easily walk to church. He didn't always go, but because of him, that gate made it easy for us to go. My father cared enough for me to have a spiritual influence that he installed a gate.

I went to church on Sunday mornings, Wednesday nights for the church supper, and on Sunday nights for choir. Mama always made roast beef on Sunday, and I would finish eating just in time to jump up, run out the back gate, and be at choir practice by five o'clock.

I've already told you about my father's struggle with alcoholism. But he accepted Christ when he was in his fifties, and we were baptized together when I was a young girl. He and my mother were planning their first trip together after twenty-four years of marriage, to Mexico, my mother's homeland, before his sudden death at the age of sixty-four from a massive stroke.

Most of us likely don't think much about it whenever we go through a gate, but now a gate always reminds me of my father's love—my earthly father, and my heavenly Father. Both fathers provided a way for me through a gate. The symbol of the gate is emotional for me now when I think of the words of Jesus: "I am the gate; whoever enters through me will be saved. He will come in and go out, and find pasture. The thief comes only to steal and kill and destroy; I have come that they may have life, and have it to the full." Jesus is the ultimate gate!

The minister at my home church would say when someone came forward to receive Christ as their Savior, "They are making the most important decision of their life." He would say it each time with the same voice inflection and the same facial expression as he stood with them on his left.

I would think, *"This is not the most important decision in life. He's just saying that because he's a minister and we're in church. That isn't the most important decision. We all know that choosing who you will marry is the most important decision in life."* The pastor's words were, to me, what I call "repeating chimes." Repeating chimes are something you hear so much that you don't really hear it at all anymore. Repeating chimes can be anything so familiar that you tune it out. It can be a book that has sat week after week on your nightstand that you don't even notice it anymore. It could be a Bible in your home!

The thing is, my childhood minister was right—only I didn't know it then.

∽

Not long after we were married, I made a new friend named Tootie. She invited me to a non-denominational Bible study, called Bible Study Fellowship (BSF).[41] Tootie and I would ride together. I knew some other people there, Lisa, Dreama, Thelma, and Sarah from Meredith College, and we all tried to sit together for the lecture part of the class.

We had weekly assignments that ideally were supposed to be done daily to get the most out of the study, but I would cram down answers about thirty minutes before Tootie would come to pick me up. I didn't want my paper to look blank if someone were to see it (not exactly the right motivation for doing a Bible study, but that's where I was at the time).

When I was a student I had always done my homework, so I would rush to put something down in my notebook after I got home from work on Monday night and then race off to class. I did not have my heart in the Bible study at all, but I did not want to look unprepared. Looking back on it, I see now that I cared about what people thought of me—not what God thought of me—and that's why I didn't want to *look* unprepared. Believe me, I was unprepared. "For they loved the glory that comes from man more than the glory that comes from God" (John 12:43). Sadly, I was not living for God's approval. Jim Elliot said he studied the Bible because he sought the degree A.U.G.—approved unto God. He took this from the words of 2 Timothy 2:15 (KJV) which state, "Study to shew thyself approved unto God, a workman that needeth not to be ashamed, rightly dividing the word of truth." I'm sorry to say I did not have a noble motivation, and was not going for my AUG degree.

I remember the class finished about nine, and I would look at my watch every time about 8:45 and think, *"Only fifteen more minutes, and I can go home, put my head on the pillow, and go to sleep."* I barely got by in the class; I was asleep in more ways than one. The class lasted from September through May, and when it was over, I did not sign up for the following year.

Years later, I couldn't remember what we had studied in BSF, even though I had been in the class for nine months. As I was telling this story a couple of years ago to a group of women, Sarah, my college friend who had also taken the BSF class that same year, came up to me and informed me we studied the book of Matthew that year. I'm delighted to tell you that I came back to BSF several years later as a Christian, with my children in the children's program. We were all wide-awake and thrilled to be part of it! I never looked at my watch either! After I had a heart change, the right attitude would come to change everything. But you'll have to keep reading to find out how that came to be.

As I sit here typing, my bridal portrait is hanging on the wall in our bedroom. Even the picture shows how I thought in our early marriage. You see, I had planned to wear my hair down for the wedding as I usually do, but when the portrait was taken weeks in advance of the wedding, the photographer took pictures both ways: with my hair down and with my hair up.

Terry said that he liked my hair down, because that was what he was used to. For my main portrait, though, I selected the picture with my hair up, even though Terry had already said that he preferred it down! So the portrait in our bedroom is a constant reminder of how selfishly I made decisions before my conversion to Christ. My selfishness caused me not to consider Terry's interests ahead of my own, as scripture calls us to do.[42] Wouldn't it be wonderful if most conflicts in marriages came from couples both wanting to please the other person? But I had never been taught what it meant to be a godly wife.

I was reminded of our early marriage debacles through my friends' recollections recently. They gave me a very nice luncheon for my birthday. There were old friends there, but also newer friends. Many of them didn't know me when I was a totally out-of-order person, before God got hold of me. Several of my newer friends had come to a class I taught a few years ago on home and time management, and they remembered that I had told them I was a recovering disaster before I began learning about self-discipline and time management. At that lunch, though, one friend reminded us all of how I once took my leftover pancakes, on the plate with the fork still stuck in them, and just placed them in the oven in order to get them out of the way. I then forgot about them—until one day about a month later when I opened the oven and discovered them. They were a ghastly sight!

On another occasion, shortly after we married, Terry had sold his car for a few hundred dollars, and the buyer paid him in cash. Terry told me that he had once heard a safety tip that burglars never look in pots and pans because they make too much noise, so he taped the money to the bottom of one of my kitchen pots. He warned me that the money was there, but I forgot. Some days later I was heating up a pot when suddenly we smelled something burning, and Terry ran into the kitchen just in time to save the charred bills!

Then there was the time Terry came into the den while I was ironing on a coffee table that he had made in his high school shop class. He was so proud of that table, and when he saw me ironing on it, he said, "You shouldn't iron on that table, but on an ironing board. That's not an ironing board." I didn't pay any attention to him, though. I thought, *"Oh, it's okay; I've got a towel down on the table, no problem."* Terry was busy in another part of the house, so I kept ironing his pants. (Don't copy my behavior on this! I didn't know yet that the Bible says that to obey is better than sacrifice.) I just kept steaming away.

I finished ironing and went to pull the towel up to put it away . . . but it was stuck to the table! You've heard of the *perfect storm*? Well, this was the *perfect glue*! The steam had mixed with the varnish and had made the perfect glue. But wait, there's more. The towel wasn't a solid-colored one: it had white flowers printed all over it. The key word here is *had*. As I peeled the towel off the table, I painfully listened to the audible sound of the white flowers—being transposed onto Terry's handmade table! I knew I was in big trouble now. I used nail polish remover and an entire bag of cotton balls to remove all the white flowers. Terry came by and discovered what had happened. All he could do was shake his head.

And I mustn't forget to mention the time I washed and dried Terry's canary-yellow dress pants with the navy-blue bath towels. I hear you domestically savvy people snickering behind the cover of this book. I know. I know.

CHAPTER SEVEN

HOUSE TORN DOWN

AFTER TWO YEARS OF MARRIAGE, disillusionment began to set in. Every Saturday morning, when Terry and I were both at home relaxing from our busy work schedules, I would start crying and tell Terry that something was missing in our marriage, and that I didn't want us to end up divorced. He didn't know what to do with me. Both of us were in our early twenties and clueless. It seemed I was all right when I was busy with work though, so we both just let it slide.

I stuffed my anxious and disillusioned thoughts about our marriage aside for the next six months, after Terry suggested that we build a new house. I reasoned that a change of scenery would be good; maybe a new house could help make me feel better. Terry had a close friend, Rudy, who was a builder, so we decided to buy a lot and draw up the plans. Building a house created a wonderful diversion from my inward struggles, so we sold our little ranch house and began construction on a 2200-square-foot home in North Raleigh.

We enjoyed building the house. We agreed easily on the decisions. I remember people saying that it must be so stressful on a marriage to build a house together, but we were having fun. I loved the peach and teal colors I had picked out for the decorating. After several months, we moved into the brand new house, but what I didn't realize was that I was about to crash lower than ever before.

Things were going very well at Xerox. I had recently been promoted to account manager in charge of sales of all Xerox equipment to all state government accounts in the state of North Carolina, including the sixteen state universities.

Xerox did little business with the state and had no state contracts, but I really wanted the position because I saw it as a challenge: I figured the only way to go was up. It surely couldn't get any worse. I began to focus in niche-market areas, specifically on our high-end, high-speed equipment. As I learned the real benefits that we uniquely offered (for example, to a university that had huge masses of paper to print annually), our sales began to rise. My job became educating the sales teams around the state in how to market to the state system. As I helped them become successful, I became successful, and as our sales rose, my income continued to escalate.

The longer I stayed in the position and the more experience I gained, the easier my job flowed. I even arranged a meeting with the governor of North Carolina to discuss strategies for improving relations between the state and Xerox. When the governor's scheduling secretary came on the line, I explained that the "Vice President of Xerox Corporation" was coming to town and wanted an audience with the governor. "Oh, when will he be here?" she asked. (My sales VP, Al, was only vice president and general manager of Xerox's coastal region and Xerox had a boatload of other vice presidents, but I didn't mention that little fact to the secretary!)

Since I hadn't spoken with Al yet nor told him of my plans, I said he would be in town the next month, knowing that if he could have an opportunity to meet with the governor to enhance Xerox's image in the state, he *would* be here the next month. The secretary gave me an appointment immediately, so in 1985, my boss and I met with the governor! From a career standpoint, I was at the top of my game. The meeting with the governor did not go unnoticed by the higher-ups in Xerox. I also began receiving phone calls from all over the United States from my seasoned counterparts in the other states, who wanted to know how I arranged a meeting with the governor. Our sales continued to escalate and with it went my income, especially after we were awarded a category on the state contract. I was eventually invited to serve on the Governor's Quality Task Force and later was awarded the Governor's highest award in the state: *The Order of the Longleaf Pine.* (I've never quite understood how or why I received that award.) Yet despite my success, a growing dissatisfaction continued to brew inside of me.

Pastor Rick Warren of Saddleback Church has said that he used to think life was a series of hills and valleys. Something good might happen, a mountaintop experience, followed by a dark period—and back and forth life goes. But after his wife was diagnosed with cancer as he was simultaneously experiencing the tremendous success of his book *The Purpose Driven Life,* he changed his thinking. He now believes that life is like a set of railroad tracks, with the bad and the good occurring at the same time. No matter how wonderfully an area in one's life may be going, there's always another area that needs help. No matter how bad life can be on one level, there is always something to be thankful to God for. God is always most concerned with our character—not our comfort and convenience. God cares more about what we are *becoming*, not so much our *doing*, and this is why, Warren says, we are called human *beings* instead of human *doings*.

Focusing on our problems is a downward spiral of self-centeredness, but focusing on God and others will fill our lives with purpose and meaning while we are here on Planet Earth. Sadly, during the early part of my marriage, I focused on me, me, me. My life. My issues. My problems. My wants.

So while I was experiencing great financial success in my career which eventually would soar to over six figures, on a personal level, I was struggling. *Was this all there was to life?* I was twenty-five years old, I had a great job, good friends, a new house, was married to a great guy who also happened to be good-looking . . . but I was miserable on the inside. I had a huge void inside of me. And my beautiful new house didn't deliver any relief from my restlessness. In fact, instead of filling the void, moving into the new house somehow made my emptiness all the more real. I knew I couldn't go on living this way, wondering for the next sixty years what was missing in my life.

In early October of 1984, just five weeks after moving into our new home, I returned from the one-week sales training seminar at the Xerox training center in Leesburg, Virginia. In my mind, I kept comparing Terry to the charismatic people I had just met who were in charge of training.

I now believe that most struggles begin with a thought in the mind. We are encouraged in the Bible to "not be conformed any longer to the pattern of this world, but be transformed by the renewing of your mind."[43] We are further spurred on to "take captive every thought to make it obedient to Christ."[44] But I was totally unaware of any practical, biblical teaching in this area, so I allowed my mind to chew on any thoughts it wanted to. A worthy and true expression says, "You can't help it if a bird lands on your head, but you don't have to let it make a nest there!" In other words, it is not a sin to be tempted, but to allow ourselves to dwell on wrong thoughts and let them settle in and make a home in our minds leads to sin.

With no bridle on my thought life, I inwardly asked myself, *"Why can't Terry be more outgoing? He's the problem in this marriage. If he would just be more dynamic and funny like those sales trainers. . . . And why is he so concerned about how I wrap the lettuce in the refrigerator and fold the towels in the linen closet? Can't he be more relational, like me?"*

Knowing nothing about the glorious differences between men and women and thinking that both sexes were just alike, I thought my concerns were worthy of more attention than his, so I selfishly ignored Terry's simple requests such as wrapping the lettuce so it would stay fresher longer and folding the towels before I put them in the linen closet. (I'm embarrassed to say it, but I was too lazy to fold them, so I would simply throw a pile of clean towels on the shelf.) Don't get me wrong. It was not an overt power struggle about who was going to get their way; I was just naturally thoughtless. I wasn't trying to be purposefully malicious; I just didn't consider what Terry would like.

> Knowing that men and women have different perspectives—on nearly everything!—could have saved us a lot of heartache.

At that time, I lived life always thinking that the *next thing* was more important than whatever I was engaged in. So I would rush off to work—*no time to put the dishes away; I gotta go. No time to eat; I'll be late. No time to record this check I just wrote—I gotta, I gotta, I gotta.* I flew by the seat of my pants, as the saying goes.

I once overheard a woman at the office who always arrived by eight mention that she made a full, hot breakfast of eggs every morning, and then put all the dishes away in the dishwasher. *How did she do all that?* I wondered. I was somewhere between being in awe and being baffled, and I felt compelled to ask her how she accomplished all of that before coming to work. So I asked her. She replied that she never really thought about it, she just got up and did it.

Just got up and did it???

I was lucky if I had time to grab a prepackaged item to eat in the car—if there was even anything to eat in the house! It seemed there always was something more important to do that would be found in the ever-elusive *next thing* (which was such a moving target that I never could catch it.)

Looking back, I now realize that my sloppiness was rooted in selfishness, as well as a lack of concern for my husband's interests.

I disregarded Terry's desire for a sense of order every time I chose to "just do it when I felt like it."

I tossed all the clothes I wore all week in a big mountain on the bed in the guest room. My solution to this mess was easy: I just shut the guest room door. Sometimes two week's worth of laundry would pile up, until I was looking for a particular item to wear; only then would I put the pile away. Sometimes Terry would have to go in that room to get something out of the closet, and seeing my mess annoyed him. He had asked me repeatedly to just hang my clothes up after I wore them, but that wasn't my style. So I selfishly did it my way, thinking that my concerns for our relationship were far more important than his "trivial details." I couldn't see that being courteous to my husband was a huge part of our relationship, and all the while I was "tearing my own house down," as it says in Proverbs of the foolish woman.

So, I concluded that there had to be someone else out there for me. Someone more like me. Terry and I were too different. I also had the false idea that there was no difference between men and women; I foolishly thought that men and women were just alike. People were just people, I thought, and all the same.

I wish I had learned earlier how different men and women are. I should have realized that Terry and I had often both witnessed the same event, yet seen it totally differently. One simple but blatant illustration that occurred early in our marriage should have made this obvious to me.

One weekend, we hitched our bikes to our car and headed for Ocracoke Island on the outer banks of North Carolina. We soon settled in to our hotel and decided to bike over to the picturesque Ocracoke Lighthouse.

Moved by the beauty and the relaxed atmosphere, we decided to get out paper and pencils and sketch the lighthouse. (We haven't sketched together before or since. Terry was a good sport in the first place in going along with my idea to do it.) There was no peeking at the other's drawing until we were done. I fully expected our drawings to match, for the most part; after all, we were only sitting two feet apart, and the lighthouse was only fifty yards away.

When we finished and turned our drawings around so we could each see the other's finished product, though, I was surprised to see that Terry's sketch of the lighthouse was from a much closer perspective than mine. In my drawing, the lighthouse was further off in the distance. And what was with the dark bold pencil bit, outlining his structure? I had made my lighthouse edges muted and undefined. Terry's drawing contained birds; several of them were flying all around the top of his lighthouse. I never noticed a single bird while I was sketching! We later matted and framed our lighthouse drawings together in one frame—two very different perspectives, yet one new combined picture.[45] (Possible story spoiler—you may want to finish reading this book before looking up this footnote.) Oh, how wonderful it would have been to have had an older, wiser mentor teaching me that this difference was so very necessary in marriage.

ᔕᔒ

Knowing that men and women have different perspectives— on nearly everything!—could have saved us a lot of heartache. For the most part, unlike with the differences I saw in our lighthouse sketches, I greatly misinterpreted Terry's differences early in our marriage by categorizing them as uncaring and done on purpose to hurt my feelings. I assumed that since men and women were both people, that we were generally wired the same way. *Wrong!* Men and women are vastly different. Yes, we both are sinners, yet each of the sexes has its own strengths and weaknesses. As Ruth Bell Graham put it, "If two people agree on everything . . . one of them is unnecessary."[46]

A good marriage doesn't mean you don't have conflict. A good marriage means learning how to resolve conflicts; it means working toward identifying a solution. The important thing is to seek unity as much as you possibly can. Keep being one in the marriage a top priority. God will use your differences for His own glory and purposes. A mature woman knows that her husband does not have to be just like her; he is a different person.

But the more I saw that Terry wasn't like me, the more disillusioned I became. The more he didn't treat me as I wanted to be treated, the lonelier I became for a deeper bond that we did not have.

I remember the first time Terry wanted to buy me a Christmas present, after we had been dating only a few months. He wanted me to go shopping for my present with him.

Can't he do this by himself? I thought. *This takes all the fun out of it if I have to show him what to buy me. How unromantic!* I had the unreasonable expectation that Terry should have learned all my likes and dislikes after only knowing me a short time. Little did I know how unreasonable my expectations were. Even though we were just dating, I had no idea that the Bible tells husbands to "try to" understand their wives.[47] I now think that's because we women are often hard for men to figure out, and the best they can do is to *try*.

So at Terry's insistence, I went with him to the mall. The longer we shopped, though, the quieter and madder I became. I can still see us descending the mall escalators in deathly silence. He had no clue why I was upset; he was just trying to buy his girlfriend a present. That's a nice thing, right? Meanwhile, I was thinking, *Doesn't he just instinctively know what to get?* I incorrectly assumed one of two things: either Terry was just like me and should know any number of gifts that would please me . . . or else that he was a clairvoyant. Why didn't I focus on how thoughtful Terry was to want to get me something in the first place? I had no idea that, in a romantic relationship, a woman's attitude is so important. Boy, did I have a lot to learn!

I eventually picked out a jewelry box that had a removable plate that could be monogrammed. And I am still aghast, nearly thirty years later, to think of the letter that I ordered to be put in the center of the monogram: an "M"—for Mikels! Here I was, not only just a college freshman, but Terry had not even proposed! That jewelry box still sits on my dressing table and is a constant reminder to me: I knew nothing about true femininity, what the Bible calls a "gentle and quiet spirit."

Unfortunately, I didn't know how precious before the Lord a humble and submissive spirit is—so precious that it is called "of great worth in God's sight."[48] I didn't know that men and women were simply different. I just kept pondering how Terry didn't understand me, and I am sure that my behavior also baffled and frustrated him.

∽

After I wrote the note telling Terry that I was leaving, I felt justified to "do my own thing," wanting to go back to being single again. I legalistically thought that I was being quite reasonable because I was not going behind Terry's back. I had informed Terry, by way of the note, before I told anyone else. Now that I was separated, I kept telling myself that I was available to date other men.

Looking back, I see how foolish I was to think of myself as unmarried only because I had written a note. Years later, I would learn about some religious leaders in the Bible, called Pharisees, who consistently demonstrated that kind of legalistic and self-justifying behavior. They would, figuratively speaking, wash the outside of the cup (i.e., their actions), while the inside was full of self-indulgence.

But Jesus told them right to their faces that they lived life backwards: He said if they would "clean the inside of the cup . . . , the outside also will be clean . . . on the outside you appear as righteous but on the inside you are full of hypocrisy."[49] In other words, when we get our hearts right with God then our motives and actions will be more pure without our even having to think about them, and then we won't have to go around justifying and excusing ourselves.

Getting right with God was the last thing on my mind. How deceived I was! The apostle Paul writes, "If any one of you thinks he is wise by the standards of this age, he should become a 'fool' so that he may become wise. For the wisdom of this world is foolishness in God's sight."[50] I knew nothing of God's wisdom; instead I foolishly trusted in my own decision-making abilities.

I never read the practical teaching found in Proverbs, such as: "He who trusts in himself is a fool, but he who walks in wisdom is kept safe."[51] Little did I know then that, when compared to our own independent thinking apart from God, "the foolishness of God is wiser than man's wisdom."[52] At that needy time in my life after I had separated, I had no idea that the Bible had so much wisdom to impart to me through the example of the lives of real people and through the inerrant Word of God.

I didn't even know that I was needy, for I had temporarily fooled myself into thinking that my restlessness could be solved by my own striving. I didn't know the life-saving words of truth such as, "Do not be wise in your own eyes," and "If any of you lacks wisdom, he should ask God, who gives generously to all without finding fault."[53] [54] I was so foolish that I couldn't have even told you where the Bible was that I had been given upon graduation from college. It was packed away in some unknown box in the attic of our new home.

❧

In those first couple weeks after Terry and I physically separated, I thought I had found the freedom that I wanted. Soon a friend at work was planning a party, and I saw it as a perfect opportunity to have a date with someone new. I think I was on an adrenaline rush, as I thought I was in for nothing but a fun time, since now I could keep my eyes open for the real "Mr. Right," who would cancel out my "mistake" of marrying Terry. So I invited a guy who was a single friend of a friend, and we went to the party, . . . but he never called me back. I was baffled, because I thought he had had a good time. Another friend from work, Charlie, had a friend he wanted me to play tennis with, so I met his friend and we enjoyed playing tennis together a few times.

But I very quickly decided I didn't want to date anyone until I could get some answers to my nagging questions. Less than two months had gone by since I had separated from Terry, yet the questions continued to haunt me. What had happened in our marriage? Why did I now feel like Terry was my brother and not my husband? (I kept telling myself that, anyway. I would say, "He's a great guy, but we should never have married.") I felt like a kite that wanted to soar, yet my string of the past was burdensomely holding me down. What I didn't know then was that cutting my string off would only cause me to crash. I needed help.

I knew I needed to talk to someone, but I didn't know who to talk to. I didn't want to talk to any of my friends from before our marriage, because they represented my life with Terry and I felt guilty for leaving him. So I decided to look in the phone book for a counselor, and I found one with a very caring demeanor who was Jewish, with a strong Hebrew accent. Her name was Naomi.

I went to psychotherapy sessions with Naomi regularly. Inevitably, I would pour out my story to her and sob. She would hand me tissues. For one hour, I did almost all the talking, then I would pay the hourly fee: eighty-five dollars per hour. I told her how empty I felt, and that I wanted to meet someone new and exciting and she said, "Vana, (with her strong accent, Juana came out "Vana") you are a late vloomer! (bloomer) You are vlooming now and you need to ex-verience!" (I cringe even all these years later at the "advice" I received. I think overall it played right into the devil's schemes, although some aspects may have been positive, such as her genuine caring nature toward me.)

I loved having someone to talk everything over with, even though I was an emotional wreck, dumping all my confusing thoughts on Naomi and crying most of the time. I remember talking to Terry once or twice during this time, and I would say, "Naomi this" and "Naomi that." I felt like Naomi was my best friend in the world. Terry told me something to the effect that he was worried I had Naomi on a pedestal, and that I felt Naomi was my only friend. He was concerned that I wasn't keeping up with my old friends. He was partly right; I worshipped the ground Naomi walked on, and I strangely looked forward to every crying session.

After a while, though, I didn't see any change for the better after all the sessions with Naomi, so I eventually stopped going to her. I wanted to find another counselor, but I was totally ignorant about counselors. I didn't even know there were secular counselors and Christian counselors. If I had it to do all over again, I would only seek Christian counseling, such as counselors registered with the American Association of Christian Counselors (www.aacc.net), or one recommended by the counselors available at Focus on the Family (www.focusonthefamily.com).

I think I went to one more counselor but changed again, this time asking Terry if we could go together. He agreed, and he and I would meet there, but we would spend our entire time in the counselor's office disagreeing! Like with Naomi, I remember

Terry and I did most of the talking and the counselor was like a spectator at a sporting event. To top it off, we again had to pay for all the "fun" we were having in this "counseling" thing.

Afterward, we would go out to the parking lot, still weighed down with our unresolved conflict; it was not a good experience. I would cry, and we would not be communicating well. It finally came to a head one afternoon in the parking lot after a typical inharmonious counseling session when Terry asked me why I wanted him to go with me to counseling. He asked me, "Can you say that you want to be married to me?" I answered, "No, I can't say that. I just want to find out what happened." He said, "Well, I am not going to go to counseling with you for the rest of my life so you can find out 'what happened'." So we quit going to counseling. I didn't see Terry for days, and then the days turned into weeks and weeks. We were living totally separate lives.

CHAPTER EIGHT

PROVIDENCE

I HAD BEEN TO THREE counselors, but I had no answers. I had grown up going to church right behind my house, and I knew that the answers must be in church. God's goodness must have been revealed to me in some way in my childhood experience, for that connection was now drawing me back nearly ten years later. Perhaps it was the godly hymns and the Bible stories that were dormant in my soul that were calling to me. So one Sunday early in 1985, I decided to visit a church where a coworker attended. It was called the something Church of Unity. It sounded good to me, so I went.

They had a panel set up front, and about four people were having a panel discussion. The longer I listened, the more it sounded like an academic class. No one prayed. No one ever said the name "Jesus." I knew enough to know that something was not right; I knew that I could cross this place off my list in my search for answers.

On a cold, winter Sunday soon after that, a small church came to my mind, so I went there. Terry and I had been there once, early in our marriage, because our friends Ken and Sarah Bowden had invited us. I remembered the pastor of that church had seemed so young. I thought a pastor would always be an older man, perhaps bald and elderly like my first pastor at our church in Richmond. This pastor was neither bald nor elderly. He seemed too young to lead a church: maybe he could lead the youth or something, but not the whole church. Terry and I had never gone back after that Sunday we visited with Ken and Sarah, until that winter day I came back alone.

The name of that small church was Providence Baptist Church, and the pastor's name was David Horner. Something was different this time as I sat in my seat. I was really listening. When he would address the Christians he would say, "Christian, . . ." and I knew in my heart that he was not referring to me. I was not a Christian; or was I? I did not know. You see, I had no assurance that I was a Christian. I remembered being baptized when I was about twelve. As I mentioned earlier, my father was baptized in the same service with me, but I couldn't say with assurance that I was a Christian.

I took the church bulletin home and read in it that the singles gathered at seven-thirty on Friday nights. Since I considered myself totally single, I thought about going, but I tossed the bulletin in the trash. As the week went by, I kept telling myself, "I need to go on Friday night." Friday night came, and I knew I had had that talk with myself about going. Soon it was almost seven-thirty, so I decided to call the church to see if they were indeed meeting that night. No one answered, and I was about to chicken out. Then it occurred to me that the phone was probably locked up in the church office. So I grabbed my purse and my keys, and out I went.

When I got there, I didn't see any cars and the church looked dark. *"Well, I guess they aren't having it,"* I told myself, *"so I guess I'll just go home."* Something inside me, though, said to go up to the front door, against all the logic I could muster. So I got out of the car and went in.

There was one girl standing there, looking kind of shy, who also seemed to be in her twenties. In a moment, another girl came in and stood in the foyer. I walked over to them and introduced myself, and I asked them if they were here for the singles meeting and if it was still on, since I didn't see any cars. Before they could answer, another girl walked in, and for some reason I started introducing everyone and chatting with them, because I could tell they were more nervous about being there than I was. Somehow in helping them, all my misgivings vanished.

Within a matter of minutes, streams of people were coming in. There was a large room just beyond the foyer, and everyone was starting to gather in there. Some guys were down front tuning guitars, and before long over sixty people were seated. I took an open seat, and met the girl who was seated next to me, Kaye Crumpler. We chatted for a few minutes. She was very friendly and confident, and when a guy down front asked the group if any visitors were here, Kaye raised her hand. She said, "This is my friend, Juana Mikels." She made me feel so welcome, especially when she introduced me as her friend.

We sang some Christian songs with the guys playing their guitars, then later broke into small discussion groups. Something felt so good, right, and natural about this. I hadn't sung Christian songs like that with guitars since I was in the youth group in high school. It felt so familiar. I knew I would be back.

I felt drawn to go back to Providence. I went on Sunday mornings, and I went on Friday nights. It did feel strange to go alone, though. When I was married, Terry and I were always going places with friends whom we had known a long time. Here I knew no one. Everyone I was meeting was new.

Then suddenly one Friday night, I heard, "Juana!" It was Florence Hassell, an acquaintance from Meredith College. How wonderful to have Florence now as a friend, for she was someone I knew through Meredith College. Here was someone who knew me! I also became good friends with Nancy Olson and Kaye Crumpler.[55] They all seemed to have a peace, confidence, and exuberance for life that I admired.

I began joining these girls for pizza after the singles meeting was over; we would get a large table for about fifteen.

No one drank alcohol, and we just enjoyed each other's company as we ate together. That was like icing on the cake to me. I liked it that no one drank, because I didn't drink. All of my friends had always had the habit of drinking alcohol at social gatherings, so I had always been like a fish out of water. In college, I drank one time the first month, felt sick for two days, and never drank again. Perhaps since my father suffered from alcoholism, I had a natural aversion to alcohol. It was so refreshing being with people who didn't have to drink to have a good time! (It is not a sin to drink alcohol.)

The Bible does command Christians in Ephesians 5:18 not to get drunk, though, but instead to be filled with the Holy Spirit. In another place it says not to be a stumbling block to a Christian who may not be as mature in the faith as you are. In other words, it is wise and loving to refrain from your freedom to drink openly so that you don't inadvertently trip up another Christian who doesn't realize we are free to do that, or who may have a tendency toward substance abuse. Oswald Chambers states it like this:

> We argue on the rational line—Don't do this or that because it is wrong. Paul argues in this way: Don't do it not because it is wrong, but because the man who follows you will stumble if he does it, therefore cut it out, never let him see you do it anymore (cf. 1 Corinthians 8:9–13).[56]

Once when I was in the small group at the Friday night singles meeting, we were discussing something about being Christians. I knew I wasn't a Christian, because I knew there was a difference between these new friends and me. I said to the guy sitting across from me, after he had assumed that I was a Christian, "Oh, I'm not a Christian." He just about choked. I guess he thought that everyone who would spend Friday nights with Christians was a Christian.

As I listened to David Horner's teaching and continued attending Providence, I felt drawn to continue coming back. I started having several burning questions, though, and I decided to make an appointment to speak with the pastor. I remember asking him if we could go to lunch, because I had several questions. David surprised me by his reply. He said he did not go out to lunch with women unless a third person went along.

That was a radical idea to me! What was it with these people from Providence? Why were they so weird? Going out to lunch with a coworker of the opposite sex was a common practice in the corporate world, where busy people combined eating with discussing whatever needed to be discussed. Looking back, I can see that God was showing me people of genuine integrity who lived out what they believed.

I later heard that Billy Graham never met alone with a woman. All these years later, I am still aghast to think that I would have even suggested meeting a pastor over lunch! I guess I'm in the weird crowd now too, but I am getting ahead of myself.

At our meeting, I asked David Horner, "Why are we all here?" He answered, "To glorify God." I was not sure what that meant, so he offered an example. He said, "Let's say there are two women. One wants to glorify God, so she wears a chaste, modest dress. The other one wants to bring attention to herself instead of to God, so she dresses in a revealing dress.[57] One lives to glorify God, one does not."

Much later I found out that Paul exhorts believers to live for the glory of God as he instructs them saying, "whether we eat or drink or whatever you do, do it all for the glory of God." We further read in Ephesians of the mystery of God predestining us to be His sons through Jesus Christ "in accordance with His pleasure and will—to the praise of His glorious grace." Later in the passage, we read that, having been chosen in Christ, God is working out everything in conformity to His will and purpose. Why? What for? What is His will? So that those whose hope is in Christ might be "for the praise of His glory" (1 Corinthians 10:31;

Ephesians 1:5–6; 11–12). I had more questions for the pastor. I asked him about marriage. He turned to the picture of his wife behind his desk, and he said, "This is my wife, Cathy. I am committed to her. Marriage is a commitment."

He then tried to give me a book entitled *Hope for the Separated* by Gary Chapman. I didn't like the title. Three times he tried to push the book across the table, and three times I pushed it back. I told him that I knew what that book was going to say and that I would only read the first paragraph and close the book. I told him he should give the book to someone who would read it.

He won the back and forth thing, and I took the book home to appease him. I did just what I thought I would do: I read the opening paragraph, closed the book, and put it up on a high shelf in the closet where I wouldn't have to look at it, much less read it.

I continued to struggle for five months. I had so many questions and so many misconceptions. For example:

- I didn't want to turn to God as a crutch. If I just turned to Him to solve my problems, I knew I would leave just as soon as everything got straightened out.

  How wrong my thinking was. God wants us to turn to Him. In Proverbs 3:6 we read, "in all your ways acknowledge him, and he will make your paths straight."

- I had the wrong notion that God couldn't want me, because I was separated, and I had left my husband.

When I could get my life together and clean up my act, I thought, then He might be able to use me.

God wants us to come just as we are, as Billy Graham has called countless sinners to Christ using the song, "Just As I Am." In Matthew 11:28, Jesus said, "Come to me, all you who are weary and burdened, and I will give you rest." We say, "I must finish this—I must go and do this first—I will do that after I get through this." Are these not mere excuses? God wants us to come to Him and abide in Him now.

- I had the misconception that if you said you were a Christian, you were indicating that you thought you were perfect.

I didn't know that Christians are NOT perfect, just forgiven! Jesus does tell us, though, to "be perfect, therefore, as your heavenly Father is perfect."[58] While God accepts us as we are, He does not keep us the way we are. We should see progress in our Christian lives as we desire to grow in maturity as we grow spiritually! Likewise, we cannot justify our poor behavior with excuses like, "This is just the way I am!"

- My biggest obstacle was that I was so familiar with all the Bible stories. I knew all *about* God—but He wasn't real to me.

Knowing all about God is very different from knowing God. If I know all about a person but have never met him, then I do not personally know that person. I know about former

President Bush, but I do not know President Bush. God calls
us to enter into a personal relationship with Him through
receiving His son, Jesus Christ, as our Savior.

Not too long afterward, I met with the assistant pastor, whose
nickname was "Moose." Moose was about 6'7". I remember the
conversation as if it were yesterday. I had asked him something
about marriage and, looking me straight in the eye, Moose did not
beat around the bush.

"You're trying to make a decision about your marriage, Juana,
and you are making the wrong decision. You need to decide what
you are going to do with Christ. You need to commit your life to
Him. The Bible says in Matthew 6:33, 'But seek first his kingdom,
and his righteousness, and all these things will be given to you
as well.' Do you want to make that commitment to Christ now?"

I knew all about God, but He wasn't real to me.

"I can't do that. Jesus is not real to me. A commitment would just
be lip service. I know all about Jesus. I know all the Bible stories, but
I can't commit my life to Him—He just isn't real to me."

But I was so confused. Wasn't the problem in my life that I
was separated and I didn't want to be married? Wasn't that the
main thing? Wasn't that the area that was causing my life to be
upside-down?

Moose was saying through the words of Matthew 6:33 that
my marriage was not the most important decision in my life. I
had always believed that it was, from back in my childhood days
when my home pastor would always tell people that making a
decision to accept Christ as Savior was the uppermost decision,

even more important than the person we would marry, and I would not believe it. Now I was being challenged to put Christ first in my life. He had never held that position, and I knew it.

For me, the dominating concern was "I must do this; I must do that; I . . . ; I . . . ; I . . ."; to put Christ first was a complete reversal of everything I knew. What kind of kingdom was Jesus speaking of that puts everything in life—every care that concerns us—second to our relationship with God? No, my greatest concern was my own life, and that ruled every decision.

We walked out of Moose's office that day and he said, "I want you to meet my wife." He opened a nursery door, and there was his petite, expectant wife playing with their small children. Seeing Moose's tenderness toward his family touched my heart, and I began to cry. Here was this huge, strong man yielding his life to the authority of Christ and loving his family. It was another stark contrast to life as I knew it and to the emptiness that was in my heart.

∞

Soon, I moved into an apartment of my own. I made enough money that I could support myself totally, while also paying for half of the mortgage of the new house that Terry and I had built. I remember well when the resident manager took me to look at available apartments. She said that she had two one-bedroom apartments available in two different buildings. She grabbed the keys and off we walked for her to show me the first one.

"This is the best one. A lot of great, fun, single people live in this building," she said.

"And the other building?" I asked.

"No single people live in that building."

"That's the one I want." Little did I know that God would soon get my full attention in the coming weeks, as all distractions were removed from my life as I lived alone in that little, quiet apartment.

Not too long after that, when I was alone in my new apartment, I kneeled on the gray carpeting and prayed, "God, if You are real, will You show Yourself to me? Will You show me who You are in a way that I can understand?" I was ready to end praying when I added, "and please, show me who Jesus is."

If you are reading this and feel prompted to do the same, then stop reading this book and pray now. If you aren't convinced, read the next paragraph and then stop and pray. God will honor your sincerity to know the one true God, even at this point if you don't know what Jesus has to do with you personally. By all means, come back and keep reading, as I am praying you will find out as I did Who Jesus is and what He has to do with you personally!

(Just a side note—As I am typing this from New York City, I had the privilege of worshiping last Sunday at the Brooklyn Tabernacle Church. Pastor Jim Cymbala gave his testimony in his sermon. He was once a young husband and father who had worldly success as a former basketball player yet was unhappy; he prayed the *exact words* I prayed to God.)

I continued to mingle with my new Christian girlfriends and their Christian guy friends. I soon became friends with Kevin Taylor, who was one of the guitar players who had a very outgoing personality. I appreciated his friendship in the group because he was my only guy friend. Kevin used to say he wanted God to send him a WOG. A WOG was a "woman of God." He later found his

WOG when he met Kelly, a lovely young journalist who had just given her life to Christ.

I went with my new Christian friends on a ski trip to Snowshoe, West Virginia. I remember on the long car ride, they would talk about "the Lord this" and "the Lord that." I wasn't used to this, and it was hard for me. They spoke of Jesus as if He was a close friend, intimately involved in their lives and decisions.

I also remember the music we listened to spoke of His love. I couldn't understand that. I thought the best love to attain was romantic love, but what was this love of Christ? Were these people all confused about love? Didn't they know that having someone to love you on earth was the highest love to attain? (Or so I thought at that time.) What I didn't know was that Kaye, Florence, Nancy, and the others were all praying for me to give my life to Christ.

I found out that Providence was going to have a Christian marriage seminar in March, led by Dr. Gary Chapman. David Horner had met Dr. Chapman when David was in college at Wake Forest University. In fact, Dr. Chapman had married David and Cathy. Dr. Chapman was a minister, counselor, and writer from Winston-Salem, North Carolina, and the author of numerous books including (some years later) his best-selling book, *The Five Love Languages.* He was also the author of the book David had given me that had gone back and forth across his desk. Even though I hadn't read the book, I decided that I should go to the seminar. After all, I had never tried Christian counseling.

The seminar was entitled, "Toward a Growing Marriage." (I highly recommend this seminar by Gary Chapman; he also has a book by the same title.)[59] It was held on a Friday night and all day Saturday. As I gazed around the room and noticed that everyone was either married or engaged, I began to feel sorry for myself. The only people alone there were the teacher and me! (Earlier today, just before I sat to work on this manuscript, I heard an ad on the Christian radio program *Family Life Today* for their "Weekend to Remember" marriage conference, a similar conference which is helping countless couples. The announcer chuckled, saying, "When you register for our 'Weekend to Remember' marriage conference, it is best to bring your spouse with you." I suppose he chuckled thinking, *"Who wouldn't do that?"* I couldn't help but break into a smile: if only he knew.)

Fortunately, I was able to sit beside familiar and friendly faces. The different modules that Gary taught were entitled:

"If My Wife Would Just Shape Up"

"I Don't Love Her Anymore"

"Communicating In Marriage"

"Who Is Going To Clean The Commode?"

"He Thinks He's Always Right"

"All He Thinks About Is Sex"

"If Only You Knew My Mother-In-Law"

"My Wife Thinks Money Grow On Trees"

I had never heard anything like this before! Gary said he had two aims in the next two days: to be biblical and to be practical.

Well, he had one more. To have fun. *It was fun!* The audience would laugh as he would give true examples of struggles in marriage and in our human nature as sinners. I remember he told a story about how his wife didn't close the kitchen drawers, and it bothered him tremendously. He even tried explaining to her how the mechanism containing a spring that allowed the drawer to roll back worked, so all his wife had to do was simply slide the drawer back after opening it. But she still didn't shut the drawers, even after her physics lesson.

He said that some things in a marriage can improve but some things just won't change, and we need to learn to live peacefully together in spite of it. We could all relate to everything he was saying. This biblical teaching on marriage all made so much sense! I didn't leave before buying a complete set of tapes of the seminar. I was beginning to get the inkling that a good marriage was not something you found, but something you made. It was not so much about finding the right person, it was about being the right person.

> A good marriage is not something you find, but something you make.

At the seminar, I also learned practical ways to communicate love to my spouse and valuable tips to breaking unhealthy patterns. I learned we each had our own primary love language: words of affirmation, quality time, receiving gifts, acts of service, or physical touch.

In the months ahead, I listened to those marriage tapes a *gajillion* times! I knew the modules so well that I practically memorized every story Gary Chapman had told, along with the biblical principle and scripture that went with it. I could have taught the class—there was only one problem: I didn't even live with my husband, nor did I want to! Little did I know that God was softening my heart as He was pouring Truth into my life.

Not only was Gary pointing us to scripture for life's answers, he was giving us practical examples and tools to help. As he was teaching, I began to envision a person beside me, someone who would want to live this Christian marriage of love and forgiveness that would be centered in Christ's love for us. But as I imagined a person in my mind, I couldn't see a face. I wondered if God would ever give me an opportunity to start again and do it right this time. Only there were a couple of big obstacles: I had not given my life to Christ yet, and I had no idea if God would allow me to meet someone who would desire to have a Christian marriage, too.

CHAPTER NINE

A TURNING POINT

ON MAY 5, 1985, SIX months after leaving my husband and five months after wrestling with God, I yielded my life to Jesus. Alone in my apartment, I prayed, "God, I'm tired of trying to run my life. Please take control. I yield my life to You, God. I don't know what Jesus has to do with my life, but show me who He is."

Several months later I read *Loving God* by Chuck Colson. In it, I discovered that Colson had a similar experience. He committed his life to God without knowledge of Jesus's essential part and what He endured for us. It was on a separate occasion that Colson realized his need to accept Christ. This encouraged my heart. As with Colson, on May 5, 1985, I had no idea what Christ had to do with me personally.

As I humbled myself alone in my apartment to God, I sensed that God was taking control of my life. I knew this because it was no less than a miracle that I had asked Him in, because for so many months it just seemed impossible for me to do it. But God had His hand on me, and I had done it! Immediately, the little bit of faith I had was strengthened. I had taken a baby step toward

God. Listen to the words of Jesus found in Matthew 13:31–32: "The kingdom of heaven is like a mustard seed, which a man took and planted in his field. Though it is the smallest of all seeds, yet when it grows, it is the largest of garden plants and becomes a tree, so that the birds come and perch in its branches." God will honor whatever little measure of faith we begin with in His kingdom!

Florence Hassell, the acquaintance from Meredith whom I had run into at the Providence singles meeting, had by now become a close friend. She had given me a beautiful, lavender, hard-back journal and on that night I wrote in it for the first time. It was the first of many journals that I would fill up with prayers and reflections of what was going on in my life at the time. Sadly, as I began writing this manuscript, I discovered I had lost that first journal.

I remember that my first entry on May 5, 1985 was a prayer I had written to God. I told Him I wanted to be a soldier for Him, and I asked Him to give me the strength to follow Him. The only Bible I had in Raleigh was a King James Version that we were presented upon graduation from Meredith College. I discovered that many people were now using a much easier to read version, the New International Version, so I went to the Christian bookstore and bought my own burgundy leather NIV Bible.

David Horner preached using the New American Standard Version. It was easy to see that many people were taking notes as he preached; I had never seen anyone do that before. I also had never seen anyone write in Bibles before. I began to do the same. When something special leaped off the page as I read the Bible, I would underline and date it. Now I was so eager to read

my Bible that I came home from work and read it like a novel! I
realized for the first time that everything in it was true! All of
those six-syllable Bible names that you couldn't pronounce were
real people who really lived! Each battle and war and city name
was like reading my own personal history for the first time, for
this was the history of mankind.

A few months later I also bought an inexpensive NASV Bible,
since that was what David used from the pulpit. It was nice having
one Bible that I didn't write in, so I could read a passage in a fresh
way without having to be distracted by what I might have written
at one time about that verse.

About this time, I started attending small group meetings
called "flock," held in a church family's home and comprised
of people who attended Providence. It was there that I noticed
an attractive woman with soft, shiny, gray hair wearing a royal
blue coat; her name was Bert. We became fast friends. She had
suffered a great trial some years before: her husband had shocked
her by walking away from their marriage. She was a committed
Christian, and she became a dear friend.

It was a busy time for me because I was rehearsing every night
after work and on weekends with Raleigh Little Theatre. I was
selected to be a singer and dancer in the secular drama, "Student
Prince." As I've mentioned, I had been in a theatre production
in my senior year in college and enjoyed it, and I sang at King's
Dominion entertainment park for a summer job before college.
I was one of three girls representing the Andrews Sisters singing
with a 1940s band, "The Kings of Swing." (To this day I do not
know how I got that job.)

That was where I got the theatre bug, and now that I had time to explore theatre again, I auditioned for "Student Prince." We had rehearsals every night for four or five weeks. Right in the middle of all that, I committed my life to God. Fortunately, it was a wholesome show! I started bringing my Bible to rehearsals because when we were idle, I wanted to read it. I remember several of us would be waiting in costume backstage for long periods of time, and no one had anything to do. I got to read love letters to me from the Creator of the universe as I read my Bible backstage! I had this strange sense that I was being given a chance to start my life all over again.

The day after I made a commitment of my life to God, I wanted to share the news with Terry. I hadn't seen him in a long time, so I decided to make him a fresh strawberry pie and take it to him and tell him the great news. I must have thought the news would go down a little easier with something sweet to eat.

I pulled up to our house on a beautiful sunny day and immediately saw Terry working outside. We converged on the front steps of our house, and I handed him the pie.

"I made a strawberry pie for you." He didn't seem overly excited to see me, to say the least, and he might even have been leery of the pie. Not that he really thought I might poison him; I think he was reserved because he was wondering what I was actually doing there.

"Thanks," was all he said.

"I wanted to come by to tell you that I committed my life to God," I blurted out, wanting to get right to the point of why I came to see him. I was hoping he would be happy for me, but he didn't seem too enthusiastic.

He nodded, didn't give much of a response, and acted as if I had just said, "So, did I catch you cutting the grass?" You see, he had seen me go on many tangents before that had never lasted long, and he had no reason to think that this was any different.

When we married, I had gone on one of my tangents looking for satisfaction by purchasing a microphone. This was not some kiddy microphone. I went to Radio Shack and purchased an expensive microphone, and a mixing board as well. When Terry would come home from work, there I would be, singing rock songs into the microphone.

Once when I was working for Xerox, I met a young lady in an elevator. I had on a sharp blue suit and was carrying my briefcase. She asked me what I did, and I told her I was a national account manager with Xerox. She said, "Wow, you must have always wanted a great career!" The elevator doors opened, and I just had time to answer her as I stepped out. I yelled out, "No, actually, I've always wanted to be in a rock'n'roll band!" I'm sure she was shocked.

The sad thing was, I was serious! I actually auditioned once with a rock band after seeing their ad for a female vocalist. Needless to say, they never called me back. (I had a perm in my hair at the time, and if I let it air-dry, it had a frizzy look that I thought would have been perfect for the band. Thank heavens I didn't get my wish!)

About the same time, I also wrote MTV and sent them my resume. How I thought a sales career with Xerox was a stepping stone for MTV, I will never know. I had watched the hosts talk on MTV and I thought, *I can do that.* Strangely, months later, I received the original envelope I had sent them, with my resume intact, marked "return to sender." Seems I had written the incorrect New York address for MTV, and as I held the returned envelope in my hand I remember cringing as I contemplated, *What was I thinking?* In a word, I was LOST! I had absolutely no foundation in my life. I was like a loose cannon. Poor Terry, he had no idea what he was getting when he married me!

I love the adage that Elisabeth Elliot's friend told her regarding marriage. She said, "None of us are prize packages, so just look for the essentials and skip all the rest!" Terry had to take a huge "skip all the rest" with me, for I was a surprise package of the worst kind! What Terry and I did not know is that we were bringing baggage into our marriage, just like everyone else does.

Ᏻ

"Macon, if our relationship were just from us, we would date for several more months before I asked you to marry me," the blond-haired young attorney said as he looked into the dark brown eyes of his friend from law school. "But I really believe this is what God would have me do. Will you marry me?"

Technically, they hadn't even dated one another when Paul proposed! They had been in mutual friends' weddings and once played tennis together. Paul would stop by the library to chat occasionally with a very tired Macon, as she would fall asleep reading her Bible and her stack of law books. The week before, they had gone to a Christmas Eve service. And now he was asking her to marry him!

It was New Year's Day, 1983, and Paul and Macon had agreed to get together to pray for God's will for Macon, as she was waiting to hear about working for the Billy Graham Evangelistic Association. Macon told Paul her goals, and Paul responded that he had the very same goals in life. As they both were on their knees in a posture to pray for God's will, Paul asked Macon to marry him.

Unbeknownst to Macon, Paul had recently asked God to give him God's thoughts toward Macon, because she looked and acted nothing like the blonde, bubbly girls he typically dated. Sometime after that prayer he began to see Macon with new eyes and found he had a desire to be with her. He knew immediately as they were about to pray for God's will in Macon's life that it was God's will for him to ask her to marry him, despite having had a date with a different girl the night before.

Unbeknownst to Paul, Macon had only the day before been praying about her life and her future. She yearned for a godly man like her friend Paul Newby, especially after receiving a note from him that revealed his heart for the Lord. However, she was willing to do whatever God wanted, even if that meant she was to be single. She knew that God was in control of her life. As she prayed, she was filled with a supernatural joy and peace. God had spoken to her heart, saying, *"Trust Me, I will show you My will."* When Paul proposed the next day, Macon knew that God had revealed His will.

After their engagement, Paul told Macon that she would have to start rising a little later in order for him to be the spiritual leader of their home. Macon had the daily habit of rising each morning at 5:30 a.m. to meet with the Lord. Paul was going to have to get up at 5:00 a.m. to beat her! Less than four months later, they were married. They have now been married for over thirty years and have raised four children to follow the Lord.

While the Newbys were starting out their Christian marriage based on biblical principles in western North Carolina, I was living in Raleigh. Terry and I had just celebrated our second wedding anniversary, and I was right in the midst of the sporadic "Saturday morning crying sessions" part of my life that were characteristic of the emptiness I felt at that time.

I had never met nor heard of the Newbys, nor did I know anything of the biblical way of life they led—a life based on a personal relationship with the living Christ, a relationship that provided daily, practical guidance, and could produce joy in spite of circumstances. More importantly, I had not personally met their Savior.

◈

Two years later, the Newbys were enjoying their second wedding anniversary, and I had left Terry seven months earlier. I had just yielded my life to God on May 5, 1985. Little did I know that God, through the Newbys, was about to provide a way for me to see something I had never seen before: a living and breathing example of a Christian marriage and home.

Three weeks after that May night when I yielded my life to God, I had gone out for pizza with a few of my friends from the singles group. Skeptics of the faith might call it "chance," but I know it was the merciful, loving, faithful hand of God that arranged for Paul and Macon to be eating at the very same restaurant. They had recently moved to Raleigh, relocating from the western part of the state. Someone in our group knew them and introduced them to me. They found out that I was new to the faith and that I was separated from my husband. That was all they needed to know to galvanize them into loving action of which I was to be the benefactor.

My path had crossed with Paul and Macon's path, and they soon became my spiritual mentors, dramatically influencing me for Christ. They singled me out and began to take me under their wing. Paul and Macon then faithfully discipled me for one and one-half years. This was before they had children, and I had them all to myself. Macon held a law degree, but had chosen not to practice.

In 1985, when I met Paul and Macon, Paul had just been appointed Assistant United States Attorney for the Eastern District of North Carolina, a position he was to hold for nearly twenty years. Paul was later elected Associate Justice for the Supreme Court of North Carolina, in 2004. That's who God sent to teach me the ways of God! For several years, I sent them a note every November 1—All Saint's Day—to thank them for their gift of sharing their faith and their lives with me. Hebrews 13:7 reminds us to "remember your leaders, who spoke the word of God to you. Consider the outcome of their way of life and imitate their faith." To me, Paul and Macon are Christian heroes I will never forget!

They had me over to dinner regularly. They lovingly confronted me about my marriage, and gently told me that God was in favor of my marriage being restored. They were deeply committed Christians and they demonstrated Christ's love for me by their genuine love and concern for me. We had many meals together, conversations together, and lots of discussion of the scriptures. They shared their life with me.

Paul and Macon also taught me to memorize scripture. The first passage they had me study was Romans chapter six. To this day, it is still embedded in my memory. The first seven verses begin (and I promise I'm not peeking), "What shall we say, then? Shall we go on sinning so that grace may increase? By no means! We died to sin; how can we live in it any longer? Or don't you know that all of us who were baptized into Christ Jesus were baptized into his death? We were therefore buried with him through baptism unto death in order that, just as Christ was raised from the dead through the glory of the Father, we too may live a new life!" The passage goes on to say in verse eighteen, "You have been set free from sin and have become slaves to righteousness."

They encouraged me to meditate on this passage and commit it to memory. They reminded me that now that I had a new life in Christ, I was dead to sin and the power that it held on me, and that I was free in Christ to pursue righteousness. When I would get upset about something Terry said to me, they would remind me that a dead person doesn't have any rights!

I remember one distinct occasion when I was with Paul and Macon. They had me over for a meal at the house of Macon's sister, Sarah. Sarah was the woman who had led the Bible Study Fellowship class that I had been in three years earlier. After Macon served us a great summer supper of fresh vegetables, we moved into the den to relax.

As we were talking that night, I began to ask them about dating. I had not dated at all except in those first few weeks after I had separated from Terry, because once I started going to Providence, I met socially with the whole group. They said, "Juana, don't you think that any Christian man who was a solid Christian would want your marriage to be healed?" I hadn't thought about that before. But there was just one problem: I didn't want the marriage to be healed.

> I had the notion that God couldn't want me,
> because I was separated.

God hadn't forgotten my sincere prayer to know who Jesus was, but I also added a new prayer about this time. I began to pray, *Lord, could it be possible that You want our marriage to continue? Could it be that You want us to have a truly Christian marriage? But Lord, how could this be? I don't understand.* I remember that I wrote that prayer down in my lavender journal. How could this be? I now felt like Terry was only my brother, and I hadn't even seen him in a few months. Surely God didn't want me to be married to someone whom I had no desire to be with and who seemed more like a brother.

I had totally convinced myself that the marriage was a mistake, and that I did not want to be married to him. In fact, when someone told me that Terry was dating someone else, it didn't even bother me. It was like hearing that a good friend from college was dating someone. A friend said, "You even know the person he is dating." I said, "Don't tell me. I don't need to know that." So I really knew very little about what Terry was even doing.

Someone recently asked me why I did not seem to care at all about Terry. I think I shut myself down emotionally toward him, enabling me to compartmentalize my life. By not allowing myself to examine how I truly felt about Terry seeing other people, I could live in an unrealistic "bubble mentality," thus helping me justify my wrongdoing of leaving my husband. I was like the determined Scarlet O'Hara in the turmoil of the Civil War in *Gone With the Wind*, who said "Tomorrow I'll think . . . tomorrow is another day."

I remember, too, when our first anniversary passed, after I had separated from Terry: it felt strange. But as I began to write in my journal asking God to lead me, it was as if He was guiding me to line up my will with His will. He was leading me to choose to be married to Terry because He was teaching me to trust Him. I didn't know how He was going to do this. A favorite verse at that time became food to my soul: "Delight yourself in the Lord, and he will give you the desires of your heart. Commit your way to the Lord; trust in him, and he will act."[60]

Please understand one thing: I continued to enjoy my relationship with the Lord and fully believed His promise that He would give me the desires of my heart, but I could not understand *how* He was going to accomplish it. Oh, but how His gentle reminder came from His Word! "Trust in the Lord with all your heart and lean *not on your own understanding*; in all your ways acknowledge him, and he will make your paths straight"[61] (italics mine—JM). It was none of my business how He chose to accomplish His results in my life. It was my job to trust. It was His job to work and accomplish the results.

I had a trip scheduled that June with Xerox to San Francisco. It gave me a chance to visit my college roommate, Andrea, who was living outside San Francisco at the time. I asked my mother if she would like to fly out to San Francisco from Richmond and meet me there, and I would extend my trip and take a vacation with her.

She decided to go. We had a great time together, relaxing and touring in San Francisco. As I sat in my hotel room, I wanted to write Terry. So I sent him a postcard from San Francisco telling him that I was there with Mama, but that I was thinking of him.

What I didn't know is that when Terry received that postcard, he had just been thinking, "Here I am dating someone new and things are finally going well in my life again. Now what would I do if Juana suddenly contacted me and wanted to get back together?" The next day, my postcard arrived, and when he read it, he became angry. He later told me that he had thought, "Does Juana think she can just walk right back into my life like this, especially when I have finally found a measure of happiness again?"

I left the day before Mama's flight and arranged for friends to take Mama to the airport, because I had committed to my friend and coworker, Charlie, that I would fly to Boston to attend his wedding. Charlie was marrying an attractive, young Jewish woman; he converted to Judaism just before the wedding.

A couple of months before, I had shared with him that I was struggling with what to do about committing my life to God. Charlie commented that he thought all religions were the same and that it really didn't matter which one you chose. You would think that his comment would have dampened my ardor in seeking God and finding who Christ was, but it did quite the opposite. Somehow in my heart, perhaps because I was already surrounded by the Truth of God's Word at Providence, I knew that Christianity's claims were unique.

For the first time in my life, I was studying the evidence for myself. The Jews said Jesus *was not* the Messiah. The Christians said Jesus *was* the Messiah. They both could not be right, because they contradicted one another. Buddha claimed no faith or belief in God. Hinduism said there were millions of gods. Mohammed said there was no god but Allah. Christians believed God was three personalities in one God (God the Father, the Son, and the Holy Spirit). Now surely any open-minded person who studied it could see that these very different beliefs could not in any way be considered the same, as my friend Charlie had commented. They could not all be right. They could all be wrong, but they could not all be right, because they were entirely contradictory.

Taken a step further, you could take Buddha out of Buddhism and you would still have the teachings of Buddha. You could take Mohammed out of the Moslem religion and you would still have the Koran. But if you took Jesus out of Christianity, Christianity would no longer exist. Jesus said that *He was the Truth*; He claimed to be the Son of God, a God-man!

And what about the resurrection? Jesus was the only one who said He would rise from the dead: that is, come back alive on earth after He was dead and buried (and the Bible gives accounts that Jesus was seen by over five hundred witnesses after His death). Buddha and Mohammed are buried in a grave just like I will be someday, but Jesus's body to this day has not

been found in a grave.[62] I think C.S. Lewis said it best in his
book *Mere Christianity*:

> "A man who was merely a man and said the sorts of
> things Jesus said would not be a great moral teacher.
> He would either be a lunatic—on a level with the man
> who says he is a poached egg—or else he would be the
> Devil of Hell. You must make your choice. Either this
> man was, and is, the Son of God: or else a madman or
> something worse. You can shut Him up for a fool, you
> can spit at Him and kill Him as a demon; or you can fall
> at His feet and call Him Lord and God. But let us not
> come with any patronizing nonsense about His being a
> great human teacher. He has not left that open to us. He
> did not intend to."[63]

Weeks turned into months, and I still wrestled spiritually with
what Christ had to do with me. I could not see the connection
with what He had to do with my life.

PART TWO
THE NEW LIFE

Man's part is to trust, God's part is to work.

—HANNAH WHITALL SMITH

CHAPTER TEN

FIREWORKS

JULY 4, 1985. WHEN I awoke that morning, I had no idea that God was about to set my anxious, wandering heart free. I had spent that evening with Beth (not her real name), the friend whom I stayed with when I first left the note for Terry. She had some other friends who were going to join us that night to go to the fairgrounds to watch the fireworks. Suddenly, the conversation turned to Terry. Beth asked, "Well, do you know who Terry is dating?"

Before I could jump in to tell her not to tell me, because I absolutely did not want to know, she blurted out her name. At that exact moment, Beth's friends arrived. They came in and Beth began introducing me, but I could hardly concentrate. I wanted to leave right away. I made an excuse that I really didn't want to go see the fireworks, and I drove immediately back to my apartment.

Once I got inside, my mind continued to race. I could not get Terry off my mind. All this time, whenever I had pictured Terry dating, I had kept my thoughts about him at arm's length. I didn't want to picture him with another woman. Somehow it falsely kept the reality of my actions and their consequences at a safe distance, emotionally. But when Beth blurted out the name of an acquaintance of ours, I could no longer keep it impersonal as I had been doing. I became extremely anxious and wanted to talk to Terry immediately. I hadn't spoken to him in weeks, but I dialed his number.

As far as I can recall, I had not called Terry during our entire separation, except when I committed my life to God in May, 1985 (when I took him the strawberry pie to tell him) and on this Fourth of July. I also did not gossip to anyone about Terry. I recommend that if you are separated from your spouse that you be very careful whom you talk to about them: perhaps only one trusted Christian friend, as I did with the Newbys.

The Bible exhorts us to "avoid godless chatter, because those who indulge in it will become more and more ungodly" (2 Timothy 2:16). A good reply when someone tries to get you to gossip about anyone is, "I don't think that's something that I need to know anything about." If they persist, you may have to walk away in order to be faithful in your desire to grow in godliness through fulfilling the 2 Timothy 2:16 exhortation.

Terry answered the phone; I was relieved to reach him and hear his voice, yet filled with anxiety over the turn of events in the last hour. I told him that I wanted to talk with him. He said he couldn't speak with me just then because he had company; he said he would call me later. I hung up the phone, and for the first time since I had written that note nearly nine months before, telling him I was leaving him, I thought, *What have I done? Why have I tried to convince myself for so long that I don't care about Terry?*

I felt so lonely for Terry. I so wanted to hear his voice again, but it was impossible tonight. He probably had a date with her when I had called him! I began to realize the full consequences of my actions of leaving my husband. I felt so hopeless. With tears streaming down my face, I cried out to God! Was there any hope? What was God going to say to me now?

Loneliness is a wilderness,
but it can become a pathway to God.

"Turn your loneliness into solitude, and your solitude into prayer. . . . Loneliness is a wilderness, but through receiving it as a gift, accepting it from the hand of God, and offering it back to Him with thanksgiving, it may become a pathway to holiness, to glory, and to God Himself."[64]

Then, I suddenly remembered that book that David Horner had tried so hard to give me. I had put it up on a high shelf above the washer and dryer in my apartment. Several months before I had wanted nothing to do with that book. Now, I was eagerly looking for it. The title spoke right to my heart: *Hope for the Separated*. I don't think I even noticed before that it was written by Gary Chapman.

I sat on the pastel comforter on my twin bed, and with the bedside floor lamp over my shoulder, I began to read every word. It was as if God was leading me moment by moment. I had been praying for God to show me who Jesus was. As I read, I became totally convicted that I was a sinner. I realized what Christ had done: He was broken, crushed, poured out. His beautiful hands were pierced by nails . . . for me. If I were the only person in the world, He would have suffered and died His grueling death for me.

I realized that I needed God to save me personally. I knelt beside my bed, and with tears I asked God to forgive me for leaving my husband whom I had vowed to love. Then I asked God to forgive me for every wrong attitude and action that came to my mind.

I thanked Jesus for dying on the cross for my sin and shame, and I asked Him to come into my life and be my Lord and Savior. His cleansing forgiveness was immediate and complete, and I knew it! Suddenly, the song "Amazing Grace" came to my mind. I had sung that song in church as a child and had always wondered who the wretch was. Suddenly, I knew that *I was the wretch!* The hymn had been another repeating chime to me, but now its words held so much meaning.

> *Amazing Grace, how sweet the sound*
> *That saved a wretch like me!*
> *I once was lost, but now am found,*
> *Was blind, but now I see.*[65]

It was as if scales fell off my eyes in an instant! I felt as if I had been locked in a prison, and Christ held the key. When He came in and opened the door, He set my wandering, anxious, slave-to-sin heart free! I was beginning God's free life!

I had been freed! I had discovered the way God meant for me to live, liberated from "bondage . . . and brought into the freedom and glory of the children of God!"[66]

Oswald Chambers said, "The Spirit of God is always the spirit of liberty; the spirit that is not of God is the spirit of bondage, the spirit of oppression and depression. He is always the Spirit of liberty. God Who made the birds never made bird-cages."

In the distance, I could hear something. Fireworks! I could hear fireworks bursting in the distance. I had begun the first hour of my new life in Christ with fireworks!

I was amazed when I later learned where the American tradition of fireworks originated. Anne Hibbard writes in her book, *Family Celebrations*: "In England, fireworks were entertainment enjoyed only by the nobility. In America, fireworks were displayed for all to see on the anniversary of our country's independence. This was a way of celebrating the importance of every individual person in our country. Ours was to be the land of opportunity, for everyone, no matter what his rank or birth."

Likewise, in Galatians 3:38 we read, "There is neither Jew nor Greek, slave nor free, male nor female, for you are all one in Christ Jesus." He came for everyone! Christ extends salvation to all people who will put their trust in Him, and we find freedom from the guilt and power of sin! How perfect that God celebrated my new found life in Christ with me with fireworks!

The book, *Hope for the Separated*, had guided me step by step in what to do. Based on biblical principles, the author suggested making a list of the areas where you sinned against your spouse, and to give him that list. I did exactly that, and God showed me seventeen areas where I had sinned against Terry. Before the scales fell off, I could not see myself as I really was: a sinner. Before that moment in time,

I had unconsciously let myself justify all my sins and instead blame Terry for everything, always thinking: *"If Terry* would just . . . ; *if Terry* would just . . . ; *if Terry . . ."* But now, it was as if someone had opened a floodgate, and a host of sins came to my mind.

> *You were taught, with regard to your former way of life, to put off your old self, which is being corrupted by its deceitful desires; to be made new in the attitude of your minds; and to put on the new self, created to be like God in true righteousness and holiness.*[67]

Here are some of the sins on my list:

- I sinned against Terry when I left him, after vowing to be faithful to him.
- I was more concerned about being loved than being loving.
- I was more concerned about being understood than trying to understand.
- I was more concerned about being heard instead of trying to listen.

I gained other concrete, practical help through the late hours of that night. Like Gary's wise advice that said, "If you are not free to marry, you are not free to date." I stayed up nearly all night, reading, praying, crying, and rejoicing. I kept thinking how I wanted to offer up my marriage to Christ, and I wanted to put it tangibly on a cross.

I didn't have a cross, so I wanted to make a cross, but I could not think how I would be able to make one, since I didn't have any wood. Then I thought of a clothespin. I took a clothespin apart, and turned the two sticks so they were perpendicular to one another. I attached a rubber band to stabilize the sticks in the position of a cross. I got a red marker and wrote on the cross the words, "My Marriage."

I was giving Jesus the permission to do with my marriage what He thought was best, surrendering to Him what now meant most to me. Ironically, it was the very thing that I had valued least in recent months, yet now it was of great worth! It was as if I had sold a priceless pearl at a yard sale for nearly nothing, as if it were mere paste—and now I had discovered it was a priceless pearl that was to be treasured and kept safe. I had behaved like Esau, who had sold his birthright for a mere pot of lentil stew![68]

> If you're not free to marry, you're not free to date.

Mercifully, God had strengthened my faith again, and had instantaneously transferred to me what mattered to Him. Best of all, He had shown me who Jesus was, and I was beginning a personal relationship with Him.

A few days later, I copied every word from our wedding vows off of an audio tape from our wedding. Other than the day we uttered the words at the altar, I had never even seen them in print form.

Augustine, the famous early church father from the fourth century said, "Oh Lord, Thou hast made us for Thyself, and our hearts are restless until they find their rest in Thee." I had been the most anxious person I knew, and now I had rest for my weary soul! I had met the living Christ! I had tried to fill the empty void inside of me with tangents, and when that didn't work, I thought it was my husband's fault that he didn't meet my needs. Where did I ever get the idea that any person could ever meet all of another person's needs? Only God can do that!

Pascal, the French philosopher and mathematician, said, "There is a God-shaped vacuum in every heart." That vacuum cannot be satisfied with any created thing. Now I knew for myself what the problem was in me and with humanity. I had been separated from God, alienated from Him by my sin. I had known there was something wrong, I just didn't know until that Fourth of July night what it was. God was not suggesting that I could improve my behavior or do better, but that He had sent Jesus on my behalf to reconcile me to God. He did it for *all people* of every race and nation!

God became a man, and walked the earth; He was real—fully God and fully man. He became hungry, tired, sad, angry; yet He never sinned. Jesus was the only one qualified to be our mediator, thereby taking the punishment that we deserve. Many ask how Jesus can be the only way? Thank goodness, we need only one way! We don't need any more saviors. One personality did it for all humanity.

A dramatic event in recent history powerfully symbolizes God's effort to rescue mankind. In the fall of 2010, thirty-three Chilean miners were trapped underground for sixty-nine days, and the whole world breathlessly watched the desperate rescue efforts, which were broadcast live on international television. The trapped miners could do nothing to save themselves—a way had to be provided for them. The miners didn't need ten ways—they didn't even need two ways: they needed *one* way. They did not think it arrogant of the driller to provide only one way of escape; they cast all their hope on *the* rescue effort. And then they had to actually get in the capsule that was lowered down to them.

There were not five paths that all led to the same surface; there was one and only one way for the miners to be saved. Thirty-three men could not in their own strength and intelligence make a way of escape, nor can the whole of humanity save itself from eternal death. We must put our faith in Jesus Christ. God reached down to us and provided one way of salvation, because we only needed one way.

Just as sin entered through one man, the first man, so it left through one man, that is Christ. Just listen to what the apostle Paul says: "Just as the result of one trespass was condemnation for all men, so also the result of one act of righteousness was justification that brings life for all men. For just as through the disobedience of the one man the many were made sinners, so also through the obedience of the one man the many will be made righteous."[69] Only Jesus addressed and fixed the real problem with humanity: our sinful nature.

I was totally humbled by God's complete act of grace. I had nothing to offer Him. I had not one thing I could boast about. I had always defaulted to giving myself credit for any accomplishments I had attained, but I could not take credit for this. God did it for me. Not because I earned it as a reward; no, His forgiveness was a gift. All I could do with the gift was to *receive* it. I had nothing to be arrogant about. I was helpless and hopeless in my state of sin. What had I to be arrogant about? As someone has so rightly put it, "Christianity is one beggar telling another beggar where to find bread." Taste and see![70]

CHAPTER ELEVEN

MARRIAGE OVER

"TERRY, ALL THIS TIME I'VE been thinking that you were the problem in our marriage, and that if you would just change, it would be so much better. I now realize that I have been wrong, and that I need to change. Becoming a Christian has helped me to see that. What I'm trying to say is, I would love to have a second chance with you to be your wife again." I had not minced words and had gotten right to the point. Terry just stared straight at me with an unemotional, neutral expression.

Terry had come over to talk at my request, after he returned my call the day after my Fourth of July conversion. He sat down on my new, cream-colored sofa that I had purchased for my single life, and I sat opposite him in the matching oversized chair. After listening to what I had just said, he paused, then spoke.

"So you think you can just walk right back into my life like nothing has happened and be my wife again?" Terry asked, seeming now a little agitated.

"Well, I have put together a list of seventeen areas where I have been wrong, and I am asking for your forgiveness," I said, handing him the list.

"Thank you for that," he said matter-of-factly, folding the one-page white sheet into multiple folds and placing it in his pants pocket without reading it. "Look, I've been doing a lot of soul-searching, and I want you to know, Juana, that I have a made a decision. I no longer want to be married to you."

Now it was my turn to stare straight back at Terry with all the attentiveness I owned, taking in what he was saying to me.

"It's over," he added resolutely, leaving no doubt in my mind where he stood.

I uncharacteristically sat quietly, waiting to see if he had anything else to say. Without my knowing, God had helped and strengthened me in my immediate time of need. The night before He had saved me from my sin, and now He was rescuing me from the *power* that sin had held on me, by preventing me from getting in the last word; which to me (and my tongue), was every bit as big as the parting of the Red Sea. He had also held back the waters—my tears, if you will—as He had held back the Red Sea. He had allowed me to show restraint. The Psalmist tells us in Psalm 46:1 that the Lord is "an ever-present help in trouble," and I can testify as living proof of that!

Terry broke the silence.

"How can you sit there and be so calm?" He was waiting for the old Juana to fall apart, retaliate, nag, cry, or complain, but the new Juana was slowly emerging from the cocoon that had opened the night before when I had prayed to receive Christ.

"Terry, I gave my life to Christ and now He's in control of it. Whatever I have to face, I know I will be okay," I replied calmly.

Then he left. I didn't beg him to choose me. I didn't chase him out the door crying or screaming. I let him go.

When the door shut and I was alone, though, I totally fell apart. I was filled with remorse for tearing down my own home, and sadness for what we could have had. It was like having to give back a present that I had never even opened. The floodgate of tears opened, and now the rush of the Red Sea over the Egyptians was released!

There is a time for everything . . .

> *a time to tear down and a time to build,*
> *a time to weep and a time to laugh,*
> *a time to mourn and a time to dance . . .*
>
> *a time to embrace and a time to refrain . . .*
>
> *a time to be silent and a time to speak.*[71]

God had allowed me to have the grace to be calm when Terry was speaking to me, but now that he was gone, I threw myself on my bed and sobbed and cried out to God. A verse from Proverbs (unknown to me at the time) best describes my state of mind: "The wise woman builds her house up, but with her own hands the foolish one tears hers down."[72]

In the weeks that followed, my life's circumstances continued to be in turmoil, yet I had perfect peace. The uncertainty in my life catapulted me into complete dependence upon Christ. The suffering I experienced was so intense during this time, but in the midst of it Christ was real to me like the calm in the middle of the storm. Having perfect peace in the midst of undesirable circumstances is attainable through His abiding presence.

I experienced loving comfort from the living God, who promises that those who mourn in sorrow over their sin shall be comforted. I had come to realize that only Jesus could give me joy—not Terry, not Xerox, not a new man in my life.

I desperately wanted to be Terry's wife again, but I had complete peace that even if Terry never allowed me back into his life, that I would be *more than* okay. I learned later that this is what the Bible describes as being "more than conquerors":

> For I am convinced that neither death nor life, neither angels
> nor demons, neither the present nor the future, nor any powers,
> neither height nor depth, nor anything else in all creation, [nor
> a spouse rejecting you, nor divorce, nor a broken family, nor
> anything else means ANYTHING ELSE!–JM] will be able to
> separate us from the love of God that is in Christ Jesus our Lord.[73]

I was sorry that it had taken months of being separated and experiencing a failed marriage, but I was so glad that God saw fit to call me to Himself. And if it took the pain of the marriage break-up to do it, I would have done it all again. I can only tell you that I was able to truly live in His presence and trust in His promises. That was more than enough! My heart continued to be uplifted daily. My hope was right where it should have been all along—in Christ Jesus.

❧

As a new Christian, I started looking at the world with fresh eyes. I was no longer in charge. I was in love with Jesus and I wanted everything I did to please Him. As a new Christian, I made opportunities to share Christ with old friends and new, and even on the witness stand in a courtroom.

When I was in college, I took the beginner's golf class, and during summer break after my sophomore year, I asked if I could take a set of the college's clubs home to practice for the summer. Those clubs traveled from Raleigh to Richmond and somehow got stuck in a closet at my parents' house that became their home for the next couple of years. The only time I laid eyes on the clubs for the next two years was when I was home in the winter and I would dig into the closet for a coat. Then I graduated, and from time to time Terry would ask me to play golf with him. I eventually transferred the clubs back to the trunk of my car, which became their new home for the next few years.

Early in our marriage, no sooner would Terry and I begin a round of golf together than he would tease me about those golf clubs. He would say, "Oh, I see you're still playing with those stolen golf clubs." I would jump right in with my answer, "Oh, no! They're not stolen; I'm just borrowing them." "You've been 'borrowing' them for five years!" he would say. *I was just borrowing them*—or so I tried to justify it to myself.

Fast-forward a couple of years later, shortly after I had become a Christian. I had been praying that the Lord would cleanse me of all known sin, and he gently reminded me about the golf clubs. Immediately I said, "Lord, I am taking those clubs back tomorrow."

The next day, I headed over to Meredith College and drove straight to Weatherspoon Gym, where I had been lent the clubs seven years earlier. I pulled my car right up front and grabbed all the clubs out of my trunk. As I approached the gym for the first time in seven years, I knew that I was a thief.

All those years before I came to Christ, I would not call my theft what it was, because that would have made me look bad. I could not admit that I was wrong. But God had given me new eyes that could see the truth about myself: I was a sinner. But He also was teaching me about restitution: trying to make the wrong, right, where possible. Repentance, after all, is turning away from sin, doing a complete about-face.

I walked up to the doors, and a security guard complete with a gun in his holster opened the door for me. He asked me if he could help me. I just said, "Yes, I'm returning these." (Well, the Lord didn't say I had to tell him everything, he just said to return the clubs!) He replied, "You can just put them over there by the door." I hopped in my car and drove away. It felt really good!

Another encouragement came in the life of my good friend, Sarah. Her marriage was hanging by a thread. Although she remained committed to the marriage, her husband left and divorce was imminent. During her struggles, I had been trying to encourage her from God's Word. Sarah, like me, had been in church during her growing-up years. I knew that only God knew the condition of her heart. And I knew that the enemy could easily fill her heart with bitterness and anger. God used our friendship for His purposes, and I was able to lead her to a recommitment to Jesus Christ in November 1985. God was working in her heart, and He allowed me to be a part of it.

At a Bible study, I later introduced Sarah to Bert, my friend whose husband had left her many years before. I had met Bert through Providence, and her transparency in our friendship was a treasure. We would meet regularly at her house for a quick lunch and to pray. To this day, when I think of a friend who is the ultimate listener, I think of Bert. The prayer support of friends such as Bert in the body of Christ meant the world to me.

Sarah's friendship with Bert was a godsend, as Bert provided Christian friendship and emotional support for her. To this day, Sarah and Bert remain incredibly close friends. Knowing that God was using me in Sarah's life was a great encouragement to me, and my faith was strengthened.

In October of 1985, Terry and I rounded the one-year mark since the day I had written the note and left our marriage. Paul and Macon continued to spend time mentoring me. They asked me to assist them in leading the youth of the church on Sunday nights.

In January of 1986, Paul suggested that I write a contract with God. By entering into a contract with God, I would be reminding myself of the decision I made to live for Christ and the promises that God offers His children. The contract would personify the rest of my life's new driving force: "I have been crucified with Christ and I no longer live, but Christ lives in me."[74] I was now His servant and His willing slave—He was my Master now, and He owned my whole life.

My contract would specifically flow out of the theme of the cornerstone passage from Romans chapter six that emphasized that, as a new creature in Christ, I was now dead to sin and alive in Christ (that first passage the Newbys had me memorize, weeks earlier). In my mind's eye, I can still hear Paul Newby saying, "Dead people don't have any rights!"

As I studied the Romans passage, I learned that I did not have to be mastered by sin, but instead, I could offer all the parts of my body to God as instruments of righteousness. That Fourth of July night, I had trusted Christ as my crucified Savior to rescue me from the guilt of my sin, and now I was learning to go on trusting Him as my living Savior to rescue me from the power of sin as I lived my life.

Hannah Whitall Smith said it best:

> *Then we believed that Jesus was our Savior from the guilt of sin, and according to our faith it was done for us. Now we must believe that He is our Savior from the power of sin, and according to our faith it shall be done for us. Then we trusted Him for forgiveness, and it became ours. Now we must trust Him for righteousness, and it shall become ours also. Then we took Him as Savior from the penalties of our sins in the future. Now we must take Him as Savior in the present from the bondage of our sins. Then He was our Redeemer. Now He is to be our Life [twenty-four hours a day, seven days a week, fifty-two weeks a year–JM]. Then He lifted us out of the pit. Now He is to seat us in the heavenly places with Himself.[75]*

Because of what Christ has done for us (that we could not do for ourselves) He now seats us in the heavenly places; we do not have to earn His favor, love, and wisdom. Once we enter a personal relationship with God through Christ, we don't have to try to climb a mountain and struggle to reach God (which we could never reach a Holy God without Christ bridging the gap)! He seats us in the heavenlies: "And God raised us up with Christ and seated us with him in the heavenly realms in Christ Jesus."[76] We can say with the Psalmist David, "He makes my feet like the feet of a deer; he causes me to stand on the heights."[77]

I decided to write the contract with God from the perspective of being dead to sin and alive in Christ. It would serve as a stake in the ground to me—a tangible reminder that I was under Christ's authority ever since I had surrendered my life to Him the previous July. When times of confusion or discouragement arrived, I could re-read my contract with God, giving me His perspective on life's priorities.

CONTRACT WITH GOD

JANUARY 1986

On this 22nd day of January 1986, I hereby make a contract with God the Father, Creator of the universe and Creator of me. I hereby died on July 4, 1985, when I became crucified with Christ and buried with Him. "I no longer live, but Christ lives in me."[78] Because I am dead, I no longer live for the reasons I was alive before. I am dead therefore, and no longer own the following items/attributes:

- *Home located at 2001 Bywood Court*
- *Husband named Terry Lee Mikels*
- *"Have-to-do-it-Now" Attitude*
- *Have to be in control*

- *Apartment located at 6733-A Six Forks Road*
- *Family in Virginia*
- *Job at Xerox*
- *A Relationship with my husband*
- *Need to be loved*
- *Need to be accepted*
- *Pride*
- *Desire for physical pleasure*
- *Need to be liked*
- *Need to be the center of attention*

These things all belong to Christ and God. In return Father, You promise to give to Juana Ruble Mikels the following:

- *A Full Life*
- *An Abundant Life*
- *Every spiritual blessing in Christ*
- *The Desires of my Heart*
- *To live with You forever*

The Desires of my heart are:

- *To have a full and meaningful relationship with a husband*
- *To be married one time only*
- *To have healthy children who love You*
- *My husband to know You and Jesus in a full and abundant way*
- *My mother to have peace*
- *Desire for my husband to enjoy and appreciate inner beauty and to see it and to tell me*

1 Peter 3:1–6

I give You, Father, a gentle and quiet spirit, dying to my forceful and loud nature, expecting in return my behavior to demonstrate purity and reverence. Because You put great worth in a gentle and quiet spirit, I do pray that You will allow my husband to see that inner beauty which will be unfading.

In You I trust not to break this contract.

This is sealed by the Lord Jesus Christ.

Signed,

Juana Mikels

As serious as making the above contract was (and it was a solemn vow I made to the Lord that I still abide by as a needed reminder that I *died to self*—especially when I try to go my own way; I don't want to underestimate its value in what I say next), reading parts of the terms sound foolish to me now. I didn't have a gentle and quiet spirit to give! Only God could do that through me. He does the work! The Bible tells us "every good and perfect gift is . . . from the Father" (James 1:17).

Nevertheless, God knew the purpose of my heart, and writing the contract was a stake in the ground that strengthened my faith. It's one that I need every bit as much today to remind me that dead people don't have rights.

Christ didn't come to make bad people good, but to make dead people spiritually alive—that we now may live alive to Christ and dead to sin.

What comfort would envelop me, as God would remind me of all the spiritual blessings that I possessed in Christ. In Ephesians 1:3, scripture tells us that God blesses us with every spiritual blessing in Christ—not some, but all! I was discovering that God cared about the desires of my heart![79] What's more, as I was learning to abide in Christ and live for Him seven days a week, the Lord changed my desires to line up with His desires for me.

A conversation while getting ice cream with my outgoing friend (I'll call her Anne) best illustrates this. Anne and I were on our way to the mountains of North Carolina. There we would both spend a refreshing weekend and time alone with God as we walked along the rushing brook near the cabin where we were staying. Anne was a coworker who had become a Christian around the time of separating from her husband. She never looked back and had no desire to reconcile with her non-believing husband. Over our ice cream cones, she asked me, "Juana, you left your husband just like I did. Can you really say that you desire to be married to him again? Come on, is that really your heart's desire?"

I tried to put into words for Anne the transformation that was taking place in my heart concerning my marriage. I told her I couldn't even separate what I wanted now from what I knew that God wanted. In other words, I wanted what God wanted so much that the two desires had become one. I was being transformed in my inner self, and the cry of my heart was (in the words of Francois Fénelon) that "I would have no other desire than to accomplish Thy will." My will was bending to His will. God was burning in my heart the things that burned in His heart.

I could say with confidence, "Yes! My heart's desire is without question to be married to Terry!" Once I made the decision with my will, my emotions followed right behind. I could link my heart up with the Psalmist David and say,

I waited patiently for the Lord;
he turned to me and heard my cry.
He lifted me out of the slimy pit, out of the mud and mire;
he set my feet on a rock
and gave me a firm place to stand.
He put a new song in my mouth,
a hymn of praise to our God. . . .

Then I said, "Here I am, I have come . . .
I desire to do your will, O my God . . ."[80]

I didn't know what the future held, but I knew the One who held the future in His hands. As the song says, "He's got the whole world in His hands. He's got the tiny, little baby in His hands. He's got you and me sister, in His hands!" I knew in my heart that my life was in the center of God's will, and that was the safest and securest place to be.

My heart was glad as I thought about the future. I lived amid uncertain and undesirable circumstances, yet I knew the time to come was bright, because God would be there with me. I knew that I was more alive than I had ever been in my life, and that I was going forward toward a beautiful promised rainbow coming after the fierceness of life's storms.

In the meantime, there was no let up in the storm—and I had no idea how long it would last.

CHAPTER TWELVE

THREE WORDS AND A TRIP

I WANT TO BACK UP just a bit to before I was married. Let's travel back to the first week I arrived in Raleigh, North Carolina, from Richmond, Virginia, in the fall of 1976 to attend Meredith College. It's important to view a few flashbacks with me just for the next minute or two—so you will understand the context of what actually happened next in my story.

I was a newly-arrived Meredith College freshman. One day I saw a large black-and-white poster in a store with a picture of the quarterback from North Carolina State on it. Only I didn't know his full name, because the poster only had the word "Wolfpack" written across it in big letters; I thought that was an unusual last name. Terry later straightened me out, explaining, "Juana, Wolfpack is the nickname of the football team!"

I had no idea that, ten years later, God would speak to Terry in a mighty way through the young man on the poster, through the sharing of three words found in scripture: "I hate divorce."

You see, Terry almost played football in college himself; he received several letters from smaller colleges who wanted him to play. But his high school coach got an assistant coaching position at State, and he convinced Terry to try out there as a walk-on. Terry had already decided he was going to attend State in the fall, so he decided to be a walk-on for the football team.

Everything changed, though, one hot summer day. Terry was enjoying an afternoon party, when a fellow football player left the party for football practice—and it was ninety degrees outside. Terry thought about it for a minute, and then decided he had had enough of long, hot afternoons practicing football. Instead, he decided to join a fraternity. This decision caused our paths to cross. (It's amazing how "minor" decisions like this one can change the entire course of our lives—which is why it's so important that we train ourselves to listen to and obey the Holy Spirit, so we can make the decisions He advises us to.)

∞

Back in the 1970s, when Terry was growing up in High Point, North Carolina, he played football with several excellent athletes who eventually played professionally. Before the football season started, the entire football team had to spend the night in the hot gym for two weeks in the summer without air conditioning. It was an effort for the team to bond during football practice, and Terry attributes his team's success year after year to the two-week stay in the gym, that included football practice three times a day.

Each player brought his mattress to use on the gym floor. Some players brought sheets, some didn't. But Terry remembers there was one guy who brought more. He was the star of the team, and he was a committed Christian. He brought his twin bed, headboard, footboard, nightstand, and lamp and placed them right by the door where a breeze came in, right where everyone entered and exited the gym several times a day. There was one more thing he brought: a Bible.

Terry said that every time he passed in and out the door, he would see the *Good News for Modern Man Bible* on the nightstand. It made an indelible imprint in Terry's mind. While everyone else pitched pennies and sometimes told coarse jokes and goofed-off all night, this guy separated himself and read his Bible. Terry has a lasting impression of this guy propped up in bed at night reading his Bible. Everyone respected him, including Terry.

He was quarterback of the team and was an excellent athlete, and was selected as an All-American in high school (only about thirty players in the nation per year receive this award). He also played on the golf team with Terry. In fact, Terry had known him as a young child, since they played on the same little league football team together and this player's father was the coach. This young man was named Johnny Evans, and he was the player pictured on that Wolfpack football poster.[81]

ༀ

Now fast-forward to early 1986. We had been separated over a year and a half, and Terry was not remotely interested in reconciliation. Terry was in his office one day and received a phone call.

"Hello, Terry?" a man's voice asked on the other end of the line.

"Yes?"

"This is Johnny Evans."

"Well, hi Johnny, how are you doing?"

"Doing well. Hey, I wanted to meet with you. Can you meet for lunch?"

"Meet for lunch?"

Terry wondered why Johnny would be calling him after not having seen him for years since their high school days. *"Was Johnny maybe into Amway?"* thought Terry. He had once had a similar surprise phone call from a relative he hadn't seen in years, and that turned out to be an invitation to an Amway meeting. Remembering Johnny's strong faith, Terry quickly surmised that it must have something to do with church.

"Sure, where do you want to meet?"

"How about tomorrow at the Governor's Inn in Research Triangle Park at noon?"

"Why is he picking a place in Chapel Hill?" thought Terry. *"Couldn't he have picked some place in Raleigh we could meet? That's not exactly on my way anywhere. What is this about?"* As Terry's mind filled with questions, all that came out was, "Sure."

Terry entered the prestigious private golf club with its panoramic, lush green setting. He immediately saw Johnny standing in the foyer of the dining facility. After being seated at their table, Johnny wasted no time chatting and instead got right down to business.

"Terry, when are you going to get right with Jesus?" he asked.

Terry can't remember what he told Johnny, but he will never forget Johnny's getting right to the point and having the nerve to challenge him straight on about Jesus.

Johnny continued: "There's a verse in the Bible that talks about divorce. It says that God hates divorce."

Terry wondered how Johnny knew the status of his marriage.

"I didn't know that," replied Terry. Through all the months of our separation, not one person had ever told him that.

In fact, everyone whom Terry had talked with had advised him the opposite saying, "Don't go back with Juana. There are plenty of fish in the sea." In the days to come, he would not be able to forget his conversation at lunch that day. The same guy who read his Bible every night by the door when the football team slept in the gym had earned the right to have a straight talk with Terry.

It was not a fluke that Johnny "just happened" to call Terry that day. Some weeks earlier, I had told our pastor, David Horner, that Terry knew Johnny Evans from High Point. I told him that Terry had told me in the past that he greatly respected Johnny. I asked David if he thought Johnny might give Terry a call, and he said he would check into it.

David did talk with Johnny, and he suggested that the three of us talk it over. We met at a pizza place for a quick lunch; it was the first time I had ever met Johnny.

It was good of Johnny to agree to meet, for he sure was busy. He told us at lunch that he was shopping for a new minivan, as he had just had his first child. And his second child. And his third child. And his fourth child. All in the same day. Quadruplets!

I briefed Johnny just a little on the past couple of years, and I asked him if he would pray about contacting Terry. I didn't feel it was my place to instruct Johnny on what to say to Terry. I only told him that I knew Terry respected him, and if he felt God's leading to call him, to go ahead. I also told him that I knew God could just have them run into each other somewhere if that's what He wanted, as I didn't want him to feel pressure to contact Terry just because I had asked.

Some weeks later, Terry called me and said, "I went to meet with someone today." Since several weeks had passed since I had met Johnny, I didn't put two and two together. He then said, "Did you ask Johnny Evans to call me?" I told Terry that I had told Johnny he could call if he felt led by God to do it. What Terry didn't tell me nor did he know—he would never be the same after meeting with Johnny and hearing those three little words: *God hates divorce.*

"I'm going to the beach to meet with God!" I blurted out of my car window on that sunny day in March 1986 to Lisa, my good friend from college. She looked baffled.

"Who's going with you?

"Just me!" I exclaimed.

"By yourself?" Lisa asked me incredulously.

"Yes, all by myself! Well, actually, I'm going to the beach to spend time alone with the Lord. I'm leaving right this minute!" Lisa's face showed concern for me. No doubt about it, she thought I had gone off the deep end. I knew it, but somehow it didn't seem to matter an *iota* to me. I really didn't expect my friends to understand what looked crazy to them. I was okay with that. All my confidence was in God, and I was eager to be alone with Him. "Bye, Lisa!" I began slowly backing out of the driveway.

"Well, . . . have fun," her voice half-heartedly trailed off as she waved goodbye to me, a bewildered look on her face.

"I can't wait to get there!" I yelled enthusiastically. There was no way to contain my excitement. I felt like I was going to meet with the president! And I was filled with the anticipation of the thought that He was waiting for me!

The Bible hadn't been taught in the home I grew up in and it had no meaning for my life—it was just words on a page to me, like when I was in that Bible study with Tootie a couple of years earlier. No wonder; the Bible says, "The man without the Spirit does not accept the things that come from the Spirit of God, for they are foolishness to him, and he cannot understand them, because they are spiritually discerned."[82]

But everything was different now! I was spiritually hungry, and it was as if a whole feast had been prepared for me. Once I became a Christian, a word or a sentence in the Bible would often seem to leap off the page to speak directly to me.

I was already learning the habit of daily quiet time alone with God, reading the Bible and praying. I had never even heard of it until I came to Providence, but there I had attended a Saturday class where we were given a sample format on spending one hour alone with God. It covered praising Him, confessing to Him, thanking Him, and lifting our burdens to Him. I remember thinking during that class, *How am I going to spend an hour with God, when I don't even spend five minutes with Him in a normal day?*

In a few short months, my desire had increased to where I now wanted to spend an entire day alone with the Lord!

Weeks had gone by since Johnny Evans had spoken to Terry, and during that time I had left Terry completely in the Lord's hands. I was learning to totally trust God in my circumstances and let Him solve them, so I didn't call Terry unless I was returning a call from him. I continued to wait to see what the Lord was going to do, since I knew that only He could change Terry's heart. I was totally at peace, even though weeks would go by without me hearing from him. I didn't know *how* God was going to resolve the unknowns in my life—I only knew *that* He was.

Then I determined that I wanted to go away for a night and a day, to fast and pray for our marriage. This was a spiritual practice I had heard about but had never done. I told Paul and Macon of my desire, and they suggested that I use Paul's parents' condominium at Carolina Beach. I was excited about my plans and purchased a large bottle of apple juice. That was all I planned to eat or drink during my time at the beach, when I would have an extended time alone with God. By abstaining from three normal meals, my concentration would be focused on prayer and spiritual things instead of on feeding my physical body.

When the day arrived, I took my apple juice, my Bible, Christian music, the book *Handle With Prayer* by Charles Stanley, and a legal pad with all my notes from Stanley's book. The Bible class I was in at Providence had just gone through Stanley's book, so I had many notes on how to pray. I was planning on going through the specific scriptures that Charles Stanley had identified for seeking God's will in prayer. I arrived at the condo and was delighted to find that it had a beautiful view of the Atlantic Ocean! I settled into bed early, so I could get up and begin my day alone with the Lord.

It had been weeks since I had spoken with Terry, and the last thing he had said to me was that he no longer desired to be married to me, so naturally I had been praying for the Lord to change Terry's mind about this. After I spent extended time praising God for who He is, though, He changed my heart's prayer. I no longer saw saving our marriage as top priority. My prayer became for Terry to accept Jesus Christ as his Lord and Savior, no matter what became of the marriage.

I had thought I was going to the beach to fast and pray for my marriage, but once I got there, the Lord reprioritized my desires. I experienced the truth of what the late Anglican bishop Charles Brent said: "Prayer is not so much the means whereby God's will is bent toward man's desires, as it is that whereby man's will is bent to God's desires. The real end of prayer is not so much to get this or that single desire granted, as to put human life into full and joyful conformity with the will of God."

Was God telling me that He would save Terry, but my marriage would have to be sacrificed in order to do it? Like Abraham sacrificing his son on the altar in obedience to God, God was asking me to leave the thing on the altar that was most precious to me in all the world: Terry. Like God Himself had done over two thousand years ago, when He left His Son on the altar. He had turned His back on His Son for the only time in history as Jesus hung on the cross to die in our place.

Jesus had asked the Father in the garden of Gethsemane that if there were any other way, to let this cup pass from Him. He wasn't saying He was not willing to suffer and die: He knew that He had come to die for the sins of the world. He was asking His Father if there were any other way besides being separated from Him. Jesus said, though, "Not my will, but thy will be done."[83] I knew that it was God's will for none to perish but for all to be saved, including Terry (see 2 Peter 3:9). So I prayed for Terry's salvation, praying "yet not as I will, but as You will," to accomplish it.

This is the beauty and power of fasting. Somehow, with distractions such as eating removed from my everyday living, and after confessing all my known sins, I was able to hear God's voice in a clear way. It had been over a year and a half since I had thrown away my marriage, and I deeply desired the opportunity to be a Christian wife to Terry. But God gently spoke to me that day while He had my full attention. Through scripture, He showed me that Terry's greatest need was not to be married to me, as much as I wanted the marriage!

So I began to pray boldly in Jesus' name against the strongholds the enemy had constructed in Terry's soul. Satan had filled Terry's mind with lies using procrastination ("maybe one day I will give my life to Christ"), doubt ("being a Christian won't be any fun and people will think I'm too religious"), deceit ("life is better now, it's much easier"), and no recognized need for a Savior ("I'm enjoying myself; I have peace and absence of conflict").

As I approached the end of my time alone with God, God directed me to a fresh passage:

> *You are the light of the world. A town built on a hill cannot*
> *be hidden. Neither do people light a lamp and put it under*
> *a bowl. Instead they put it on its stand, and it gives light to*

everyone in the house. In the same way, let your light shine before others, that they may see your good deeds and glorify your Father in heaven.[84]

God was providing me concrete instructions with what to do as I waited for His will in my life to be made known: to let the light of Christ shine as I did the work He gave me to do. I underlined the passage, dated it March 20, 1986, and wrote, "All I do!" Every detail about my life mattered to God. As I drove back to Raleigh, I was filled with joy to be able to live for Him.

CHAPTER THIRTEEN

NOT FREE TO DATE, IDOLS, AND EASTER

MARK (NOT HIS REAL NAME), our new product trainer at Xerox, was tall, dark, handsome, ambitious, intelligent, single, and a Christian. He would fly in from Atlanta, train our sales teams on a new product for a couple days, and then fly off to the next city. He exuded confidence and purpose, and I was impressed with this man from the moment I was introduced to him in the hall at work. *"Where did this guy appear from?"* I wondered.

Mark later peered into my cubicle when we had some time between training sessions. He saw a Bible on my desk and struck up a conversation.

"So, are you a Christian?"

"I am," I answered.

"I am too!" He exclaimed enthusiastically.

"That's great, we need Christians working here." I replied, thinking, *"Is this guy the total package, or what?"*

"Yeah, my mom led me to the Lord back home in Tennessee. She had come to know the Lord through some painters who were painting our house. She got so excited she couldn't contain it. She shared her faith with me, and I got saved."

"That is such a great story. I love to hear how people came to faith in Christ."

"I hear you are separated. Do you think you'll get back with your husband?" Mark asked, changing the subject.

"I don't know what will happen, but I have total peace about it. I came to know the Lord through my marriage separation. I left my husband, then I became a Christian, and God has changed my heart toward my husband. So now the ball is in his court."

"Is your husband a Christian?"

"No."

"Does he want to get back together?"

"No."

"And you want to be married to him?"

"Yes, I want the chance to be married to him now that I'm a Christian. God has given me a love for Terry that I couldn't have had before. The Bible says if the non-believing partner wants to stay, let him stay. So now I'm just waiting, because it's not completely resolved."

"Do you date?"

"No."

"Not at all?"

"No. People have been so nice trying to fix me up with someone they know, but since I'm not free to marry, I'm not free to date."

"How long have you been waiting like that?"

"About a year and a half."

"What if it goes on for years, and you're still waiting: are you going to date then?"

"All I know is I'm not free to date until God makes it clear what the outcome of the marriage will be."

"That's amazing. I have never heard of anything like this before. You must have a really strong faith. I admire you."

"Oh, it's not me! I am weak, but God helps me!"

I didn't see Mark for some time after that. Then several weeks later, he was back in town for training. I was in the supply room, and heard his voice in the hall. When I heard his voice I immediately felt excited. Just then he walked in, gave me a hug, and seemed eager to talk.

"Hi, Juana!"

"Hi! How are you doing?"

"Good, how is everything going with you? How is everything with your husband? It's Terry, right?"

"Yes; it's the same."

"How long have you guys been separated now?"

"Almost two years." And I thought, *"Yeah, the last thing Terry said to me was he doesn't want to be married to me—not exactly the romantic kind of words a girl wants to hear from the man she wants to be married to!"*

"And you still won't date?"

"No." I thought, *"Help me, Lord Jesus. I love my husband, and I want to do Your perfect will which You have already shown me is to wait upon You and not date. Help me Lord, not to do or say one thing to open the slightest, teeniest crack in the door that would deviate from Your plan for my life!!!"* (I prayed this even though Mark had given me no reason to think he was the slightest bit interested in me.)

"That is awesome. I admire the position you've taken." I thought, *"Yeah, well, you're not making this easy."*

"I'm dating this girl that works with Xerox in Virginia."

I thought, *"Oh, I hate that he's dating someone! I'm so disappointed! Wait, what am I thinking? I couldn't date him, much as I would like to! Date Mark? What am I saying? He's not the slightest bit interested in me anyway."*

"Really?" I said. But I thought, *"I have no reason to think he ever has had any interest in me. But even if he has, I love and am totally committed to Terry, and I am waiting for him to decide about our marriage! I want the opportunity to love my man unconditionally."*

"Her name is Christine [not her real name–JM] and she's a real 90s woman."

I thought, *"I guess he means she's a knock-out, and a stellar salesperson: . . . articulate, smart, ambitious, the works; but let's see if she shares Mark's faith in Christ."*

"Is she a Christian?"

"No, that's sort of a problem. She's got these way out ideas. I mean she is soooo off-base." I thought, *"Good. That figures. She's not the total package like him. He oughta get out of that relationship."*

"I've got a great book that talks about this. I can bring it in for you."

Mark later told me that he was no longer dating Christine. I gave him the book I had mentioned, which contained a chapter on finding a wife. It expounded on the passage in Genesis 23 that provides a great model for seeking a wife. I handed the book to Mark and told him a little about what that chapter was about.

He was very interested, so I told him a little more about the Genesis passage. I explained that it was about Isaac's servant going to find a wife for his master. He went to Isaac's homeland to find her among his own people. The Bible is clear that believers should not enter into marriage outside the family of believers. Mark was genuinely appreciative of the book and seemed eager to know what the Bible had to say in Genesis about finding a wife.

∞

One day Mark was in town, and he came by my cubicle.

"I've got some news," he said softly with a hint of excitement in his voice.

"What's up?" I asked.

"I'm leaving Xerox to go into business for myself," he continued quietly. "I'll be joining another friend in a new area of technology."

While I was happy for him, I was saddened that he would not be around anymore.

"I'm heading out now, but I'll be back in Raleigh one more time before I leave the company. I'll tell you all about it next time. Can you join me for dinner?"

"Sure."

He picked a Japanese place, and he excitedly drew his business plans on the napkin to show me how the new technology he would be marketing would be configured. It was a quick dinner, and then he drove me home.

As we pulled up to my apartment, a war was going on inside my head. Part of me wanted to ask him to come inside. It was not that I was lonely. I loved my quiet apartment, where I could shut the door behind me and spend time alone with God, or read a great book. I never even once turned the television on for noise the entire time I lived in that apartment as I had done every day when I was first married.

But how I longed for male companionship! I liked that God came up with that boy-girl thing. Plus, I didn't know anyone else like Mark. It was just enjoyable knowing him and sharing commonalities. Other than the bizarre fact that he cared to go out with someone who wasn't a Christian, he was someone who had it all together, and he was a Christian!

But another voice inside me said, "Just wish him the best." I swiftly made the decision and, with the car still running, I told him I wished him the best, then I quickly hopped out. My body was getting out of the car, but my emotions were screaming, *"Don't cut off the male companionship, it feels so good!"* After I had gotten out of the car, I felt like I had won some kind of victory, yet I was sad too. It was all very surreal, but in some strange sense I knew it was all part of something that God was doing in me to get me to trust Him.

> God was asking me to leave on the altar what was most precious to me in all the world: Terry.

God was working supernaturally in my life, allowing me to wait for the *right* male companionship. I knew that He had something else in mind, and that He had me in a waiting period in my life. God's grace prevailed and got me through my weaknesses, and my faith was strengthened.

I didn't see Mark again until several years later. I was sitting on an airplane, and I was reading my Bible. A voice overhead said,

"So, you're still reading your Bible." There stood Mark—tall and handsome. I was reminded of how normal I had felt desiring male companionship, and how God had delivered me in temptation.

Through it all, I hadn't lost my sense of humor. I love to take bubble baths to relax in the wintertime. I was relaxing in a hot bath in my apartment one day, and I was having a conversation with the Lord in my mind. I said, "Lord, you know that I was married for over three years, and I really miss masculine companionship!"

About that time, I glanced up and my eyes fell on the box of "Mr. Bubble" bubble bath soap. A big smile came across my face. "I know everything is going to be okay, Lord, since we can laugh about this together! I guess Mr. Bubble will have to do for now!" To this day, I truly believe that God loves to laugh with us, and that it is like ointment for the soul, for in the Bible we read: "a joyful heart is good medicine" (Proverbs 17:22 NASV).

For those who *have not yet married*, the Bible makes it clear to "*not* be yoked with unbelievers. For . . . what fellowship can light have with darkness?"[85] God isn't trying to prevent us from having any fun, but quite the opposite. He knows the heartache that will result if only one spouse is a Christian and cannot share the most intimate relationship they have with the Living Lord with an unbelieving spouse.

Scripture uses the metaphor of a yoke. Picture a wooden yoke with metal rings. If two cattle were unequally yoked, they would not be able to go in the same direction together. That would be like trying to get a horse and a cow to bear a yoke that is unevenly fitted for their use, causing great pain to both partners as the metal rings would inevitably bear down on their necks. How different from two cattle, both of the same bent in size and stride, who are able to accomplish so much more as they cooperate in the same direction. The yoke becomes their friend to work on their behalf! Such is the analogy of two Christians, walking in stride together in Christ.

The Bible provides concrete direction for those of us who are believers who are already married to nonbelievers. Just as in the times of the Corinthians, one spouse would get saved, and direction was needed as to whether they should stay with their non-believing spouse. "If any brother has a wife who is not a believer and she is willing to live with him, he must not divorce her. And if a woman has a husband who is not a believer and he is willing to live with her, she must not divorce him . . . but if the unbeliever leaves, let him go. A believing man or woman is not bound in such circumstances; God has called us to live in peace. How do you know, Wife, whether you will save your husband? Or, how do you know, Husband, whether you will save your wife?"[86] Your godly witness may draw him or her to Christ.

I cannot explain why a woman as weak as me was able to hear God's voice so clearly and continue to have joy in the midst of total uncertainty and rejection, other than it was supernaturally provided by the Lord. God tells us in His Word that He "chose the foolish things of the world to shame the wise; God chose the weak things of the world to shame the strong" (1 Corinthians 1:27). That way, we know there is no other explanation possible except that it is God at work. He will do that for anyone who puts their complete trust in Him, repents of sin, and obeys Him. Trust. Obey. Trust. Obey. Trust. Obey. God works.

Jesus said: "What is impossible with man is possible with God" (Luke 18:27). I have nothing to offer God—no abilities; it is all His grace. If He chooses to remove His grace and use someone else, I have nothing to complain about. As God works through me, He gets all the glory, for as Paul wrote: "Christ in you, the hope of glory" (Colossians 1:27).

I could face anything with Jesus in my life, and I counted it a privilege to suffer for Him. It would soon be two years since our physical separation, but I had not received any divorce papers from Terry. Someone once said, "You have to stand on your head as a Christian, because the world is totally upside-down from the Christian worldview." I was living proof of that statement, as I sought to purposefully live for Him amidst a life that was filled with uncertainty. One thing I knew: I knew Who held the future, and it was bright because He was in it.

※

"He doesn't love you, don't you see? Get a divorce! What are you waiting for?" Mama would passionately declare across the long distance phone lines to me.

I would answer her by saying, "Mama, I'm not waiting on Terry, I'm waiting on God. I'm waiting to see what God is going to do."

"But he doesn't love you!" Mama persisted. "Can't you see that? How long are you going to keep waiting?" Exasperated that her daughter was waiting through what looked like a hopeless situation, she would by now be nearly shouting through the phone. Looking back, I don't fault my mother for her unrestrained delivery of her emotions; she came from a culture of loud talkers who all talked at the same time, as I told you in an earlier chapter.

But I was learning to filter all voices that vied for my mind through the lens of scripture. "They will be divided, father against son and son against father, mother against daughter and daughter against mother, mother-in-law against daughter-in-law and daughter-in-law against mother-in-law" (Luke 12:53). How clearly I was living this out, but God's Word gave me the clear direction I needed. "You may often see Jesus Christ wreck a life before He saves it."[87]

> An idol is anything a person puts before God.

I was learning a very important biblical principle. Christians cannot have two masters: we can only have One. "No one can serve two masters. Either you will hate the one and love the other, or you will be devoted to the one and despise the other" (Matthew 6:24). Jesus Christ wants to be the Master and Lord of our lives, and He was on the throne of my heart. I loved my mother, yet I knew where my first allegiance was: to the Lord Jesus Christ.

Christ wants to hold such a supreme position in our life that by comparison the Bible even uses the word "hate" for other relationships. "If anyone comes to me and does not hate father and mother, wife and children, brothers and sisters—yes, even their own life—such a person cannot be my disciple" (Luke 14:26). There is a high cost to be a disciple of Jesus!

God tells us that He is a jealous God and He wants us to have no other gods before Him.[88] Anything put before Him will separate us from Him, and that is sin. Sin will not bring about the godly, full, abundant life God desires for us. When we love something (you can even substitute the word worship in some cases)—beautiful violin music, spectacular sky diving, superb ice skating, another person—we must tell someone about it with the utmost praise of what has captured our affection. God wants our *highest praise* to be reserved for Him, and Him alone!

The God Who created us wants to receive our highest worship. He doesn't even want our affection to be in our striving to know Him; He wants our supreme affection to be *for HIM.* Would you want your lover to love you, or to love the process of chasing after you? Your lover wants you to love him above all. So it is with the Author of love. The Bible says that God is love.[89]

Simply put, the Bible tells us, "He must increase, but I must decrease."[90]

We must have no other gods before Him, because that would be serving an idol. An idol can be anything: things that appear bad and things that appear good. An idol is anything a person puts before God. Many potential idols are not bad in themselves— they can be good things. But the good can be the enemy of the best if they are put before God. As Christians, our loyalty must be first to God. We must resolve this firmly, so when the temptation comes, we will be able to stand up under it.

Idols can appear in any form: exercise, parents, children, spouse, ministry, education, money, a godly family, alcohol, work, applause, or accomplishments. Seeking God's will to the point that you are running ahead of God can even become a distraction from really worshiping God and truly keeping Him first. We must not become so busy, even in ministry, that we lose our love for Christ as uppermost in our heart.

We are in a very dangerous position when we have an idol before God, because we can become totally insensitive to the things of God. We can become callous toward people who we naturally do not like, instead of interceding for them. Instead, we need to "Consider how far you have fallen! Repent and do the things you did at first. If you do not repent, I will come to you and remove your lamp stand from its place."[91]

There have been times in my life when I have put idols before God. Most recently, I did this with the writing of this book. My husband had asked me to exercise to take care of myself, but I wouldn't listen. It made no sense to me to stop working, for I was working against a deadline and had so much to do. I just wanted to finish my manuscript changes for my publisher: I had made that my god.

Then God arranged for me to get very sick for ten days. At first I resented getting sick, and I asked the Lord why He would allow me to get so sick when I was trying to do this ministry of writing my story out for Him. I told Him I couldn't take care of my family or finish my writing while sick in bed! Then, as the days wore on with migraines and nausea, He finally had my full attention.

God showed me in this involuntary fast (for I could barely eat anything, only drink) that I had put ministry ahead of Him. Since I wasn't spending any time eating, I had nothing but time as I lay there on my bed. As I began to put myself in a spiritual and emotional position to hear from God, by reading my Bible and the godly testimony of a man named Brother Yun, I read Revelation

2:5, the verse about repentance I just quoted. I got on the floor and, while I didn't have any tears (I was too weak and exhausted), on the inside I cried to God in repentance.

God loves a repentant heart. He longs for us to come to Him and repent and do what He says. In an instant, He showed me several areas where I was not obeying Him.

I immediately knew that God wanted me to walk. To walk with Him daily, yes—but He was also saying that I was to walk physically, just as my husband had been encouraging me to do for so long. He also showed me that I was to email a woman who needed help: I had been deaf to her pleas, thinking someone else could help her at my daughter's school. I had rationalized that at least I was one of only seven out of a hundred parents who attended the parents' meetings on rainy, cold nights, and that someone else of the ninety-three who didn't show up could help her.

God tapped me (on the inside, not physically) as I lay on the floor in repentance. He was calling me to do the secular job to help this woman. It was as if He was saying, "I want you to do that job, Juana. There is no such thing as secular work for the Christian who offers their work unto Me. That work will be sacred when you do it in My Name." I repented of not being willing to help, for I knew my over-fascination with finishing my book had hardened my heart. It had prevented me from hearing the simple things He had for me to do.

The very first thing I did when I got up from the floor was email the woman who had asked for help, to tell her that I would be happy to take over the fundraiser.

I continued to be sick afterward, but my spirit began to soar! My faith grew stronger than ever, even while my body still hurt and was weak. My spirit was being fed huge meals of His Word as I read scripture and praised God. Jesus reminded me that He brought the Father glory on earth by finishing the work that *the Father gave Him to do*.[92] It was as if Jesus had told me Himself:

> *I have food to eat that you know nothing about. . . .*
> *My food . . . is to do the will of him who sent me and to finish his work.*[93]

I got better, and my husband asked me to take walks and relax and not work on the manuscript. This time, I listened and obeyed. I had God's peace again, and felt His power resting on me after I repented and turned from my selfish, independent ways. I realized that earlier I had listened to the enemy and made ministry an idol.

I spoke in an earlier chapter about the enemy who seeks to destroy us. We will face opposition, so we need to expect it. The Bible says, "all who will live a godly life in Christ Jesus shall suffer persecution" (2 Timothy 3:12). When we face opposition to what God has clearly shown us, we need to recognize that its source is not so much the person standing in front of us—or on the phone as in the case as my mother—but it is a spiritual battle with an unseen enemy.

We need to be prepared, as we never know when the opposition may attack. We can prepare by putting on God's armor daily. Listen to what Paul wrote to Christians:

> *For our struggle is not against flesh and blood, but against the rulers, against the authorities, against the powers of this dark*

world and against the spiritual forces of evil in the heavenly
realms. Therefore put on the full armor of God, so that when
the day of evil comes, you may be able to stand your ground,
and after you have done everything, to stand. Stand firm
then, with the belt of truth buckled around your waist, with
the breastplate of righteousness in place, and with your feet
fitted with the readiness that comes from the gospel of peace.
In addition to all this, take up the shield of faith, with which
you can extinguish all the flaming arrows of the evil one. Take
the helmet of salvation and the sword of the Spirit, which is
the word of God.

– Ephesians 6:12–17

It is dangerous not to know who your enemy really is, or you
may try to engage in the battle in your own strength. Putting on
the armor and taking the battle to God in prayer are your weapons,
not your own understanding and strength.

I wrote so much here about having no gods before God because
it is so easy to do, especially in America where we materially have
so much. Clearly, our dissatisfaction and unhappiness in life
comes from not giving God His due praise. I can personally attest
to that from my life before I met Christ, and even as recently as
when I put this manuscript before God.

When once we truly put Him on the throne of our lives—not
just being saved Christians living however we want to live but
truly placing the living God on the throne of the daily decisions
of our lives—then we can truly experience God every day.

∾

I have often heard people say, "God never gives you more than you can handle," but that is not a biblical statement. He tells us to cast our cares and anxieties on Him. In my life, He has given me way more than I can handle, and He desires that I give it over to Him. He wants to handle our burdens for us.

I couldn't help but write out for you all three stanzas of the beautiful hymn "What a Friend We Have in Jesus," by Joseph Scriven. I love that Scriven included the phrase *needless pain*, as that is so true!

What a friend we have in Jesus,
all our sins and griefs to bear!
What a privilege to carry
everything to God in prayer!
O what peace we often forfeit,
O what needless pain we bear,
all because we do not carry
everything to God in prayer.

Have we trials and temptations?
Is there trouble anywhere?
We should never be discouraged;
take it to the Lord in prayer.
Can we find a friend so faithful
who will all our sorrows share?
Jesus knows our every weakness;
take it to the Lord in prayer.

Are we weak and heavy laden,
cumbered with a load of care?
Precious Savior, still our refuge;
take it to the Lord in prayer.
Do thy friends despise, forsake thee?
Take it to the Lord in prayer!
In his arms he'll take and shield thee;
thou wilt find a solace there.

We must leave our burdens with God. Every time we find we are fretting over them again, we must take them back to God for Him to carry. Cares and anxieties can make a person physically ill. Many times in my life I have foolishly tried to bear the load of some heavy responsibility or worry that has taken away my sleep and my appetite, and even produced migraines. (After thinking I had given it to God, only to take my troubles back again!) We must take them to the Lord, and *leave them with Him.* (You do realize that I'm talking to myself, too, as I write you?)

We must give not only our burdens, but also our whole self to Him! We must give all that we are, have, do, and suffer to Him, daily. We can give ourselves anew to God each morning.

Make a daily, definite consecration of yourself to God. Get alone if you can and say it aloud in the room, or perhaps as you rise and your feet touch the floor. If it helps you, write the following prayer on a 3x5 card and place it on your nightstand or in your Bible for easy reference:

Lord, I give myself to You anew today, along with my will. I give
all that I am, all that I have, all that I do, and all that I suffer

to You. I'm willing to be made willing about all You want me to do.[94] *Thank You that I don't have to worry about_____ [Fill in the blank; I used to fill it in with my marital uncertainty, and have filled in the blank with hundreds of other worries over the years.], for You carry the weight of my burdens. I hand over to You every care and every temptation. Thank You that I don't have to handle them, but I can hand them to You! Thank You Jesus for doing Your part in my life perfectly. I confess the sin of _____. [Insert whatever comes to your mind since the previous day or time, allowing time for God to show you those sins: worrying about how long your marital separation will be or if you will ever be married, fretting about your daughter, talking rudely to your husband, etc.] Work in me to will and act for Your good pleasure. I put myself entirely in Your hands and that is where I will stay. I trust You.*

I've tried to make this prayer a natural part of my quiet time, by giving myself and my burdens to Him before I begin the day. I don't always do it, but when I do, I have a greater trust and confidence in the Lord no matter my circumstances, and my faith is strengthened. "Do not be anxious about anything, but in every situation, by prayer and petition, with thanksgiving, present your requests to God. And the peace of God, which transcends all understanding, will guard your hearts and your minds in Christ Jesus."[95] You will discover that even though your situation may not have changed, you can have perfect peace right in the storm you are facing.

Whatever trouble you are going through (God knows all about it) moves from your problem to His problem when you consciously and deliberately hand it over to Him. I love the story that Amy Carmichael told from her early days as a missionary. She and another older missionary couple were held up in Japan because of some type of boat problem. The boat continued to have problems that went on for days, and Amy was distressed because they couldn't get on to do the work they were called to do, as other missionaries were fully expecting them. One of the older missionaries wisely told Amy, "God knows all about the boats." Since becoming familiar with that story, I have made "God knows all about the boats" a catchphrase in my life, to remind me of God's sovereign leading.

Oswald Chambers said:

> *Faith never knows where it is being led, but it loves and knows the One Who is leading. It is a life of faith, not of intellect and reason, but a life of knowing Who makes us "go." [Or stay, wait, hold up the boats, etc.–JM] The root of faith is the knowledge of a Person, and one of the biggest snares is the idea that God is sure to lead us to success.*

God's Word continued to speak to me personally to give me guidance. I knew unequivocally that my loyalty now was to Christ. My dear mother was a slave to her feelings. As the tables had completely turned, and now Terry was rejecting me, Mama may have even been reliving the pain of her divorce—the enemy reminding her of when her first husband had rejected her.

It is natural to be tempted in this world by so many voices that are not of God. Remember, the Bible says that the enemy of our souls masquerades as an angel of light. Even our parents can unknowingly give us bad advice. As my mother did, parents often (and often mistakenly) try to prevent or remove suffering from their grown child's life. But that suffering may be the very tool God is using to mold them into Christ's character, and so the parent may actually be interfering with God's purposes to mature their child. If you are reading this book and have just realized that you are struggling through a myriad of disguised voices of even well-meaning friends, family, or coworkers that the enemy has used to pull you away from a deep, abiding faith in God—don't fall for it!

Stay in God's Word, which is like ammunition for your soul! When thoughts enter your mind trying to rob you of your joy in the Lord, say, "I take captive every thought to make it obedient to Christ" (2 Corinthians 10:5). When nagging thoughts would creep in of mistakes I had made, like leaving my husband, or even small mistakes that could still cause agony in my heart and mind, I would remember to boss myself around using God's Word, saying, "I take that thought captive and make it obedient to Christ. Jesus, thank You for dying for my sin. Thank You, Jesus, that You have covered my sin completely!" When the nagging reminder would return, I would say it all over again. If you have to say it 100 times a day, say it.

We must remember who is the author of doubts and discouragements: they are not from God; they are from Satan. Just as with an alcoholic, it cannot be given up little by little; it must be wholly given up at once. At the very first suggestion of a doubt, temptation, or discouragement, we must hand it over to God to manage on our behalf. It must be done immediately when the thought enters our minds, with full trust in the Lord to take it. Pay no attention to it and do not let it settle into your mind.[96]

Martin Luther said that we can't stop birds from flying overhead, but we can stop them from making a nest there! What a great analogy of not yielding to temptation. *It is not a sin to be tempted.* If it were so, Jesus would have sinned! He was actually led into the wilderness *by the Spirit* to be tempted by the devil![97]

When you are tempted and the thought first enters your mind, think of temptation as nothing more than walking by a group of dangerous hoodlums and overhearing their conversation. It is not a sin to hear it; you must keep on walking (figuratively and in some cases physically), though by all means, do not indulge in the conversation! You may need to pack your bags and get out. Joseph literally ran out when Potiphar's wife tried to tempt him.[98]

Did you know there are no new temptations? Mankind faces the same, common temptations we always have. Did you also know that our faithful God provides a clear way out when you are tempted? Will you take the escape route? How is your story going to be written in the face of temptation? "No temptation has overtaken you except what is common to mankind. And God is faithful; he will not let you be tempted beyond what you can bear. But when you are tempted, he will also provide a way out so that you can endure it."[99] Oh, that we would be women (and men!) of God, pursuing a lifestyle of godliness and faith![100]

In the battle, when doubts (or temptation or discouragement, for that matter) attack your mind, simply repeat (and mean it) what Hannah Whitall Smith said.

"We must simply say, I dare not doubt. I must trust. God is my Father, and He does love me. Jesus saves me. He saves me now." Those three little words, repeated over and over, "Jesus saves me, Jesus saves me," will put to flight the greatest army of doubts that ever assaulted any soul. I have tried it many times and have never known it to fail.

Pay no attention to your doubts. Treat them with the utmost contempt. Tell Jesus that you trust Him and that you intend to go on trusting Him.[101]

Oh, that we would all live as totally sold-out Christians: truly putting God first, denying ourselves, following Him unreservedly at any cost, and being able to say with the apostle Paul, "for me to live is Christ." I wish we could all grasp that "faith means putting our full confidence in the things we hope for, it means being certain of things we cannot see" (Hebrews 11:1, Phillips).

❧

By an act of my will—not my feelings—while I was waiting and hoping for the Lord to change Terry's heart, I was holding fast "to the pattern of sound words that you have heard from me [Paul], in the faith and love which are in Christ Jesus" (2 Timothy 1:13, NAS). God was assuring me that even in our weakness, although "we are faithless, He remains faithful" (2 Timothy 2:13). We must believe He is faithful and there is no unfaithfulness in Him, not because we can feel the faith or can touch, hear, smell, or see it, but because He said it! Oh, how many times Paul and Macon said to me as a new believer in Christ, "God is faithful!"

On my first Easter after having become a Christian, Paul and Macon wanted me to go to the beach with them. They were concerned that it wasn't wise for me to go to Richmond where my mother was completely unsupportive (due to her agony over my situation). With the ongoing uncertainty regarding my separation circumstances that appeared to have no end in sight, she vehemently wanted me to seek a divorce. I think too, as my mother, she hated having a daughter in limbo and suffering through marriage problems.

I didn't know what the outcome would be either, but I could say with the apostle Paul, "For this reason I also suffer these things; nevertheless I am not ashamed, for I know whom I have believed and am persuaded that he is able to keep what I have committed to him until that day" (2 Timothy 1:12). I was drinking in God's Word, day by day, and being strengthened in my inner person. As I said in an earlier chapter, I had perfect peace amidst my undesirable circumstances.

So that first Easter as a new Christian, I went to the beach with Paul and Macon where we attended a sunrise service, and it was glorious! The Bible tells us, "if anyone is in Christ, he is a new creation; the old has gone, the new has come!"[102] Everything was new to me. It was my first Easter after entering into a personal relationship with Christ, and it was so meaningful to me. As Lee Strobel, Christian author and apologist, says (in one of his books, I can't remember which) of his own conversion, it was as if I had been viewing the world through a small black-and-white television when I could have had a big, full-color, surround-sound, high-definition system!

Oh, how all the hymns came alive for me too. I had sung them as a child and knew all the verses, but now I sang them with tears and conviction, as the words held so much meaning for me now. I had rattled off those hymns as a child and never had given the words much thought. Oh! How I now loved "Trust and Obey," "O Worship the King," and "Rejoice, the Lord is King."

Years later, Elisabeth Elliot introduced me to her favorite hymns, a few of which we sang with her in my home: "Beneath the Cross of Jesus," "Great is Thy Faithfulness," (I knew that one), and "And Can it Be." (They always ended hymn singing in their home with "And Can it Be.") When I once asked Elisabeth what her favorite hymns were, she replied, "I have about seventy." In one breath she rattled off seven titles that I wrote down.

She was deeply concerned that the church of this generation was abandoning hymns—which were often theologically deep and whose verses were a logical progression of thought—in favor of praise songs, which she found to be "thin," theologically speaking.

On Elisabeth's earliest visits, she played the piano. In her last visit in January 2014, over a decade since the onset of dementia, she was unable to sing with us except through her big blue eyes.

I have had the privilege of having Elisabeth play hymns for me on the piano when no one else was around and I was flat out sick on the couch of the President's home at a seminary. I have also had the privilege of singing beside her—standing and rejoicing in hymn singing in church. (I foolishly held the hymnbook in front of her for her reading convenience, not realizing that she needed no prompting for the words—she never looked at the page, as she had all the stanzas committed to memory!)

Oh! How my soul was fed by hymns during my marital separation. My personal favorite as a new believer was "Crown Him with Many Crowns"—the words rolled off my tongue as they came back from my childhood at Derbyshire Baptist Church. How I adored (and still adore) the words "matchless King," as now I claimed Him as my *matchless King!*

Crown him with many crowns,
the Lamb upon his throne,
Hark! how the heavenly anthem drowns
all music but its own.
Awake, my soul, and sing
of him who died for thee,
and hail him as thy matchless King
through all eternity[103]

I was also finding out that familiarity opens us up to the very real possibility that we won't pay any attention to what we are saying. Samuel Taylor Coleridge said, "There are truths which are commonly considered so true as to lose all the powers of truth, and they lie bedridden in the dormitory of the soul." The truth had been tucked away in me as a child, but was now no longer dormant! The words were no longer repeating chimes to me. How thankful I now was that my parents had taken me to church, for I had so many of the words already in my head.

Chances are, if you are like me, you have said some commonly known prayers without giving it any thought. It's easy to do with formal, repetitive prayers such as the Lord's Prayer. It was the Lord Jesus Himself who gave us the Lord's

Prayer as the model to follow, when the disciples asked Him to teach them to pray. We can invest that repetitive prayer with our own sincerity as we pray, with acknowledgment of the mystery of God to answer our prayers. We can use the prayers of others to help us pray; we don't have to pray only spontaneous prayers. They all count when they are prayed from a genuine, clean heart in Jesus's name! (I credit Elisabeth Elliot for the ideas in this paragraph.)

I also use the prayers we find in scripture that the apostle Paul prayed for his friends. What meaningful prayers to pray for our loved ones! Instead of praying a blanket prayer that God would "bless them," we can copy the kingdom prayers that Paul prayed for other people. For example, I pray for Terry that "God would work in him (Terry) that good will which is pleasing unto Him."[104] I pray that Terry would walk in a manner worthy of his calling, and that he would have a "knowledge of the will of God."[105] I pray that we will have a "growing love for one another."[106] (I also to this day pray many of these prayers for my children and for close friends.) See appendix 1 for prayers that I use as my template when praying for my husband that you can use with your husband, inserting his name.

❧

Getting back to my story: from time to time Terry would want to meet with me. Things would start off amicably, but often he took the opportunity to vent his feelings. He was angry with me for leaving him, and he had not forgiven me. He didn't even realize that was what was happening, and it played out by him telling me all the things he didn't like about me. Sometimes I would simply sit there and listen, but often I didn't, and I hurled back insults.

Later, I would realize that I had blown it, for Terry didn't even know the Lord yet, but I did! Where was my forbearance? I would pray for God to give me yet another chance to not be so easily insulted, as it says in 1 Corinthians 13—the most common "love chapter" read at weddings. I knew the Bible spoke of love as being "patient . . . kind . . . not easily angered." Ouch! I had to give up my right to be offended, because I was now buried with Christ and free to live solely dependent on Christ for my identity. Christ was my rock, my ultimate support.

Jesus's outpouring of unconditional love in spite of my ugly self was more than enough for me. His love sustained me. Maybe that's why the Bible says of faith, hope, and love, "the greatest of these is love."[107] I longed to be more like Christ! He was a friend like no other!

CHAPTER FOURTEEN

LOVE MUST BE TOUGH

"WILL YOU TAKE YOUR WEDDING ring off?" Terry suddenly asked me as we were out on a date together. "Don't you understand the pressure that puts on me, by your wearing that ring?"

"Okay, I didn't know it bothered you," I replied. I sure didn't have to guess where Terry stood while we were dating again! One thing was for sure: he did not want me wearing my wedding ring.

Not too long after that date, my phone rang.

"Juana, I've been thinking, and I've come to a decision. We don't need to date anymore, because it's not going anywhere. It's over between us."

While I was calm with Terry on the phone, as I had been several months earlier when he had said the same thing in person with me the day after my conversion, I immediately telephoned Macon with a sudden feeling of desperation. My old spirit of anxiousness had reared its ugly face, casting a darkness that seemed to hang over me on that night. Macon was there for me, though, praying with me over the phone and pointing me to the Truth of God's Word. She came over to my office the next day and brought me a book.

Terry went back and forth in his mind over a period of months, wrestling with what to do about our marriage. It was a roller coaster that would last for well over another year. He was deeply hurt when I left him, and he did not want to open his heart up to hurt from me again. He still hadn't forgiven me for leaving him in the first place. All of this led to more confusion in his life about what to do.

∞

As I continued to memorize Scripture and pray over those long months, my faith was strengthened. God's ways were a mystery, but I accepted them. Now when I became suddenly upset after talking with Terry, I no longer had the need to call Macon. Instead, I was learning to go directly to God with my sorrows, and He would calm my spirit and heart as I would turn to Him.

I drank in His presence, knowing that I was secure in the hands of the One who made me and loved me and called me by name. "He calls his own sheep by name and leads them out."[108] The preceding verse says that his "sheep listen to his voice." I was learning to pick His voice out of the crowd of noise and other voices that tried to compete with His. God desires to speak personally to us!

Paul and Macon had given me a tape with a collection of hymns on it. In my lowest points, when darkness would settle into my soul after a disturbing phone call or visit from Terry, or when someone would tell me they saw Terry somewhere, I would put on my favorite hymn from that tape. It was "Turn Your Eyes Upon Jesus." I must have played it a hundred times, as I would kneel alone in my apartment on that gray carpeting. With tears streaming down my face I would sing:

Turn you eyes upon Jesus,
Look full in His wonderful face,
And the things of this world will grow strangely dim
In the light of His glory and grace.[109]

I had surrendered my life to Christ, and now it was time to trust Him. My life was still in turmoil, but I had peace in the center of the storm.

⟷

The phone rang in my apartment.

"Hello?"

"Juana, this is Terry."

"Hi, how have you been doing?" It was so good to hear his familiar voice! I hadn't spoken with Terry in weeks. I knew the ball was supposed to stay in his court, so I didn't contact him even when the days turned into weeks.

"I'm good. Look, I have two tickets for State's basketball game on Saturday night, and I was wondering if you would go with me."

"Sure, that'd be fun," I replied, thinking, "*You have no idea just how much I want to go! I cannot believe you called me! This is wonderful!*"

"Okay, now, it's just a basketball game; don't read anything into this," Terry said.

"Oh, it'll be fun to watch State play," I said. But actually, for me, this was "girl meets boy" all over again, and I couldn't wait!

When Terry came to pick me up, he had never looked so good to me. All these years later I can't tell you what he was wearing, but I remember thinking, "*This feels so strange dating the man I was married to, who doesn't want me to consider this a date, but whom I want to be married to. And technically, since we never divorced, I <u>am</u>*

currently married to him. This is the strangest thing I have ever done! But I was going to have to take what I could get, so to speak, to meet Terry where he was. Believe you me, I did not say one single word about his earlier vow that everything was over between us.

I had to exercise total restraint on my words, for I *wanted* to be so much more than just a date for Terry—I wanted to be his wife! By God's grace, though, I knew it wasn't God's timing for me to say a word about our future together.

After that game, Terry asked me out again.

I had to settle for dating the man to whom I wanted to be married. Only I *was* currently married to him! But I knew—for our relationship to progress—it was going to take time for him to forgive me and trust me again.

Unfortunately, no sooner would we have a few dates and things would appear to be going well, than Terry would call everything off and not want to see me anymore. This happened several times. I found out years later why this kept happening, but when we were going through this, I didn't question Terry on what he was feeling and thinking.

As you may recall from an earlier chapter, Terry had finally moved on with his life several months after I left him. By that point, he had no hope from me that we would ever reconcile, so he began dating someone else.

The woman he was dating had never done anything to hurt him, and they seemed to always laugh and have a good time together. With me, Terry had to deal with the anger he harbored against me for leaving him. This made Terry's life complicated. Often, while he was on a date with me, he would find himself thinking that it would just be easier if he started fresh with the other woman. ("Start fresh" is a misnomer, though, for he would have taken all his unresolved emotional baggage into the "fresh" relationship, and that would have affected them eventually.)

Each time Terry would have a negative change of heart toward our relationship, I would go back to God, asking Him to give me patient endurance as He unfolded His will. I was not waiting on Terry; I was learning to wait on God to show me His will.

∾

Terry now believes totally differently on the subject of dating while separated. He believes that introducing a third person only muddies the water and adds confusion and chaos into the mind of the newly separated person, nor is it really fair to the third person. He believes now that his dating another woman ultimately delayed our reconciliation, and he does not recommend that people date while they are separated.

Terry now advises people in similar situations to wait it out. He believes that doing so allows both the spouses the opportunity to cycle back at the same time, although it may take a good bit of time for *both spouses* to cycle back to the same page: hence the need for a waiting period while abstaining from any outside dating.

In many separations, adequate time is not allowed by both spouses to allow the opportunity for this to occur. It requires forbearance. Our society doesn't like words like self-control, restraint, patience, endurance, and forbearance. The Bible speaks much of patient endurance, though, and God can instill forbearance in you. It had so much to say about waiting that encouraged my soul.

Wait for the Lord; be strong and take heart and wait for the Lord.[110]
I wait for the Lord, my soul waits, and in his word I put my hope.[111]
Blessed are all who wait for him![112]

And my absolute favorite verse on actively waiting on God:

Those who wait for the Lord will gain new strength;
They will mount up with wings like eagles,
They will run and not get tired,
They will walk and not become weary.[113]

What beautiful words of hope sent by God Himself to us!

The book Macon brought to my office amid my anxiousness and discouragement the night after Terry had said on the phone that "it was over," was entitled, *Love Must Be Tough*, by Dr. James Dobson. The book jacket said that James Dobson was the host of a daily Christian radio program named "Focus on the Family."[114] I had no idea that book would not only give me the immediate practical advice that I needed to hear, but it would introduce me to a lifelong source of encouragement for Christian families under the ministry founded by James Dobson.

What I remember most in the book was a diagram showing a pair of fists, labeled Fist A and Fist B. Each fist represented a spouse in the marriage. The first drawing was of the two fists held equally high in the air, about six inches apart. The next diagram emphasized that when one spouse (i.e., fist A) tries to get away from the other wounded spouse in a broken marriage (i.e., fist B), the tendency is for the wounded spouse (i.e., fist B), to try to grab a tighter hold on the spouse who is moving away (i.e., fist A), to retrieve them and not lose them. This makes the other spouse (i.e., fist A) want to go further away.

Another set of diagrams showed one hand trying to separate from the other hand, but this time, the second hand did not try to smother the first, pursue it, or grab it. The second diagram represented the "love must be tough" application, indicating that if you let your spouse go, you are letting them have the freedom to choose. (And that by giving them the respect to make their own choice by not chasing them down, you actually increase the chance of the marriage being rekindled.)

Now I had the direction I needed! I simply had to give Terry the freedom to walk away! I didn't have to do anything; I simply needed to let him go. Amy Carmichael once said, "Anything that is really ours, is ours forever." So if we let it go, if it is really ours, we can rest in the knowledge that it is ours forever. I resolved as I read Dr. Dobson's book that I would subscribe to the "love must be tough" concept.

I resolved once and for all in my heart and mind that the ball was now totally in Terry's court. He chose me once, and if he ever wanted to marry me again, he would have to choose me a second time. Terry would have to do that as a clear choice of his own free will. Little did I know that, in the days that were about to follow, the "love must be tough" philosophy would cause me to take a defining action that I would never have thought in my wildest dreams I would ever do.

For several months after Terry had told me there was no hope for our marriage, I heard nothing from him. While for the previous many months he had already been vacillating, it really did seem that this last time he meant it for good. This was the longest period of time I had gone with no contact from him, and it was over one and one-half years since I had left the note. Then the phone rang one night.

"Juana, this is Terry."

"Hi! How are you?"

"I'm doing okay. Look, I can't make you any promises, but if you're willing, I'd like us to try to date one more time."

We began dating immediately, and once again I had to put all my desires to be his wife on the shelf and be willing to just spend time with him on his terms. We had a few dates, and things seemed to be going well. Then late one night, my phone rang again.

"Juana?"

"Yes?"

"I'm sorry to have to tell you this, but I've made a decision. Everything is off. It's really over this time. No more dating; I've made up my mind once and for all. I can no longer date you, see you, or have any contact with you. I'm sorry, but this is how it *has to be*. Juana, I'm telling you that this is the end. *It is finally over.*"

I hung up the phone.

"Juana, this is the end. It is finally over."

In the book of Psalms we read that God has assigned "my portion and my cup; you make my lot secure."[115] Looking back, I can see that my "lot" (my destiny, my portion, my assignment) included receiving that phone call. God's loving hand was behind it just like a mother's hand is behind the bottle that contains the bitter-tasting medicine for her child. It tastes bad, but it is needed. God may have to hurt us, but He will never harm us. His love governs everything, and it was ruling my destiny.

Make no mistake: there was suffering associated with being rejected. Terry had experienced it as a result of my choice to reject him, and now I was experiencing it as a result of his rejecting me.

No matter what comes to us, good or bad, as a result of someone else's choices (and most of us consider suffering as "bad"), be they purposefully done or not purposefully done—we need to receive it as directly from God the moment He allows it into our life. Listen how E.B. Pusey so beautiful states this principle (he writes from the 1800s, but we can understand today):

> *This, then, is of faith, that everything, the very least, or what seems to us great, every change of the seasons, everything which touches us in mind, body, or estate, whether brought about through this outward senseless nature, or by the will of man, good or bad, is overruled to each of us by the all-holy and all-loving will of God. Whatever befalls us, however it befalls us, we must receive as the will of God. If it befalls us through man's negligence, or ill-will, or anger, still it is, in every the least circumstance, to us the will of God. [underlining mine– JM] For if the least thing could happen to us with out God's*

permission, it would be something out of God's control. God's
providence or His love would not be what they are. Almighty
God Himself would not be the same God; not the God whom
we believe, adore, and love.[116]

I wish I could tell you that I had a conversation with God immediately after hanging up with Terry. Oh, that God would be our first response in our joys and in our dissapointments! I had a conversation all right, but I'm sorry to say that I left God completely out of it. It was as if I had unconsciously responded, "Step aside, God, I want to talk to Satan." (Not a wise move. I am so thankful for God's mercy over my ignorance when He knew the overall spirit of my heart was to follow Him. Today looking back, I would not recommend for anyone to converse with Satan other than to quote scripture, as Christ did in the wilderness. Nevertheless, God is merciful, and He can still lead us in spite of our foolishness.)

Perhaps it was also a rare moment of righteous anger; I can't say for sure. Righteous anger is the only kind of anger that Jesus demonstrated. Jesus got angry when the moneychangers were making a mockery of God's house by changing "the temple from a place of prayer into a place of corrupt commercialism."[117] He even overturned their business tables, but that was clearly righteous anger and of course not sinful.[118] Righteous anger is not capricious, unlike the anger that can suddenly emerge from human tempers, which if not kept in check with the Spirit can easily turn into sin. (For example, not getting my selfish way, such as when someone else gets "my" parking spot.)

After I hung up the phone with Terry, I marched around my room, treading more heavily with each step. As I did so, I spoke aloud with keen determination, directing my words to the author of confusion himself: Satan.

"You think you are so smart! Well, I have a thing or two to say to you! You can just get out of here right now! You are nothing but a lying, scheming deceiver and I have had all of you I can stand! You prance around like you are an angel of light, but you are nothing but a source of darkness, confusion, and destruction, and I'm not falling for it! Oh, you have really ticked me off good, so just watch what I'm going to do about it! I am packing up my stuff and I am MOVING HOME!"

As I continued walking around my apartment—well, it was more like stomping—I gathered energy, intensity, and resolve as I spoke out loud. I didn't shed so much as a single drop of a tear this time. I wasn't sad; I was mad! I wasn't even angry at Terry. I could see things for what they were, and I was furious at the enemy for causing such total confusion in Terry's life. Yes, I had left my husband nearly two years before, but I had confessed all that as sin and had not wavered once since the day I gave my life to Christ.

I knew where this confusion had come from: it was evil and satanic. It was exhausting and confusing for Terry. I made a *love must be tough* decision: I was moving back home!

You see, several months prior to that night I had I met an older Christian couple: very good friends of Paul and Macon's who were visiting them from out of town. Paul and Macon had the most united marriage I had ever witnessed, and they had told me that Jerry and Dee's unity was their model, so naturally I wanted to meet them. I left quickly after only briefly speaking with Jerry and Dee, though, as the four of them were leaving to play tennis.

Later, Paul and Macon told me they had related my story to Jerry and Dee after I left: my leaving my husband, my coming to Christ, my desire to reconcile, Terry's rejection of the reconciliation, and the ensuing confusion. Jerry said, "She left him initially? And she moved out? Well, sounds like the tables have turned now, and the shoe is on the wrong foot. Juana has repented, so she needs to move back into the house. Let him move out now if he wants, so the shoe will be on the right foot."

When they first relayed Jerry's opinion to me, I was shocked. There was no way I was going to even suggest that to Terry! Move back? That sounded crazy, and I was surprised that Paul's friend Jerry, whom he admired so much, would even suggest such a preposterous idea. It sounded to me as if I would be dishonoring Terry all over again.

But that night, when Terry called me in such utter confusion for what seemed like the tenth time, the idea to move home came to my mind instantaneously, and it had never looked so good. I was so mad at the enemy that I decided that was exactly what I was going to do! If Terry wanted to move out, that was his business, but I was going home! My unsaid quest was sort of an "as for me and my life, I will serve the Lord" ambition.[119] I decided to start first thing in the morning toward the goal of moving home.

I did have a sense of peace about what God wanted me to do, however crazy it seemed. I had been praying fervently for His will. Then it struck me that night in an instant of crystal-clear clarity . . . Jerry's advice coming back to me, combined with the "love must be tough" principle I had learned. Yes, crazy as it sounded, the Holy Spirit was leading me home . . . literally.

It was in that instant that God's will came as a claim upon my conscience. It didn't have to make sense to me. My part was simply to do it. It was hard for me to perceive my course of action as a sacred and God-blessed task—it was so different from familiar Christian tasks such as assisting in the church nursery or making soup for a sick friend—but the carrying out of it was the very design of God. I did not have to understand in order to obey.

The knowledge that returning home was God's will for my life gave me great determination and courage in spite of my fear. How I felt about it really didn't matter anyway. I didn't have to feel anything to obey. We read nothing about what the great saints of the Bible felt when they obeyed God. They simply obeyed. Noah obeyed. Daniel obeyed.

The next day, I called the utility company to have my power disconnected at my apartment. I contacted a moving company and provided them my current address and my "new" address. It felt odd as I spoke with these strangers on the phone about my plans as if they were common, everyday, next-step decisions from a new customer. Far from it. This was a top secret mission! I hadn't told a soul. And what's more, Terry knew nothing of it.

Christ alone set my heart at peace with each step I took toward returning home, but each step of trust and obedience made the next step easier. When apprehension resurfaced, I cast myself fully on God yet again. "God is our refuge and strength, a very present help in trouble" (Psalm 46:1, KJV).

Had I been more mature in my spiritual life, I perhaps would have told trusted friends such as Paul and Macon, or maybe, as Queen Esther had done, asked them to pray and fast for me for three days before I made this bold move. Queen Esther and I had a lot in common. Like Esther, my husband had not requested to see me in weeks. She was entering her husband's personal space without first receiving her husband's request to do so—which in her case was punishable by death, if her action did not please the king. What was I risking to come home without an invitation? It could be the final death of my marriage. In my heart, though, I believed it was the right thing to do. If my marriage perished, it perished.[120]

I met with the apartment manager to tell her that I was moving out. (The same one I mentioned in an earlier chapter, who recommended I be placed in the building with all the "fun single people," to which I responded to put me in a quiet building.) She was single, too, and she knew I had been separated when I moved into my apartment nearly two years earlier. She asked me where I was moving, and I told her "home."

She replied, "Oh, are you and your husband back together?"

"Not exactly," I replied.

I didn't tell anyone else of my plans. Moving day arrived, and late that Saturday afternoon two large men appeared at my apartment with the moving truck. My stomach was filled with butterflies, like when I used to wake as a child on the long-planned and long-awaited day when our family was departing on a camping trip—only this was like a secret mission planned in record time. I was filled with anticipation of the day that lay ahead of me, as if I were about to watch the conclusion of a movie—only I didn't know if I was in a romantic comedy or a horror film!

I only knew I was filled with a strong inward sense that this action was exactly what I needed to do. The two strong, unassuming movers were, unknowingly, crucial accomplices in my life's drama, and in a role they hadn't even auditioned for. I knew for sure, though, that I couldn't follow through on the move without their muscles! They loaded everything up: my sofa, my chair, my kitchen table and chairs, washer, dryer, my twin bed, lamps, accessories, clothes, and other items. They had my house address on the paperwork, and I was to meet them there.

I had no idea if Terry would be home when the moving truck pulled into the driveway. I don't remember if the men told me they were going to stop to eat or if they headed straight to our house. It was only about a five-mile trip to our house, and by now it was almost sunset.

As I drove my car west down Falls of the Neuse Road, with the clear, bright, setting sun pouring into my windshield, I felt like I was being filmed in a movie. But this was no movie; this was real life. It was a surreal experience. Could I really be doing this? Was I crazy? Had I lost my mind? What was I doing?

Was I crazy? Had I lost my mind? What was I doing?

I wanted to pull my car over, for I desperately wanted to get alone with God and be still with Him for even just a few moments. I turned into a familiar Kentucky Fried Chicken and went into the restroom. I remember that no one else was in there, and as I recall, it was one of those smaller, single bathrooms. I stood right in front of the sink, bowed my head, and lifted my heart up to God. *"Oh, Dear God! Please help me!"*

I pulled up to the house. I don't remember if the movers got there first and were waiting for me, or if they arrived a few minutes after me. I can tell you that there was no sign of Terry. I unlocked the house and noticed that his car was not in the garage. I had to pay no attention to any doubting thoughts as they tried to dart into my mind. Instead, I gave focused concentration to the movers, as they began to alternately ask me, "Where do you want this?" As the movers constantly exited and re-entered the house with their dollies, they were totally unaware of the magnitude of what they were doing.

I told them where to put everything. We disassembled a card table that Terry had put in the kitchen, and replaced it with our oak kitchen table and chairs that Terry had stained for us when we first got married.

Everything was neatly put back where it had been nearly two years before, and then the movers left. I can't remember how much I gave them for a tip, but I probably gave them the biggest tip of my life.

I was so relieved that the move-in was finished—and finished without incident. But more importantly, I had made full restitution for leaving my husband. I had completed the work that I believed God had given me to do, by fully repenting for leaving Terry, and I had become more and more convinced that this strange action was God's will for me. With each step I had taken to move (other than when I was driving into the sunset earlier that evening, when my emotions were welling up and I had to turn my eyes to Jesus in that bathroom), I knew that this decision was the right one.

I was *home.*

CHAPTER FIFTEEN

HOME

I ENJOYED JUST WALKING AROUND the house for a few minutes, smelling the fresh paint and carpet that somehow had retained its familiar and welcome scent almost two years later. It was nearly dark now, so I turned some lights on downstairs. There was our teal green and cream-colored carpet on the stairs that I had carefully planned out when we were building our house. Oh! How many wallpaper samples I had looked at before deciding on the simple, contemporary peach and teal geometric print in the kitchen that seemed to recognize me, too, as I gazed upon it like an old friend.

I looked around upstairs in the quiet, wondering for a few seconds which room I should take. I didn't have to wonder long: I took our peach bedroom. Of course! How I loved our carved rice pattern on the pencil post of our dark, mahogany, king-sized bed against the contrast of the light peach-colored walls! I was home, and I couldn't wait to crawl into my own bed. This was where I belonged. Only one thing was missing: Terry. With butterflies still in my stomach, I went to bed.

Sometime later that night, I heard noises downstairs, like doors shutting and footsteps, and I sat up in bed. I can't remember what I was thinking at that exact instant, but if I had to guess, it was probably the biggest, *"Oh my goodness, here we go!"* moment of my life. I knew this was the moment when I would discover Terry's response. I heard his footsteps coming nearer.

"Juana?" Terry called out my name while walking upstairs.

"I'm here," I answered in the dark.

He opened the door and flipped on the light. "What are you doing here?" Terry asked, incredulous, staring at me in his bed.

"Well, I've come home," I answered nonchalantly, as I looked at his dumbfounded face.

"I can see that, but *what are you doing in here?*" Terry asked, with a totally confused expression on his face.

"I just decided that it was time to come home. I was wrong to leave, and so I'm back."

"But I'm not ready for this. You can't just do this!" His face began to take on an angry appearance. "I'm not ready to be married to you again; you cannot force this on me!"

"I just knew it was time for me to come home . . ." I interjected, escalating in volume.

"So you think you can just come home, and everything will be like you want it? This is not right! I am not doing this!" Terry blurted out. He continued, "You can stay in this room, but I'm staying in the guest room! Good night!"

Visibly agitated, he quickly shut the door behind him.

"Good night!" I retorted.

❦

Here is Terry's perspective on that infamous night:

I pulled up at home and saw lights on. Seeing Juana's car in the garage, I thought, "What is Juana doing here?" When I walked into the kitchen, I noticed our kitchen table and chairs were back where they had been before Juana took them when she moved out. I realized that Juana had moved back home, and I was totally confused. I was just as bewildered when Juana came back home as I had been when Juana left home! I felt dumbfounded, but I was also angry. The ironic thing is I had gone to an automobile race in Charlotte that day. The last time I had gone to a race was nearly two years ago, when I came home and Juana was gone. The whole thing was strange. I knew one thing, though: I was not staying.

❦

Deep inside, I had hoped that Terry would stay, but I wasn't in the least surprised. I hadn't come home to try to force him to be married to me; I came home so that our living situation would more accurately reflect the truth of our relationship. I had initially rejected Terry and sinned against him by leaving him and choosing to separate. But I had repented. I had done a complete turnaround.

He had done an about-face as well. For nearly one and a half years, Terry had rejected me. He now had to make a concrete choice: his actions would reflect if *he* now chose to separate from me. My love had to be tough, allowing Terry to reach a crisis of decision. As Jerry had wisely said, "the shoe had to get on the right foot."

The next morning I jumped up to make some coffee for Terry. I didn't drink coffee, but I knew he liked coffee early in the morning. He came down, left, and didn't touch the coffee. I didn't see him the whole day. When he finally came home, he said he wanted to speak to me.

"Look, Juana, you cannot force this marriage on me," Terry calmly told me.

"I know that."

"I can't live here if you're here, so I am moving out."

"Okay."

"You just can't force your way on me, so I'm going to move in with Craig. It's going to take me a couple days before I can move, so in the meantime, I'll continue sleeping in the guest room."

I was disappointed, but again, not too surprised.

For those next couple of days, I wanted to make the most of my opportunity to show Terry kindness, since I had never lived with him as a Christian. I knew my time was short, since he would only be there for two more days. I made him coffee those mornings, but he made it clear that he did not want me doing anything for him, including making him coffee. He rejected anything I tried to do for him.

Boy, was the shoe on the other foot now! I was the recipient of his rejection, as he had been the object of my rejection when I left and would not even let him come talk to me.

⁓

Terry moved in with a single friend from college, Craig Adams. We continued to live independently, and I adjusted to life back in the house we had built together right before we had separated. I missed Terry terribly. We had planned every part of the house together, and now I was back, but he was gone. I also had to carry around the knowledge that I had torn my house down with my own hands, and, although I had found complete forgiveness in Christ, I still had to face the consequences of my actions. As I said in an earlier chapter, I continued to be reminded that I was living proof that "the wise woman builds her house up, but with her own hands the foolish one tears hers down!"[121]

> My love had to be tough, allowing Terry to reach a crisis
> of decision.

During this time, Terry would have conversations with me. As in our earlier dating conversations while we were separated, he would tell me all the things that he didn't like about me. I was on to this pattern in our conversations, so I prayed for patient endurance before we would get together to talk. I also had Christian friends praying for me when they knew Terry and I were getting together.

Sometimes I let him just get it off his chest, but I am sorry to say, there were several times when I would dish it right back. Afterwards, I hated it when I did that, because I wanted Terry to discover the love of Christ. "I pray that you . . . may have power . . . to grasp how wide and long and high and deep is the love of Christ, and to know this love that surpasses knowledge."[122]

I wanted so much to have the opportunity to be Terry's wife again, only this time I wanted to be a Christian wife. I had been studying for over a year and a half what God's Word had to say to wives. I knew the difference Christ was making in my life, and I wanted Terry to know how deep Christ's love was for him. I wanted to be a strong witness for the Lord, but many times I retaliated against Terry's criticism and blew it once again.

Kneeling alone by my bedside in our peach-colored bedroom, time and time again after I had blown it with Terry, I would confess my vindictive attitude to the Lord.

I was tempted to say, "But what about his attitude, Lord?" But God would gently remind me that I was only responsible for my own sin, and that I was not the moral custodian of my husband. He was pleased with my brokenness over my own sin, and He allowed me to leave Terry with Him. It was none of my business; it was between Terry and God.

The real underlying issue was that Terry had not forgiven me for leaving him. But how could he truly understand how to forgive, until he knew Jesus Christ personally? Once we meet the Savior, He teaches us how to love and forgive. I was the one who was the Christian, and I needed to reflect my Savior's character.

I needed to be forgiving, if I wanted to be forgiven. "For if you forgive men when they sin against you, your Heavenly Father will also forgive you. But if you do not forgive men their sins, your Father will not forgive your sins."[123] I continued to gain strength from God to sustain me as we continued to live in uncertainty.

ᚷ

I wrote Terry a short letter telling him that he was free to go. I wrote it instead of telling him face to face, because that way I could say exactly what I wanted to say. Speaking it to him would have opened me up to saying all kinds of things that I might have regretted. "The one who talks much will for sure sin, but he who is careful what he says is wise."[124] The letter said something like this:

Terry,

I wanted to write you to tell you that I have been doing some soul searching, and I now realize that I have been wanting to hang on to you against your will. I know now that cannot be done. I want you to know that you are free to go. I can no more force you to be married to me anymore than I could have forced you to marry me the first time you chose to ask me to marry you. I want you to know that I will be fine. I told you a year ago that I had committed my life to Christ. I know that He has been with me this far, and I know He'll go with me in the future. I am thankful for all the good times that we shared together.

I will always wish the best for you in the years ahead,

Juana

Notice that I did not begin, "Dear Terry," nor did I end with, "Love, Juana." That was intentional. I did not go on and on about how I would always love him—on the contrary, I didn't mention a word about loving him. Oh, don't get me wrong. I did love him! If I had followed how I *felt*, I would have told him so in this note, and probably more than once. But I was not following my feelings.

If I had followed my feelings, I would have said things like, "I love you, I will always be here for you, I will wait for you as long as it takes, etc." I might have even met with him face-to-face to be able to be with him.

But that is exactly what I chose not to do. The "love must be tough" approach gives the spouse who wants out and feels pressure to make a decision the freedom to choose for himself—what James Dobson describes as "opening the cage door." God had provided me the practical help I needed straight from the pages of *Love Must Be Tough*.

I knew with confidence that God was guiding my every step. I wrote that letter by a sheer act of my *will*, convinced it was the right thing to do. It was not at all what I felt like doing or saying, but I had made a total surrender of my life to God, including my emotions. My emotions tried to manage my life for me, making me wonder at times if I had really made a complete surrender to God, so I couldn't question the matter for even one moment with my emotions.

How different my mother's response had been, all those years ago, from what my response now was. Hers was totally based on emotion, because she too longed to have her broken marriage restored. I knew that in her case she did the best she could during a dark time of chaos and confusion in her life, as she tried to navigate her way through her deep struggles.

How different my life now was! Once I was also controlled by my emotions, and I left my husband because of them. I had spent a year and a half crying on Saturday mornings as a newly married wife and I had cried regularly in each session with Naomi. What had my emotions done for me? I had belonged to myself for twenty-six years, and during that time my emotions had their turn at managing my life—and had failed me miserably!

We can trust God with His timing. He is never late; He is always right on time.

I knew I had made a complete surrender to God, and that He was now in complete control of my life. My will had to hold firm and steady, though, and I couldn't allow my emotions to debate if I had really done it. I *had* surrendered my life utterly to God. Now I could say with the apostle Paul, "For to me, to live is Christ,"[125] and that was settled in my will. "It is your purpose God looks at, not your feelings about that purpose. And your purpose, or will, is therefore the only thing you need to consider."[126]

I had learned the secret that obedience lies in the will. So many women are just like I was, slaves to their feelings. Oh! There is freedom from being a prisoner to our feelings! If we follow our feelings, we will be deceived! "The heart is deceitful above all things and beyond cure. Who can understand it?"[127] If we wait to feel good about a decision, we may never make the right decision. I need to know this truth to this very day. I would not even get out of bed each morning if I followed my feelings. Obedience to God lies *in your will!*

If I can do this, so can you. Since you have read this far, you know I am a misguided, foolish, unspiritual, emotional woman who needs direction. Pray and obey God implicitly. Do what He tells you to do, or stop doing what He tells you to stop doing. Feelings follow faith—faith doesn't follow feelings. You will have the joy of knowing you obeyed God and did the right thing.

The safest place to be is in the center of God's will! When opposition comes (expect it) and it is difficult, you will have God's peace in knowing that you are totally in His hands, right where He wants you to be.

◌

In Terry's confusion, he had been asking his family and friends what he should do, after I had become a Christian and had made him aware of my desire to reconcile. Everyone advised him the same thing: "don't go back with her; you aren't compatible with her," and "there are more fish in the sea out there." Not one of the people whom Terry asked for advice professed to be a Christian. No one suggested that he try to reconcile.

Unknown to me, on three different occasions Terry drove to the county courthouse to begin paperwork to file for divorce. Many years later he told me that each time he arrived at the courthouse, he waited his turn in line to get assistance. When he got to the front, he could not go through with it, and he just walked away.

On the third time as he was waiting in line he said to himself, *"Okay, I'm going to wait my turn again to get the papers to file for divorce. If I get to the front of the line, and again I can't do it, then that's it. That's it for good—I am not coming back."* He waited as the clerks assisted each person in front of him. Finally, he got up to the front of the line, but was unable to continue—he walked out of the courthouse for the last time.

◌

A couple of months later, in October of 1986, twenty-four months nearly to the day after leaving my husband, Terry had to have some minor surgery. God ordained that surgery. Terry called me and asked me if I would come to the hospital. I visited with him in the hospital and stayed by his side. As I helped him and leaned over the bed, he affectionately held my hand.

Unlike when he didn't want the coffee I had made him when I first came home, he now allowed me to serve him. I could get him water, fluff his covers, but mostly I sat beside him to give him companionship. We were taking baby steps in the right direction.

When it was time for him to be discharged, he told me he wanted to go home, to our home. He asked me if we could go home together. My answer was "Yes!"—he did not have to ask me twice! There was not a lot of fanfare in his asking me, nor a lot of fanfare when I answered, but somehow I think there might have been a few angels rejoicing overhead. My heart overflowed with joy as I knew I was experiencing God's faithfulness.

Just recently, I read that Microsoft founder Bill Gates said in an interview that he thought it made sense to believe in God but "exactly what decision in your life you make differently because of it, I don't know."[128] What decision do you make differently??? Are you kidding me? For starters, how about all of life's big decisions and little decisions?

I tremble just thinking of all I would have missed had I not waited on God and sought after Him twenty-eight years ago. I would have missed out on so many blessings God had in store for me. God knew exactly what it would take for me to come to the end of myself and to be receptive to meeting His Son. He knew the suffering I would have to endure to grow in perseverance. "We also rejoice in our suffering, because we know that suffering produces perseverance; perseverance, character; and character, hope."[129]

He knew how much I would need perseverance and hope for things that were to come later. Without perseverance I would not have learned to depend on the Lord for my total sustenance. I would not have known that His presence alone was more than enough to see me through anything that I would have to face in the future. Through my trials, God equipped me to be a better wife and a better mother than I would have been otherwise. As I told you earlier, I'm not a different kind of Christian because I'm a woman—I'm a different kind of woman because I'm a Christian, and that has made all the difference.[130]

As I continued to enjoy my relationship with Him, God was equipping me for the challenges that were yet to come: with Terry's blessing, voluntarily leaving my six-figure income (at Terry's worst time, financially) to be a full time wife and mother; waiting on God to change Terry's heart so we could teach our children at home; and serving Christ by accepting the challenge to teach my children at home for the next thirteen years.

Had I not waited on God during my time of marital separation, I would not have learned to recognize His voice among all the other voices calling for our attention. I would not have been able to deal with what was really going on in my heart—I would still be trying to carry the weight of my sin, which I was incapable of doing anything about. I would not have known what it meant to wait on God. I would not have had His daily instruction, but would have been left to my own devices to "guess" and follow my misguided feelings.

And just think: I nearly threw it all away.

I would not have known the joy that comes from facing difficulty in relationships in life by honoring my marriage commitment, and finding God's plan for a man and a woman as He had in mind from the beginning. I would not have known the joy that comes from having a clear conscience before God. I would not have reconciled with my husband nor desired to—I would have thrown away the opportunity to continue to build on all the history we had lived and built together that began when I was a skinny seventeen-year-old freshman and he was a good-looking nineteen-year-old sophomore in college.

I would not have discovered that genuine restoration can only come through Jesus Christ and the power of forgiveness. Corrie ten Boom, that great saint who during World War II hid Jews in her home at her own family's risk and whose sister and father died under the hands of the Nazis, said that those who were able to forgive were the ones best able to rebuild their lives. I am living proof of that. What a different life I would have had, had I not taken the less-traveled road and entered into a personal relationship with the living Lord through the narrow gate.

Seven years after I became a Christian, Terry gave his life to Christ. Two years after we reconciled, our daughter Blair was born. Five years after we reconciled, our son John was born. Seven years after we reconciled, our son Alex was born. Eight years after we reconciled, I taught my first class on Time and Home Management, eager to share with women how our homes can reflect the order of our Creator's design. (Think of it: me, a recovering slob!)

Ten years after we reconciled, on April 5, 1997, our daughter Mary entered the world—surprisingly, born totally blind—having been born without any eyes whatsoever. Our relationship with Christ equipped us on the inside to be able to deal with the outside with an inner peace, and an acceptance that God was still in control. Having our souls in perfect peace in undesirable circumstances is entirely possible and attainable—with a childlike trust in God. And His amazing grace continues to pour over our family. I wouldn't change anything that I have been through, for it all worked together to draw me to the Savior and—ultimately—to draw our entire household to the Savior.

When I look at my four beautiful children—Blair, John, Alex, and Mary—I sometimes weep when I think of how different my life could have been had I continued on the path of selfish desires that I was on. I will be forever grateful to the Lord for reaching down and touching my life and rescuing me from myself, for surely "the broad road leads to destruction, and many enter through it. But small is the gate and narrow the road that leads to life, and only a few find it."[131]

All of our children have personally received Christ as their savior. Fourteen years later, on the National Day of Prayer, 2001, a local news team picked our family of six out of the crowd of hundreds. They interviewed me as to why we came to the steps of the state capitol building for such an event (located one-tenth of a mile from the courthouse where Terry had been unable to file for divorce fifteen years earlier). We were able to take a public stand for praying for our nation as an entire family committed to Christ. Nineteen years later, in the fall of 2006, Terry began leading Fellowship of Christian Athletes at Daniels Middle School in Raleigh, with all four of our children and me serving with him at his side—joining Johnny Evans's team as a volunteer.

I have listened in amazement to Terry describe (after he became a Christian) how he saw the unraveling of our marriage. To hear him tell it, it sounds like it was all *his* fault for neglecting his wife; from my perspective, I had been the one destroying my home.

But I've concluded that when a person truly yields to God's working in their life, he or she takes responsibility for the damage from their side. When Christ takes hold of a life, He gently convicts us individually through the Holy Spirit so that we will know the Truth. It is a place of liberation, for Jesus said, "You shall know the Truth, and the Truth shall set you free."[132]

In recent years, God's faithfulness and grace have been poured onto our parents. After being widowed for twelve years and in her late seventies, my mother married a committed Christian man whose wife of forty-six years had died. How sweet to watch him lovingly tie Mama's tennis shoe laces: he is a humble man who loves to serve others. Terry's parents began attending church in the sunset years of their life after receiving a golfing friend's invitation, and they have begun to grow in the Lord.

Does Jesus Christ make a tangible difference in my life? Yes! In fact, when I consider the whole of my life, I consider everything to be either Before 1985 or After 1985, since 1985 was the year that I began my personal relationship with Jesus Christ. God is the God of second chances!

God performed a miracle in my heart when he gave me a second chance in life, by making me a new creation on that Fourth of July night when I confessed Jesus as my Savior. And then He gave me a second chance in my marriage! That was twenty-eight years ago, and on April 4, 2014, we celebrated our thirty-third wedding anniversary.

Trust in the Lord with all your heart,
and lean not on your own understanding;
in all your ways submit to him,
and he will make your paths straight.[133]

∾

God does answer prayer. Sometimes He says "Yes." Sometimes He says, "No." But most of the time, He says, "Wait." Whatever answer He gives, we can trust Him. We can trust Him with His timing. He is never late; He is right on time. He tells us that, "All things God fits into a pattern for good, for them that love God and are called according to His purpose."[134] And His purpose is always to conform us to the image of His son. I can thank the Lord that His will is being worked out in my life. I can thank Him that one day He is going to show me the pattern, and I will see that He fulfilled His promises.

God is knitting each of our lives together into a beautiful tapestry. At this point, though, all we can see are the knots and loose threads on the back side, and they can look like a chaotic jumble. But on the front side of the tapestry a stunningly beautiful pattern is being woven, that we will one day get to view.

THE WEAVER

My life is but a weaving
Between my Lord and me,
I cannot choose the colors
He worketh steadily.

Oftimes He weaveth sorrow,
And I in foolish pride
Forget He sees the upper
And I, the underside.

Not till the loom is silent
And the shuttles cease to fly
Shall God unroll the canvas
And explain the reason why

The dark threads are as needful
In the Weaver's skillful hand
As the threads of gold and silver
In the pattern He has planned.

Author Unknown

And so you have come to the end of this part of our story. Many years have passed since the events described in this book, and since then many more colors, threads, and knots have been woven into the pattern. As I am now an older wife, I am asking God for more exuberance and enthusiasm for life; I desire to grow younger at heart as I grow physically older. Jesus Himself said, in Matthew 18:3–5, that to become a mature believer is to become like a little child. There is something marvelously youthful that occurs when you invite Jesus to help Himself to your life: you grow younger instead of older.

I know that without God continuing to work in my life, my natural tendency would be to become the very opposite: old in spirit. As I said before, He could remove His grace at any moment, and choose to use someone else; I would have nothing to complain about. It is all about His grace in our lives—it is nothing special about us.

As J.R. Miller wisely points out, I cannot stop the wrinkles from surfacing and the gray hairs from growing, but I can live as a young woman and even like a playful child, having fun in my aging "house." Instead of being marked with frowns, frets, unattractiveness, dullness, complaints, whines, worries, and strife, I pray that God will give me a simple, youthful spirit and joyfulness as I move toward old age here on earth.

I cannot stop the aging process of my body, but there is nothing to keep my spirit from being young![135] Jesus tells us in Matthew 9:14 that the kingdom of heaven belongs to those who are like children. Oh, that smiles and laughter would abound from my face like those of a happy young girl! Wouldn't we all like to be the wives of happy husbands as we grow old together, before we go into the life everlasting? How about you? Will you join me in this prayer by God's grace? Will you go to God to be renewed day by day on the inside?

The events I've described are barely part of Terry's and my memory now: they are like an old, faded dream. Like Jacob who worked seven years for the woman he loved, yet "they seemed to him but a few days,"[136] those days of our early troubled years seem like a distant memory compared to the solid Christian home we love and enjoy today. Those traumatic old events were only the birth pangs of the adventures in the life of our new *Christian* family. All my children have ever known is a Christian home, to God be the glory! The old is gone, and the new has been created!

It's not that we never face difficulties now, but now we know we can face anything with our Savior's abiding presence: He has taught us how to love and forgive!

It's not so much the question of *can* I (and you) establish a Christian home, but *will* I (and you) establish a Christian home?

We have a gold plaque mounted beside our front door, and on it are inscribed the words of Joshua 24:15: "As for me and my house, we *will* (italics–JM) serve the Lord." If we are now serving Him even after our messed up beginnings, then so can you. Every home faces trials, and you can get through yours. It is always possible to do the will of God! Say with me: "I *will*, by His grace, live in obedience to what God wants me to do." I'm talking to myself, too, even all the way at the end of my story. We all need encouragement. It is always possible to do the will of God!

Our homes can be mini-embassies for the kingdom of God. We are Christ's ambassadors as we trust and obey Him in the kind of woman we are, the kind of wife that we are, the kind of mother we are, the kind of sister we are, the kind of daughter we are, and the kind of friend we are. All you have to do is ask Him! "Ask and it will be given to you; seek and you will find; knock and the door will be opened to you. For everyone who asks receives; the one who seeks finds; and to the one who knocks, the door will be opened" (Matthew 7:7–8).

So much more happened after all these events, but that's another story: the making of a Christian family. Come find me later, and I'll tell you what happened next.

And just think: I nearly threw it all away.

∾

Will you join me in the words of St. Francis of Assisi, the theme of whose prayer God put on my heart that Fourth of July night over twenty years ago?

Lord, make me an instrument of Your peace,
Where there is hatred, let me sow love;
Where there is injury, pardon;
Where there is doubt, faith;
Where there is despair, hope;
Where there is darkness, light;
And where there is sadness, joy.

O divine Master, grant that I may not
So much seek to be consoled as to console;
To be understood as to understand;
To be loved as to love;
For it is in giving that we receive;
It is in pardoning that we are pardoned;
And it is in dying
That we are born to eternal life.

PART THREE

THE LIFE OF FAITH AND MARRIAGE

A man's true progress consists in denying himself and the man who has denied himself is truly free and secure.

—THOMAS À KEMPIS

CHAPTER SIXTEEN

WHAT FAITH MEANS

BY NOW, YOU HAVE SEEN that Terry and I came a long way from where we started in our marriage. There is no question in my mind that we would have ended up divorced had I not taken a U-turn on the road of life. I would have missed all the joy and future blessings that God had prepared in advance for me, had He not drawn me to Himself.

It is still amazing to me, and I am humbled when I think of God reaching down and touching me and making a way for me to *know* Him, through what Christ did for me on the cross.

For what else would cause a woman to go from leaving her husband and wanting her own way, to desiring her marriage back and praying for harmony and unity with the husband of her youth—wanting to make his life as easy and pleasant as she can?

We don't need to find ourselves—we need to lose ourselves! In losing our lives, we find our lives. Remember the contract I wrote with God? We die to ourselves. Denying ourselves, we find immeasurable freedom. My life for yours. It is the mystery of God.

On that never-to-be-forgotten October night when I left Terry, little did I know that that one night—which I would later describe as the worst night of my life because it bore the worst decision of my life—would lead to the best decision of my life.

The worst day of my life . . . somehow would be forever strangely linked to the best day of my life. I had no idea that things were going to change forever and never be the same again. It reminds me of another day that, before I was a Christian, I never gave much thought to—except when it gave me a day off from school.

Good Friday. The day when Christians all down the ages from all over the world commemorate Jesus's death on the cross. It seems a strange name for such a sad day. But in my old life, it didn't really mean anything to me personally at all.

Good Friday. The worst day in all human history, yet looking back now, strange to say, knowing what I know now—it's the best day in all human history. The day that Jesus was killed—the only One who never did anything wrong. Some alleged criminals are imprisoned unjustly, I know, but Jesus *never* did anything wrong. The Bible says He was without sin. Crucifixion was a grueling way to die, reserved for criminals and renegades. Over His head at His crucifixion was written an inscription: "Jesus of Nazareth, The King of the Jews"—the charge for which He was dying. He was crucified between two real criminals. They were robbers.

One of the robbers admitted that they were getting what they deserved for their wicked deeds, saying of Jesus, "but this man has done nothing wrong."[137] As Jesus hung on the cross, with the criminals one on the left and one on the right, He said, "Father, forgive them, for they do not know what they are doing."[138]

But what did Good Friday mean to me when I was twenty-six, except perhaps a long weekend? My thoughts and actions showed where I stood: I knew nothing of Calvary's love.

Cross necklaces. Silver ones. Gold Ones. Large ones. Small Ones. A bizarre choice for a decoration to beautify one's neck. The cross: the symbol for an instrument of torture. When Jesus Christ said, "It is finished," he bowed his head, lowered his neck, for you and for me, and died.[139] His body hung, lifeless, on the cross.

"If I have not compassion on my fellow servant even as my Lord had pity on me, then I know nothing of Calvary love."[140]

If I have not compassion on the man I married even as my Lord had pity on me, then I know nothing of Calvary love.

I did not write my story just to tell you a story, but to tell you the *ultimate story*. For Christ died to pay the debt for *me and for you.*

One author has stated, "Sin will cost you more than you wanted to pay; it will take way more than you ever planned to give and it will lead you further than you ever wanted to go." Just think of the emotional cost of divorce—let alone the financial, spiritual, character, and future costs.

Perhaps you, like me, had to enter a place of great difficulty in your life to show you your need for the Savior.

Could it be that your marriage is the very thing that God wants to use to bring you to complete dependence upon Him?

In this life, God gives us far more than we can handle. He wants us in return to hand the problem over to Him: to the One Who can handle it. It then becomes not our problem, but His problem! He wants us to trust and obey Him, and He will do the work. That is the life of faith. Hard? No. Difficult? No. Impossible? Yes! The

Christian life is impossible. It is only by God's grace working in us that we can live it. The Bible tells us that Jesus said, "Apart from me you can do nothing."[141] But the good news is—we don't have to live apart from Him!

Sadly, I didn't know any of this when I was twenty-six. I was placing my confidence in confidence and in myself. One of my favorite movies is *The Sound of Music*, but when Maria sang the words "I have confidence in confidence alone," she, like me, was placing her trust in absolutely nothing. Even placing our faith in faith is meaningless. For the Christian, it is all about the *object* of our faith—the risen and living Lord Jesus Christ.

When I separated from my husband, seeking the Truth was the furthest thing from my mind. I was set on a course toward a wasted life. And I didn't want anybody telling me what to do. I wanted to do what I wanted to do.

We don't need to find ourselves—we need to lose ourselves!

I was set on a course seeking freedom and comfort and happiness, yet I knew nothing about what it meant to follow Christ, who is the only way to true freedom and true happiness. It would be years before I would become familiar with the words of Christ (often written in red in Bibles). Words such as "seek first [God's] kingdom" became a love letter to me during my separation, as if they were personal instructions from Jesus to me.[142] These words were contrary to my every thought in that autumn of 1984. That was my own fault, though, since even then I had at least three Bibles in my house. (Although, sad to say, they were probably in a box in the attic.) But what now qualifies me to point you to the life hid with Christ is that in the years since I have been reconciled to Terry, I have had a lot of biblical teaching and I've learned a lot. I have desired and continue to desire to apply to everyday life the Truth I've learned, and to pass on to you what I have learned.

My foolish and self-centered reluctance to open the Bible and read even a small amount of it reminds me of the stubborn folly and pride of the parents of English poet Elizabeth Barrett Browning, who married the writer Robert Browning. Elizabeth's parents disapproved of the marriage so strongly that they disowned Elizabeth. In response, for the next ten years Elizabeth wrote her parents love letters. Finally, one day, a package from her parents arrived at her home. It contained all the love letters Elizabeth had written them—tragically, unopened. Perhaps if her parents had simply opened her letters and read them, Elizabeth's love for them would have wooed them toward reconciliation. But they wouldn't even read the letters. The Lord of the universe has written a love letter to you and me called the Bible, to woo us into a loving relationship with Him through Christ.

IF YOU WANT TO FOLLOW CHRIST

Our love for Him is to be first in our life, even above our closest human relationships. Christ said He did not come to bring peace but a sword—and a sword severs and divides. In some cases, followers will be thought of as hating their families, for loyalty to Christ must come before one's loyalty to one's own family.

I could not have been going in any more opposite of a direction before I became a follower of Jesus. Not only was I not looking for Jesus, I was looking for the best possible *earthly* relationship I could have—to find someone to live with for the rest of my life.

Jesus instructs His followers: "If anyone would come after me, he must deny himself and take up his cross daily and follow me. For whoever wants to save his life will lose it, but whoever loses his life for me will save it."[143]

Christ is inviting us—*if we want* to follow Him—to deny ourselves and follow Him, daily. The King James translation says, "if any man will," the New American Standard states, "if anyone wishes to come," and the New International Version puts it, "if anyone would come."

Do you hear that?

We don't have to be His disciple.

We don't have to be a Christian.

We can go our own way.

He said, "*If* you want to be His disciple, *then* . . ." He doesn't force you to follow Him; it is completely voluntary. Yet once decided upon, the cost is clearly given. Three conditions apply: the disciple must deny himself, take up his cross, and follow Christ.

Christ-followers are clearly required to follow Christ's example of a life characterized by self-denial. Christ Himself said to the Father, "yet not as I will, but as You will," concerning His upcoming and never-before separation from His Father to pay for the sins of the world.[144] By "denying oneself," followers must seek the good of others above their own good.

We are all bombarded with messages from the world around us telling us that we have to be our own person. These messages shout that we have to look out for number one, and make sure our needs are being met.

I learned that the true Christ-follower lives diametrically opposed to the ways of the world. At the core of the Christian faith is the giving up of your rights—your way. It's a giving up of putting "me, myself, and I" first, to putting someone else first. The selfish, self-centered part of "I" must be killed: put to death, so to speak.

> Christians are called to die little deaths day by day to
> our selfish ways.

And a biblical marriage means that we must constantly be willing to sacrifice our wishes for the good of the other person. The thought I mentioned in my bridal portrait story bears repeating: Wouldn't it be great if all the conflicts in marriage were about both spouses wanting to sacrifice for the good of the other? Nevertheless, I'm talking to women. I'm talking to myself. So let's begin with us. As the song says, "Let there be peace on earth, and let it begin with *me*."

Being a Christ-follower means giving up your life for others. Put plainly, it is being considerate of others. It's thinking about other people first: What do they need? "Do nothing out of selfish ambition or vain conceit, but in humility consider others better than yourselves. Each of you should not only look to his own interests, but also to the interests of others."[145] It means being thoughtful of those you live with, and those around you.

I had no earthly idea how much of my life and conversation was in slavery to myself. The things I wanted to talk about. The things I did. The things I felt. The fact is, we all love talking about ourselves. We don't need to vote for any idols, because we already have one: self. Remember what Janet Erskine Stewart said: "If we get our own way, we nurse a hideous idol called self. But if we give up our way, we get God."[146]

A simple story from normal, everyday life shows this. I walked into a quick-take-out Chinese place to pick up some food for dinner. Several people were standing around waiting, so I walked up to the counter and placed my order for the usual large chicken broccoli and hot-and-sour soup.

As I was pulling my wallet out to pay, I could hear a woman over on my right huffing and puffing. I continued to pay, thinking, *"Boy, they must really be taking a long time on that woman's order. She is one upset lady."* She shuffled back and forth and huffed and puffed some more as I thought, *"They are really busy tonight. It might take a long time to get my food; I'm glad I got my order in."*

I stepped away from the counter to wait for my food, when I noticed that woman step up to the counter, still huffing and puffing, and place her order. *"Wait,"* I thought to myself, *"she was already here when I got here, which means . . ."* I had jumped right in front of her and placed my order ahead of her. She was upset all right: at *me!*

I told the Chinese server that I felt terrible about my mistake, but he replied, "She's always like that."

It's more true I'm the one who is always like that. But it shouldn't be that way.

I wish I could tell you that events like that are rare. But the other day I was paying for my groceries in the "twenty items or less" lane. I was searching in my pocketbook for my checkbook, which was hidden among the pile of receipts. Oblivious to anything going on around me, I suddenly heard a man's loud voice. An elderly man seated in a motorized assisted device who was next in line behind me (whom I hadn't even noticed was there), bellowed at me.

"T-H-E-R-E'S PEOPLE IN LINE BEHIND YOU!"

"Oh, I'm paying right now!"

"IT'S TAKEN YOU F-I-F-T-E-E-N MINUTES!"

Ouch.

Common courtesy in the everyday affairs of life.

I'm talking about being aware of what others are doing, and not holding them up.

Noticing other people.

Making other's lives as easy as we can—especially our spouses (I need to hear this too.)

Humbling ourselves by being a servant.

Offering the first cookie on the plate to someone else before we take one.

Sadly, the people we treat the worst and take for granted may sometimes live in our own homes. One man I interviewed who got attention in another woman's arms told me he basically felt ignored by his wife in favor of her work and her television programs. Something is very wrong here. Some wise person has said that "the house that has no time for courtesy will always have time for rudeness." If we treat our family members with love and respect, we will treat others the same way.

Unfortunately, so often it is reversed. Christians, of all people, should be the most courteous on the planet. Jesus said,

"By this all men will know that you are my disciples, if you love one another."[147]

One hymn title says it best: "They'll Know We are Christians by Our Love." No one accidently develops into a lady or a gentleman; it must be learned in the home. The world will not go to church or read the Bible, but they will watch a Christian family. Our lives need to be dramatically different from the lives of our neighbors. If they aren't, it can mean only one of two things: either our neighbors are walking close with Christ, or we are not.[148]

I can tell you that before 1985, I was not.

The thing was, I loved getting my own way. Leaving my husband wasn't exactly considerate, to put it mildly! I wanted to do what I wanted to do, and nobody was going to stop me.

∽

Jesus is our model as our servant leader, and He even washed the disciples' dirty feet after the last meal He would have with them. He said:

> Whoever wants to be great among you must be your servant, and whoever wants to be first must be your slave—just as the Son of Man did not come to be served, but to serve, and to give his life as a ransom for many.[149]

What kind of worldview is this in which the first is last? The greatest is the humblest? The goal is to be the servant of all?

Read what a woman named Judith Lakes wrote, who paraphrased the "Hall of Fame" passage in the Bible regarding Jesus's life and attitude of servanthood. She rewrote it from a wife's perspective:

A Wife's Commitment

I, being made in the image of God a believer, a woman, and a wife, having equal worth in God's sight and equal access to the Lord as my husband, I choose not to grasp after a position of equal leadership with my husband, which is not my God-given place. Rather, I choose by God's grace to make myself nothing—taking on the very nature of a servant, which was the attitude of Jesus.

Desiring with all my heart to be humble like Him, I choose to be obedient to God's command and submit to my husband and die to myself. I understand that this decision will cause pain and suffering at times.

But in those moments, may I all the more identify with my Lord. When the cross is hard to bear, I pray for the will to give Him the burden of my heart and learn to rest in Him.

I trust God and His Word and am confident that He will exalt me in hearing of one of His own who obeyed His will. By His grace I will receive my reward worshiping Him in His presence forever—confessing Jesus Christ as Lord to the glory of God the Father.[150]

What a solemn commitment to contemplate. What an example of giving one's life for someone else, as Christ did for us. This commitment describes a radical life that I knew nothing about when I got married. True discipleship means following Christ wherever He may lead you.

In the book *Stepping Heavenward: One Woman's Journey to Godliness* by Elizabeth Prentice, the main character starts out blaming everyone else for what happens to her. Everything is someone else's fault—before she is slowly and genuinely transformed as a Christian.

I was just like her.

I was on the path of trying to gain the world and, in doing so, to lose my soul. One of the most wonderful things about Christianity is that it rescues us from wasting our lives on ourselves.

And a self-centered life is a wasted life.

There was a young American woman in the 1930s who was not much younger than I was when I stood at that crossroads that October night in 1984. At that time, she stood at a crossroads in her life too, but unlike me, she chose to fully surrender to Christ, to deny herself, to take up her cross and follow Him. Did she know the cost she would one day have to pay for her decision to follow Christ? Listen to what Betty Scott wrote in the days of her youth, in a prayer to Christ:

> *Lord, I give up all my own plans and purposes*
> *All my own plans, desires, and hopes*
> *And accept Thy will for my life.*
> *I give myself, my life, my all*
> *Utterly to Thee*
> *To be Thine forever.*
> *Fill me and seal me with Thy Holy Spirit.*

Use me as Thou wilt.
Send me where Thou wilt
And work out Thy whole will in my life
At any cost
Now and forever.

When Betty was only two years older than I was the night I stood in my kitchen and wrote my totally different note, she had married John Stam; they had a little baby girl, and they were missionaries in China. In 1934, they were captured by Chinese Communists, stripped half-naked, and paraded in the streets. Before they were captured, John had written a note. He had hidden the letter in the baby's clothing telling what had happened. He then wrote, "Philippians 1:20: 'May Christ be glorified whether by life or death.'" Betty had to watch as her husband was beheaded. Moments later, Betty had to put her head on the chopping block.

A young girl named Elisabeth copied Betty's prayer into her own Bible when Elisabeth was only twelve years old, because she had met Betty when hospitality had brought Betty to her home to share a meal with her family. Some time later, Elisabeth's father read the news in the paper that Betty had been murdered. Elisabeth learned at a young age the high cost of being a Christian, but it only increased her desire to one day become a missionary. It was from her that I learned about Betty's prayer. Elisabeth did grow up to become a missionary, and eventually our lives crossed. I didn't meet her until eight years after that October night when I left my husband. Her name is Elisabeth Elliot.

A self-centered life is a wasted life.

As she mentions in her foreword to this book, Elisabeth and I became friends in the earlier years of my Christian walk. I had been a Christian for seven years. She would come to have a great impact on my life, mentoring me and teaching me what it meant to be a Christian wife and mother. She wrote me over thirty-five letters, which I treasure, and she has visited me in my home on several occasions. Last month, my daughter and I were invited to visit Elisabeth and her husband, Lars, for several glorious days with them in their home by the sea. I was so honored when she invited me to speak on her radio program: she seldom had guests. All God's grace!

Elisabeth had much to endure in her life: her first husband, Jim Elliot, was murdered on the mission field. Betty Scott and John Stam, and Elisabeth and Jim Elliot suffered for doing the right thing—and it all came from faithfully following Christ and where He led them.

For most of us, God does not ask us to give our lives to Him as the Stams and Jim Elliot had to do, but we are all called to die little deaths day by day to our own selfish ways, as we seek to live for Him. We need to be obedient wherever He has called us to live. How about you? Will you obey Him and ask Him to make you into the Christian wife, parent, child, sibling, friend, and (sometimes) stranger that He calls you to be?

CHAPTER SEVENTEEN

REFLECTIONS ON MARRIAGE

REMEMBER THAT, WHEN I LEFT my husband, I began a quest to find my true soul mate? I wanted to chase romance, thinking the grass was greener with someone else. Why wouldn't I change what I could, to be spared living my entire life only to learn too late that I could have changed it for the better, long before?

My thoughts mirrored, almost down to the words, what Governor Mark Sanford of South Carolina said to his wife before they divorced. "Do you want to wake up when you are eighty and know you never had a heart connection?" His wife, Jenny, was shocked to hear him say this, as she had believed that they already shared a "heart connection"![151] I discovered the governor's comments when I was writing this book, as I read Jenny Sanford's memoir, and I cringed when I learned of the severe consequences that flowed from his choices—the loss of his marriage and family.

When I left Terry, I had no one in the wings waiting to spend his life with me as Governor Sanford had—but I foolishly wished I did, and I was planning to do all I could to find him. I longed to find my one true love, whose love would last a lifetime! Someone who would be crazy about me, and me about him. I was looking for the kind of love that Nicholas Sparks writes about in his bestselling novels. I went to hear the famed love-story writer speak. Someone in the audience asked him if he felt each person had one unique soul mate on earth, to which he hesitated before saying a resounding: "No!"

Looking back, I can see that it was only by God's grace that I did not become entangled with someone else. This "find my one true soul mate" mentality was a common thread among a number of the individuals I interviewed for the book—and it ultimately helped to destroy their marriages. In my own story, by God's grace I discovered the ultimate and only *true* soul mate for the entire human race: Jesus Christ. I now see that both the Governor and I were troubled with a restlessness that only Christ can calm, because no person on earth can satisfy those deep longings of the human heart.

Your true soul mate is the living God who made you and knows everything about you. God loves you more than anyone on earth is capable of loving, with a complete, unconditional love. This is a mystery. A gift. And He offers Himself to you.

But what about this term, "soul mate?" How many times I have heard in the news that a prominent person justifies their infidelity to their spouse because they have met their true "soul mate." Listen what one wise woman, whom I'll call Susan, told me in an interview. Susan had an adulterous relationship with her boss. She later repented and recommitted her life to Christ, and then remarried her husband, whom she had divorced as a result of her unfaithfulness:

> *I have come to despise the use of the word "soul mate." I don't use it in my marriage, even though I feel more connected with my husband than anyone in the world. We've lost who our soul mate is. The person I was in an adulterous relationship with kept telling me that we were meant to be together, that we were "soul mates." How could that be, if it was going to hurt our own children so much? How could it be that we were meant to be together, disallowing our commitment to God? I was playing with fire. The term soul mate is so stupid: our souls belong to Christ.*

Oh, how I wish that myriads of other people could know what Susan had to learn through severe pain and anguish. We need to entrust our soul to the true keeper and lover of our soul, Jesus Christ, while remembering that there is an adversary who stands in direct opposition to our soul.

OUR SOUL'S ENEMY

I wrote in Part One about the enemy of our soul. He does not come calling to us in a blatantly evil voice—or he could blow his cover. Remember the crafty sound of his voice as he whispered his lies in the beginning of my story? No, the enemy of our soul is a master of disguise, and one of his primary techniques is deception. We buy into it, and the rest is history.

In the third chapter of Genesis, we find the story of creation and the beginning of the earth and mankind. In the Garden of Eden, Satan appeared to the first woman in a disguise. He entered her mind with a thought as he spoke to her disguised as a serpent, and deceived her (by creating doubt) into thinking that God did not have her best intentions in mind, and that she could be like God (if she went against Him). How foolish our Grandmother Eve was to fall for the enemy's trap!

The essence of Eve's part in the Fall, when she partook of the one fruit that was forbidden, was not in her being deceived. She was deceived, make no mistake, but the root of the problem was her sin of usurping Adam's authority. You see, Eve was clearly made the vice-president in the relationship, and Adam was the president. The vice-president (Eve) has important responsibilities and is in a position of high value and influence, but the buck stops with the president (Adam) so he must be the one to make or approve all major decisions.

Eve was subordinate to Adam, but subordination does not mean inferiority. The president is not chosen president because he is a better person than the vice-president. Being president is an office, an assignment. Our husbands have been assigned an office by God (not by us!). And subordination is divinely inspired from the very nature of God. The Bible says that the Holy Spirit willingly serves and glorifies Jesus, and Jesus willingly serves and glorifies the Father. Jesus completely obeyed the Father and made Himself what the Bible calls "a little lower than the angels," when He took on the form of a man.[152]

"Subordination is not inferiority," wrote P.T. Forsyth. "It is divine. The principle has its roots in the very cohesion of the Eternal Trinity . . . To recognize no lord or master is satanic . . . I insist on the Christian principle, drawn from the very nature of

God and essential to the masculinity and femininity which He has made. Without the spirit of subordination there is no true piety, no manly nobility, and no womanly charm."[153] Forsyth goes on to say: "Such a concept is vehemently opposed to the world today. But if we insist on equality, we refuse the divine order which brings harmony."[154]

Reversing her and Adam's roles was Eve's big mistake: which we wives still do today whenever we try to control our husbands and call the shots.

Subordination does not mean inferiority.

We wives often think we would never have fallen for that trap, as Eve did, but hold on; not so fast. We do fall for it. Every time we believe the enemy's lies that come through deception—or fall for his crafty tactics, such as self-pity, doubt, discouragement, or trying to control our husbands—we are giving him territory in our lives. The Bible says he prowls around "like a lion," ready to devour its prey. The problem is that he appears to be only an irresistible kitty cat—but he has the teeth of a piranha.

Remember that Satan's promises never come true, and disobeying God's Word is never wise. Beware of thinking that you would never fall for Satan's trap as Grandmother Eve did, for nowhere do we have more opportunities to feed our own sinful desires than in the closest of all human relationships: marriage. Two sinners coming together for a lifetime—fully exposed.

MARRIAGE MEANS BEING EXPOSED

My kitchen window faces directly into my neighbors' kitchen window. Now I have some of the nicest neighbors around who we consider not only neighbors, but good friends, and we are very friendly with each other. Even so, it seemed that each time I was at my sink I was looking right at them, and they could look right at me! I felt so exposed that I got my husband to put up blinds. Who really wants to be exposed?

We have a little problem, though. We are never so exposed to another human being as we are in marriage: . . . naked . . . sick . . . well . . . cross . . . patient . . . impatient. Mike Mason, in his book *The Mystery of Marriage*, says that marriage is like having a huge tree growing right through the center of one's house. The other person is always there, like the oak tree in the middle of the room![155]

The Bible teaches Christians that we are to love others as we love ourselves. We are to regard them as every bit as important as we think we are. There is no other relationship on the face of the earth where we are confronted with this more than in the marriage relationship.

God's Word tells us that man was created in the image of God. Since that is so, we are led to conclude that there is nothing on the face of the earth so dear to God as a living, breathing, human being.

Because He loves us, God wants to sharpen and refine our character, and there is nothing that can sharpen us as "iron sharpens iron" as much as the marital relationship. Like sandpaper, our spouse can be used to sharpen us, but the sandpapering process can hurt. Wouldn't it just be easier to remain alone? (One woman whom I interviewed for this book, who got a divorce from the father of her children, is now in a marriage she finds equally difficult. She had the integrity to tell me that she wasn't so sure she made the right choice. In another interview, a man told me that he was equally miserable in the new marriage that was created out of his infidelity to the first marriage.)

God created marriage. It was not a human invention that was developed at some point in history. "[Marriage] is not a mere human arrangement, something that sprang up in the race as a convenience along the history of the ages. It was not devised by any earthly lawgiver. It is not a habit into which men fell in the early days."[156]

Marriage is a divine institution that was created by God in the beginning when He created mankind. Marriage is God's idea to complete the man, by bringing him the woman in holy marriage. It is to be the closest and holiest relationship on earth. If the union fails to bring joy and blessing, the problem is not due to God's holy institution, but with those who enter into it.

God created marriage to be a blessing to those who enter into it. It is to be a source of joy. It was designed to bring two people together to form one new union. The two are to leave their father and mother (despite the parent-child relationship being as close as it is) and cleave to one another.

From that point forward they are to consider the best interests of the other above their own. It is meant to be one man and one woman sharing life together as one unit for a lifetime. I recently met parent expert John Rosemond who told me: "Children don't need two parents—they need parents of *one mind.*" Being the best wife or husband you can be takes precedence over all other relationships. Being the best spouse you can be actually is the best thing you can do for your children. All other considerations are now second to the marriage union. Parenting is temporary—marriage is permanent. Each spouse seeking the good of the other person for a lifetime!

> Only God can truly meet our needs—we need to look to
> Him for that, not our husband.

But there's a thing we have, called an *ego*, that gets in the way. The reality is we don't always treat other people as we should. Being married was a designation designed by God for our ultimate blessing, but sad to say, our sinful natures get in the way and at times we even look at our marriages as if they were an annoyance to our day.

We care so much about ourselves that we become our own biggest obstacle to a more satisfying marriage. We decide that it couldn't be our fault, though, and instead we say things like, "If only he (or she) would [fill in the blank].

But for the one who has found new life in Christ, it doesn't have to be this way. In Christ, we have the help of the Holy Spirit working in direct opposition to our sinful nature, shaping us into the image of Christ. Giving us, in a word—the heart of a *servant*.

Think of it. A *servant*, not a nagger!

Did you know the book of Proverbs says that "a quarrelsome wife is like a constant dripping"?[157] The Bible is blunt, isn't it? A nagging wife seems to have no tact—apparently no restraint on her tongue. I once heard nagging defined as repeating something more than once. Ouch.

So why do I think I need to repeat myself to get a point across? Do I not believe that my husband can hear me the first time? Don't I want to be a good wife? We also read in Proverbs, "He who finds a wife finds what is good."[158] Wives are intended to be a gift. Gifts are things we like. Maybe next time, just before I'm tempted to repeat again what I have already said once to my husband, I can pause and ask myself: "Will saying this again contribute to my acting like a gift to my husband?"

We can assume, then, that marriage can be really bad—but it can also be really good. When it's really good, it's like money in the bank! But when it's really bad, it can be like a nagging toothache. Such a mystery. A paradox. But whoever said life was going to be easy?

The book of Proverbs concludes by saying that a virtuous woman is hard to find, but once found, is worth more than what money can buy—bringing her husband good, all the days she is alive.

Even now (it's been over twenty-eight years since I became a Christian), if I make my husband dinner, and he comments that he would like some Italian seasoning in the meat, I may *feel* like saying, "So that's the thanks I get for making supper! I'm just as tired as you are, but at least I made something. You can just sprinkle that little bottle on your own food!"

But I can replace those defensive thoughts by an act of my *will*, reflecting on my identity in Christ, contemplating, "I have done this for Christ! What is done for Christ lasts! Thank you, Lord, for giving me a faithful, hard-working husband to cook for! Teach me to not be so easily offended and help me remember that Terry likes Italian seasoning!" I don't always respond the right way, but I can't say that I don't know what God wants. He wants to make us less selfish and more loving. Remember how we talked earlier about being dead to self? Remember that contract I wrote with God? Dead people don't have any rights!

Let's follow the ways of the Proverbs 31 woman and, with God's help, let's *aim* to bring our husbands good. But I can hear you saying, "But what about my needs?" Only God can truly meet our needs—we need to look to Him for that, not our husband.

The very points where men and women see things differently can become the closest points in marriage, as we learn to appreciate our spouse. J.R. Miller states it this way:

> *Some are disappointed and discouraged by the discovery of these points of uncongeniality, these possibilities of discord, concluding at once that their marriage was a mistake and must necessarily be a failure. Their beautiful dream is shattered and they make no effort to build it again. But really all that is needed is wise and loving patience. There is no reason for discouragement, much less for despair. It is entirely possible, notwithstanding these points of friction and uncongeniality, to realize the highest ideal of wedding life.*

That was something I didn't know as a new bride. No wonder I was dissatisfied! Plus, I had never heard that, for most married couples, there is a slight dip in satisfaction in their early marriage. Hold on: "dip" means that it rises back up. Do not despair! The marriage can still be what God intended it to be—a blessed union. There is hope.

NORMAL DIP IN SATISFACTION AFTER WEDDING

I never knew there was normally a dip in satisfaction not too long after the wedding. Perhaps knowing that could have helped me endure the "tree growing in the middle of my house" and to try watering it in the early days of my marriage. (I'm writing to women, but let's not forget the men also have to endure the tree growing in the middle of their house, which is us wives!)

Sociologists have studied trends in marital satisfaction. In marriages lasting over thirty-five years, they discovered that there is an initial slow descent in satisfaction after marriage, but as time passes, the couples' level of satisfaction rises again and later surpasses the highest level of satisfaction to that point (the highest level to that point being immediately after they married, before the slow decline downward.)[159]

> Most married couples experience a slight dip in satisfaction early in their marriage.

Author J.R. Miller compares a wedding, life, and family to a mountain stream. The stream begins as a tiny thread: as a frolicking brook among flowers (the wedding). Sometimes the stream plunges into a gorge where the sun never shines (deep burdens or responsibilities). More streams join it (the children) before it eventually goes out to sea (life everlasting). I love this analogy taken from God's natural world. "There are times of sorrow, when the peaceful current is broken, when the stream plunges into the gloomy chasm. Every home has its experiences of trial. But through these it passes, emerging again, and flowing on, calmer, deeper, more majestic, in richer, fuller life than before."[160]

I want to point out that just because the sociological trends in marital satisfaction show a decrease in satisfaction as life's demands increase, that doesn't mean everyone *has* to go through them. I know now that help is available to change the natural progression to drift away from one another; God's grace and power is always available to us to make the hard but right choices.

MAKE THE IMPORTANT THINGS IMPORTANT

Neither Terry nor I knew then the importance of establishing good routines in marriage to keep the lines of communication open. I'm talking about doing simple things together to allow time to talk with one another, such as regularly taking a walk together alone. Investing time and effort into our marriage on a regular basis beforehand would have helped us focus on what was important, rather than merely responding to urgent issues. We should have made our relationship a priority when it was only "important" and not a crisis.

I have since learned that rarely do the important things *have* to be done on any given day or week. Instead, we crowd them out by defaulting to the urgent things. This can be a slow marriage-killer.

But the urgent things too often take precedence. They cry out for immediate attention: things such as responding to a friend's invitation, answering the phone, planning events with friends, and attending optional business social events. Those things in themselves were not wrong; they were good things. We didn't know then to say "No" to the good things so we could say "Yes" to the right things. I never knew that *good things can be the enemy of the best things*. With a sense of loss, I can look back and see that Terry and I pushed the important things in our marriage aside.

COMMUNICATION IS CRITICAL

After Terry and I were reconciled, I decided to make him fresh-squeezed orange juice every morning as a special treat. I bought oranges by the bagfuls, and used a manual juicer and my wrist to squeeze them; four squeezed oranges yielded one delicious cup of juice. I happily did this every day for the first four months we were back together, as a loving service to Terry.

One day, Terry was standing, barefoot, in the kitchen. He asked me if I had ever noticed the bits of nachos and dirt on the floor that stick into your feet. I told him, no, I hadn't noticed. He then said, "I really appreciate your squeezing me fresh juice in the morning, but I actually don't want any fresh-squeezed juice. I'd much rather have a clean kitchen floor."

Here I had been squeezing four oranges every day by hand, for four long months, thinking Terry was just loving that orange juice— and all along what he was wanting me to do was sweep the floor!

I told this story to an acquaintance, who replied, "What horrible communication! That is the worst communication I have ever heard of!"

I thought it was excellent communication. Better to learn in four months time what could have taken us decades to learn! I learned a lot that day about communication, as well as about doing what pleased my husband instead of what pleased me. And simply talking about it made all the difference.

LITTLE THINGS

Do the little things in life really make that much of a difference in a marriage? Yes! They do. A little inconsiderate remark. An intentional jab. A harsh criticism. A public contradiction.

Things such as nagging, watching television when your husband is talking to you, talking while your husband is trying to watch the game, texting when your husband is talking to you, using the excuse of headaches for not being intimate, procrastinating with a simple request, leaving hair on the bathroom floor, criticizing your husband in public. Need I go on? You can add your own "little things," I'm sure.

Over time, little things such as nagging can wear a person out. My husband's friend commented that he avoided going home until late at night just so he wouldn't have to face his wife's constant nagging.

Some "little things" may even show up quite innocently. When we were first married, we ordered a beautiful rice-patterned, pencil-post, queen-sized bed from Terry's Aunt Carol, who worked for a furniture manufacturer. Somehow there was a mix-up and the manufacturer accidently shipped us a king-sized bed. It was too much trouble for them to replace it, so we were able to keep it.

How nice, right? We thought so. Before we got the king-sized bed, though, we slept much closer together. But since we now had so much more room with the new bed, we began to spread out, and we got accustomed to it. If we traveled and had to revert back to a queen bed, we not only found it hard to sleep, but we began to desire more of our own space! All because of a delivery error, a subtle little thing that at first made us feel like we had made out like bandits, ended up robbing us! Not good for the beginning of a marriage, as the two are learning to become one. That physical distance was a foreshadowing of what would happen to us emotionally.

❧

I know that early in our marriage I struggled with what I call the "I'll do it later" syndrome; that got on Terry's nerves, I'm sure. The problem was, "later" never came until Terry would ask me to wrap the lettuce better or put my dirty dishes in the dishwasher.

I always justified it to myself: "What's the big deal? I can do it later. I'm in a hurry now." Why didn't I notice that I regularly said I was in a hurry and that it was an annoying habit? How was it that I didn't notice that I was responsible for contributing to a slow drift in an unhappy direction?

I'll give you one more example of an annoying habit I have that I'm still trying to kill. Terry will sometimes tell me that he has already told me something—for example, that we're having a Young Life meeting at our house that night, with an extra sixty-five kids or so who'll be showing up in an hour. (This actually happened.) If I don't remember him telling me that I'll reply, "Where were we standing when you told me that?"

If there's one thing Terry hates, it's for me to go into my "where were we standing when you told me that?" routine. When I am being that annoying, the conversation is usually over pretty fast. About the only habit Terry hates worse is my not shutting the kitchen drawers while cooking; he despises the crumbs and drips that find their way into the open drawers. Little annoyances can rub like a sudden fingernail on a chalkboard, only for what seems like the hundredth time. This is not good for our marriage, and it is definitely not endearing Terry's heart toward me.

As I was writing this, I was reminded of something else we continually disagree on. When Terry is driving, he likes for me to tell him at stop signs if I see anything coming from the right-hand side. He looks too, but he wants my perspective from the passenger seat for double caution. I foolishly (writing this makes me see how annoying I can be!) fight him tooth and nail on this point, saying that no one I know asks for a "front seat driver," to which he replies, "But I'm asking you to tell me if you see a car coming from the right."

Why don't I just do my best to make his life easier and tell the man if I see a car coming, instead of discussing back-seat drivers each time, and going on and on like a dripping faucet? How many seconds would it take? One? Two? Versus six minutes of the repeated conversation that we both despise. My sinful nature makes me talk far too much when I need to keep my mouth closed, and not enough when my husband is asking me to speak up. With God's help, I am not going to be argumentative on this point anymore. Surely, little things (such as one second!) can be used for bad or good.

But early in our marriage, I didn't know any of these things. It would be years before I met Christ and learned the difference He could make in my life, giving me the capacity to change on the inside. I needed help. I also knew nothing of the practical resources that were available: Focus on the Family resources, Family Life Today retreats, the wonderful spiritual teachers of our day like Elisabeth Elliot, Gregg Harris, and others, along with people who lived right in my own city.

> God wants to sharpen and refine our character like "iron sharpens iron"; nothing else can do this like marriage can.

Probably the biggest area of difference between Terry and me in the little things is on the subject of order. Okay, I am order-challenged, but my husband is not. He hangs his clothes up when he takes them off. He puts things back where they go when he's finished with them. His car still looks not too unlike the day he bought it. He's not neurotic about it—he just formed good habits early on, thereby not forming poor habits that have to be undone. Sometimes he hangs his pants on the bedpost or a chair until later on, but it wouldn't occur to him to toss them in a pile, wrinkling them up and thus creating more work later on (which is still a struggle for me all these years later! Remember my pile of clothes from when I first married, that I called "the mountain"?)

Just today, our maid service cancelled this week's bimonthly appointment to clean our house, for the second week in a row. I told my husband they could come next week, especially since we would be out of town. He disagreed and wanted them to come at their next available day, which was today. In fact, he said he wouldn't mind if we scheduled them to come weekly. I'd be fine if they only came once a month, because I like to work at home without interruptions.

After we had said, "I do," I think I had the misconception that Terry and I would agree on everything! When I married, I covered leftovers with nice, shiny aluminum foil. I just put it right on top of the cooking pot. If you're wondering why I didn't just put the lid on the pot, to my way of thinking it was a whole lot more trouble to go searching for a lid that I probably couldn't find anyway, so the aluminum foil sounded good to me.

Wrong. Wrong, because my husband hated that foil. He said you never knew what was behind it because you couldn't see through it. His mom transferred leftovers to nice, matching Tupperware, and Terry hated the way a pot looked in the refrigerator.

But no, for some reason I dug my heels in deeper, by conveniently ignoring his requests on how to best package food. Before long, our leftovers looked more like science experiments. (I must admit, nearly thirty years later, that a cold pot in the refrigerator doesn't look that appetizing.) Little things like this—and huge things like disrespecting your husband—can actually lead to a divorce.

Now I do love a clean, organized refrigerator with colorful fresh fruit, the yogurts all lined up in a row, and the pretty pink and regular lemonade. But let's be realistic: do I keep mine like that? No! I stuff things in there, shut the door, and head out. I'm going to work on this, though. (You'll be happy to know that later this very day I stopped and cleaned the refrigerator! I'll probably need a weekly phone reminder, though, so I won't go weeks until this occurs again!)

THE "LITTLE WAY"

In Christian circles we hear a lot about "ministry" and people being involved in Christian "ministry." But what is "Christian ministry," really?

Ministry is doing what God wants you to do, the way a Christian should do it, when God wants you to do it. So at this moment, writing my manuscript is a ministry. In just a minute, I am going to match my husband's socks, and that is a ministry. I spend a lot more time folding socks, making salads, and doing housework than I do writing books. Is one more important to God than the other? Does God care more about the writing because I am writing on spiritual matters? No! Not according to the definition of ministry that I just gave you: doing what God wants you to do, the way a Christian should do it, when God wants you to do it.

My husband likes me to keep my hair off our bathroom floor. I have long dark hair, and we have a white tile floor. Even though sometimes there is so much hair on the floor I have wondered how I could possibly have any left on my head, I can get tunnel vision and actually not even notice it. Terry asked me for years to get it up, but I was very slow in responding—always thinking that something else was more important, and I didn't put his interest ahead of my own. (I'm embarrassed to admit that I've even justified my actions with, "Well, the maid is coming in three days.")

One day, I was listening to Elisabeth Elliot teach about the fruits of the Spirit. As she read the words of Galatians 5:22–23, my lack of self-control in not stopping to pick up my hair was so evident to me. I was convicted of my sin of ignoring my husband's request; I was ashamed of myself. I immediately turned the radio off, got on my knees, and repented. I even wrote Elisabeth to ask her the best way to get the hair up!

I still don't vacuum it up every day, but I now realize that getting my hair off the floor is important to my husband, so it should be important to me, and I now vacuum up my hair much more than I otherwise would have. With the Holy Spirit's leading, this habit has turned into a conviction. Now I am committed to getting my hair off the floor regularly.

You may be thinking that getting my hair off the bathroom floor is such a tiny little thing. But it is in the little things that God wants us to die to ourselves and obey Him. Jesus is not right beside me, or just ahead of me, *He is in me.* If we are going to be His followers, we are going to suffer. We need to give up our way in the tiny ways, and in the big ways. I'm not allowed to be annoyed or irritated by the things that annoy and irritate me, because I am to take up my cross and follow Jesus.

Jesus wants to work in and through these little duties that are unpleasant to us. One person has described the taking up of the cross as the continual daily practice of small duties which are distasteful to you. Put that way, when offered to God, menial work such as getting the hair off the bathroom floor can be viewed as spiritual work. It is ministry, and every bit as important as writing a book or singing in the choir—maybe even a little bit more! When offered to Him, God can take what would have been meaningless and transform it into a pathway to joy. Amazing. Unbelievable.

I have a quote posted in my home where I can see it and be reminded often: "Beware of allowing yourself to think that shallow concerns of life are not ordained of God; they are as much of God as the profound."[161] Whatever we do— the tiniest little thing or the great big thing—we should do for God's glory!

In Richard J. Foster's book *Prayer: Finding the Heart's True Home*, he speaks of being ready to serve God in the little things. He tells of a very simple woman named Thérèse of Lisieux. She helped many by her prayer-filled approach to a humble life of growing in Christlikeness through what she called the "Little Way."

> *This Little Way, as she called it, is deceptively simple. It is, in short, to seek out the menial job, to welcome unjust criticisms, to befriend those who annoy us, to help those who are ungrateful. For her part, Thérèse was convinced that these "trifles" pleased Jesus more than the great deeds of recognized holiness. The beauty of the Little Way is how utterly available it is to everyone. From the child to the adult, from the sophisticated to the simple, from the most powerful to the least influential, all*

can undertake this ministry of small things. The opportunities to live in this way comes to us constantly while the great fidelities happen only now and again. Almost daily we can give smiling service to nagging co-workers, listen attentively to silly bores, express little kindnesses without making a fuss.

We may think these tiny, trivial activities are hardly worth mentioning. That, of course, is precisely their value. They are unrecognized conquests of selfishness, We will never receive a medal or even a 'thank you' for these invisible victories in ordinary life—which is exactly what we want.

An incident from Thérèse's autobiography, The Story of a Soul, underscores the suddenness of the Little Way. One uneducated and rather conceited sister had managed to irritate Thérèse in everything she did. Rather than avoid this person, however, she took the Little Way straight into the conflict: "I set myself to treat her as if I loved her best of all.' Thérèse succeeded so well in her Little Way that following her death this same sister declared, 'During her life, I made her really happy.'"[62]

The woman (who annoyed Thérèse so very terribly) felt so loved by Thérèse that upon Thérèse's death the woman could make the claim that she had made Thérèse very happy! Thérèse would have been delighted, no doubt. What a challenge to us: to resolve by God's grace to demonstrate unconditional love even when our husband may be acting unlovable. Don't we want love shown to us when we don't deserve it? Isn't that the way God loves us, in that while we were yet sinners Christ died for us? Let's pray together right now for God's help. I know I need it.

Lord God, help us to humble ourselves under Your direction, and to serve our husbands and You by doing the mundane tasks that are required. Help us to do the little thing You want us to do: to seek out the menial job, to welcome unjust criticisms, to befriend even when we are annoyed, and to help even in response to ungratefulness. It is in Your power and strength that our confidence rests. Amen.

What little thing is God calling you to do for your husband that goes against your preferences? God cares about the little things. In Zechariah 4:10, the Lord specifically warns us not to despise the day of small things. This verse has been an encouragement to me for years, because it says that God is watching to see who will be faithful in the little things. In Luke 16:10, Jesus states that the person who is "faithful in a very little thing" (NAS) shows that they can be entrusted with more important things. Will you serve Him in the little thing you know He wants you to do?

OBEYING OUR HUSBANDS

Now for where the rubber meets the road. I want to say a word about what the Bible says about a woman obeying her husband. In case you've been on an island somewhere and haven't heard all the broo-ha-ha that's been going on, the Bible clearly tells us that the wife is to obey her husband. I know: in our day and time, a lot of people don't want to hear that. People want to do what they want to do, and they don't want anyone telling them what to do.

But I'm just telling you what the Bible says. There is no confusion in what it says, as you are about to see. The definitive passage on this is found in Ephesians 5:22–25, 32 (KJV).

Wives, submit yourselves unto your own husbands, as unto the Lord. For the husband is the head of the wife, even as Christ is the head of the church: and he is the saviour of the body. Therefore as the church is subject unto Christ, so let the wives be to their own husbands in everything. Husbands, love your wives, even as Christ also loved the church, and gave himself for it; . . . This is a great mystery: but I speak concerning Christ and the church.

So there we read that wives are to submit to their husbands. Not if your husband asked nicely. Not if you want to or if you feel like it. Not if you agree with him. Not if your husband has proved himself worthy. Not if your husband is acting like a Christian. Not most of the time. Not some of the time. It says to just plain submit to your husband. At least you can say that you are not confused with what it says.

Now I would be the first to tell you that I love the idea of doing what God says. I love His Word. I love that the Lord provides us the exact direction we need. I love that He tells us we are to obey our husbands in the divine order according to God. I actually prefer being told what to do (most of the time). I like clarity and direction. I love God's plan for husbands and wives.

Now, real life enters in. Obeying is not always easy. It is one thing to love God's Word and His ways, and another thing altogether when a tiny thing comes up in life that has to do with my obeying my husband, and I don't like it. I don't always want to obey my husband. I surely do not always do it cheerfully. I'm a sinner, and I don't always act and think the way I wish I did.

> We can do with Him what was impossible without
> Him—I am living proof.

We wives have a difficult calling to obey our husbands, but if we truly love the Lord (and we sure love to say we do and sing that we do), we will do what He says. He says for us to submit to our husbands *as unto the Lord.* Is the Lord ever impatient? Is the Lord ever wrong? I know our husbands are fallible, but we are to submit to our husbands as if they were the Lord. The Lord is always loving, kind, and patient with us. By obeying your husband, you are actually obeying Jesus Christ. The Lord doesn't ask us to do anything that He will not enable us to do! We can do anything He asks us to do, not by our own strength, but in His strength. (Okay, right now I've been put to the test. My husband just arrived home for lunch, and he likes me to join him, or at least sit with him. But I've already eaten and I want to finish my thoughts here. But if I do what the Bible says I should do, I'll stop. To obey my husband in this instance means to adhere to what I know he likes or wishes. So I'm stopping, and I will be back later. . . . I'm back. And you know what? I was all worried that I would lose my train of thought, yet I'm right back to where I was. God allowed me to remember what I was talking about, so I'll get right back to it.)

Now our husbands have an equally difficult problem. The Ephesians passage above also says that the husband is the head of the wife, just as Christ is the head of the church. It says that in the same way Christ gave Himself to die for the church (sacrificially), so husbands are to love their wives. It doesn't say husbands are the head because they are smarter than you. Because they are stronger than you. Because they deserve to be the head. Because you are so sweet all the time. It just says they are the head. Period.

It also says they are to love you as Christ loved the church. How did He love the church? He loved the church so much that He gave His life! Now that's a tall order for the husbands to follow, is it not? Is my husband always going to do this perfectly? Of course not. He's a sinner, too.

"If we insist on equality, we refuse the divine order."
–P.T. Forsyth

He's going to make mistakes. We both need to give the other one a whole lot of grace, if we too, want grace when we make mistakes. For let's not forget, we are a sinner too—not just our husband! (How easy it is to expect near-perfection from our spouse, and forget that we mess up too.)

Now I ask you, is there a wife on earth anywhere who has obeyed her husband perfectly? Is there a husband anywhere who has loved his wife perfectly? I don't think so. We are both sinners; that is all there is in the human race. There was only one perfect One, the Lord Christ Himself, the only One who was fully God and fully human. Yet the Bible clearly says the husband-wife relationship is to reflect the relationship of Christ and the church.

No wonder scripture goes on to say that marriage is a great mystery, for it mirrors the mystery of the bond between Christ and His church! So the next time someone asks, "Does the Bible really say that wives are supposed to obey their husbands, and husbands are to love their wives?" You can say, "Yep, it sure does. It also says it's a mystery." And leave it at that. Mysteries are not always supposed to be solved: often they are simply to be acknowledged as such. (I'm so grateful that Elisabeth Elliot taught me these concepts on obeying my husband.)

∾

It's amazing to think that marriage is one man and one woman coming together to live for a lifetime. Two sinners hoping to have a happy, long life together! An unbelievable quest? An impossible dream? I wouldn't dream of going back to life without Christ. He is the glue that binds us together and shows us how to love. We can do with Him what was *impossible* without Him—I am living proof.

CHAPTER EIGHTEEN

YOUR STORY BEGINS HERE

MAYBE YOU'RE LIKE I WAS—LOOKING for purpose and meaning in life. We all have a spiritual void inside of us that no person can fill. Our family, friends, possessions, and even unimaginable success cannot help us fill the emptiness that exists at our core. Only a personal relationship with the living God, found only in Jesus Christ, can save us from our sin and satisfy our soul.

Perhaps you're like I was—knowing *about* God, but not *knowing God* through a personal relationship with Him. You can enter into that relationship with Him before you shut this book. If you want to be His disciple, you can trust Christ right where you are. Come to him just as you are; you don't have to do a single thing first.

I remember when I worked at Kings Dominion amusement park; we had a huge replica of the Eiffel Tower. While it was one-third the size of the original, it was still tremendous, rising over 275 feet in the air. As I would stand at the huge base of one of the legs of the tower with the Hanna-Barbera characters I was to escort around the park, inevitably a guest would come up to me and ask, "Do you know where the Eiffel Tower is?"

They were standing right at it! With all the distractions and attractions, the characters, food, music, and crowds—they had neglected to look up. All they had to do was look up! As I would point up to the Eiffel Tower from the very place we were standing, the guest would immediately know they were where they wanted to be. They came seeking! Listen to the words of Acts 17:27: "God did this so that men would seek him and perhaps reach out for him and find him, though he is not far from each one of us."

I implore you now to look up. Look up into the throne room of heaven from right where you are this very moment, to seek the One who made you!

I also remember the day I was escorting Yogi Bear and the Flintstone characters through the park, when a man came up to us who seemed to care very deeply about the characters and the impression they were making as they walked through the park. I looked at his name tag. It said, "Joseph Hanna" . . . as in Hanna-Barbera, the cartoon company. This man was their creator! I was meeting the characters' creator, the man who designed them. Of course he cared deeply about them: they were his idea, and he wanted them to reflect his purposes for them! How much more does our Creator God care about you whom He designed for His glory?

❧

Do you know Christ personally? Why not take that first step toward Him? Please continue reading, so you will discover how to enter into a personal relationship with the living God. You can know Him, and you can learn to trust Him!

Take that step; don't be afraid. Did you know that we each possess a measure of faith? Romans 12:3 tells us that God has given each one a portion of faith: "think of yourself . . . with the measure of faith God has given you." Is God speaking to your heart?

Each one of us has been given a portion of faith by God. We were made to have faith. We exercise faith daily without even thinking about it. Think of it. Every time we go out to eat, we trust the chef, do we not? If we didn't, how could we eat the food? If we didn't have faith in the chef whom we don't even ask to see, we could think he had poisoned the food.

What about getting on an airplane? If we didn't have faith in the pilot, we would never step onto the plane. But people fly on planes constantly, and no one checks to see how many hours the guy behind the wheel has, or even if he stayed up too late the night before. Surely we can make a decision to entrust our lives to the One who made us, the one Who is the God of the universe! Now I want to tell you exactly how you can know Him.

HOW TO KNOW GOD

Here's what to do if you want to know God.

Admit that you are a sinner. The Bible says that "we *all* have sinned and fall short of the glory of God" (Romans 3:23). There is only One who was without sin, and that is the Lord Jesus Christ. He already knows our pitiful condition, but it helps us to see ourselves as we really are (we're the wretches, remember?) and to admit to Him that we are a sinner.

Believe that He died on the cross for you personally, and that He is the only way to salvation. It is not enough to just believe. The Bible says that even the demons believe (see James 2:19). Many say, "Oh, I believe in God. I believe in Jesus. I believe Jesus is the Savior." But do you believe that He is *your* Savior?

There was an amazing Frenchman in the 1800s named Charles Blondin. Blondin was a tightrope walker. He once stretched a tightrope over the gorge at Niagara Falls and walked back and forth across it. He balanced a chair on the tightrope, and then made an omelet and ate it. He pushed a wheelbarrow across the tightrope. He asked the audience if they believed he could do it again. They all cheered to show they believed Blondin could do it. Then Blondin asked if someone would get in the wheelbarrow as he pushed it across the tightrope. That was altogether a different matter! Did they believe he could do it *for* them? That is the question for you about Jesus: do you believe He died *for you* personally and forgives *you* of your sin?

Jesus bore your sin when He hung on the cross. If you were the only person in the world, He would have done it for you. He wants to be your personal Savior. "But God demonstrates his own love for us in this: While we were still sinners, Christ died for us" (Romans 5:8). "Salvation is found in no one else, for there is no other name under heaven given to men by which we must be saved" (Acts 4:12).

Confess with your mouth that He is Lord and receive His forgiveness. "If we confess our sins, he is faithful and just and will forgive us our sins and purify us from *all* unrighteousness" (1 John 1:9). Know that you will spend eternity with Christ forever. He loves you with an everlasting love! (Deuteronomy 33:27).

Know that God will never leave you. "The Lord is with me; I will not be afraid" (Psalm 118:6). "Never will I leave you; never will I forsake you" (Hebrews 13:5b). In the original Greek, that "never" translates to five "nevers." "Never, never, never, never, no never!" Do we get it? God promises to *never* leave us, not even for a moment! He will not forget you. We read in Isaiah 49:15b–16, "I will not forget you! See, I have engraved you on the palms of my hands." You are always in His thoughts!

Here's a simple prayer you can say:

> *Dear Jesus, I know that I am a sinner. I believe You died on the cross for me personally. I ask You now for forgiveness, and I repent of my sin, and ask You to come into my life at this moment. I receive Your forgiveness now. Thank You, Lord!*

Welcome to the family, my new sister or brother! You are now a new creation in Christ!

For anyone who already knows Him, but has walked away: come back home! You may have turned aside from the path, but the right path is always there. It has not been changed or removed by your leaving it. You can get right back on it. You don't need to receive Him as your Savior again, you already have Him as your Savior. You have a personal relationship with Him, but your fellowship has been broken.

Come back to Him right now. Admit your sin and turn away from it. Start going in the opposite direction from the one you've been going in. Receive His loving forgiveness, and come home! His grace is there for you. Take it and start serving Him right where you are. Always remember that He will never leave you nor forsake you. Resolve to keep on keeping on, by trusting Him one moment at a time.

ON TRUSTING GOD AND THE HOLY SPIRIT

As I quoted in the preface to my story, Hannah Whitall Smith said, "Our part is to trust God; God's part is to work."[163] God always takes possession of a surrendered will, and He will accomplish the results He desires. He will do the work. Remember, though, that His way may be very different from the way we would have chosen. Our part is to surrender and to trust. "Every act of trust makes the next act less difficult."[164] But we must put ourselves into His hands completely. There is much work to be accomplished!

I've already said this, but it bears repeating; this is just too important to miss. We have bad habits that must go. We have poor attitudes and desires that are wrong. We need a changed heart and mind. We need a total transformation! The Lord is the One who does the work entrusted to Him. He accomplishes it, and He always wants to make us into the likeness of His Son. Continue to pray, "Thy will be done," as it says in the Lord's Prayer, knowing that His will "is always the will of love."[165] His will is not to harm you, but to do good to you.

"Ask the Holy Spirit to show you all that is not of Him in your heart and life."[166] If He shows you anything, immediately yield it to God. If He doesn't show you any waywardness in your heart and life, accept it. As Oswald Chambers says, sometimes there is no sin to repent of and nothing to change, and you can focus on your relationship with Christ. Rest in the knowledge that you have given yourself to Him fully. Don't wait to feel accepted by God, just know in your heart that He sees you under the blood of Jesus and He accepts you. Then, leave it with Him.[167]

Learn that the Holy Spirit will not speak to you in vague terms, and He will never condemn you. Those are darts coming from the enemy to tear you down. Don't fall for it for one second! For instance, the enemy may whisper, *"You're a bad mother, and you will never change."* or *"You are a horrible wife and God won't ever be able to use you."* Some Christians, who don't know better, might mistake this voice for the Holy Spirit—but it is not!

Remember: whoever believes in Jesus is not condemned. The enemy of our soul, the "prince of this world," stands condemned, and he knows it.[168] If you belong to Christ, don't listen to the enemy's condemnation. If I had listened to his condemnation, I would never have believed that I, a woman who left her husband, could repent and be used by God!

> Hannah Whitall Smith simply stated, "Our part is to surrender and trust. Every act of trust makes the next act less difficult."

The Holy Spirit will correct you, but never angrily or condemningly. He convicts us with a specific message so we can do something specifically in response to repent. The Holy Spirit might say something like, *"What you just said to your husband was uncaring."* or *"When you raised your voice at your son, you were unkind."*

Another one could be, *"You were impatient with that postal clerk."* You see how specifically the Holy Spirit speaks?

The Bible says the Holy Spirit will convict the world of guilt.[169] But we can respond to the conviction in sincerity with, "Lord, I am sorry for my unkind attitude, and for what I said. Thank you that you died for my sin." Often the Lord wants us to tell the other person we are sorry—and mean it. (Not an insincere, "SORRY! Or "I *SAID* I WAS SORRY!"). Be sensitive to the specific leading of the Holy Spirit's voice in your life, which is for your own good. Sometimes, the Spirit may lead you to only tell the Lord you are sorry and not the other person.

God desires for us to mature in Christ. Consider the clay and the potter. The pot is created by the master for his own use. It is subject to the bending and turning and shaping of the potter's hands, so that he can design what he has in mind. The pot's job is to allow the potter to have his way. At any time, the pot is right where it is supposed to be in the pottery-making process, even though it is not yet a finished piece of pottery. It doesn't look today as it will look tomorrow.

To give another illustration of accepting our growth and maturity in the Lord, think of an apple. An apple in June is not what the apple will be in October. A June apple is what it is supposed to be in June. It is not the same apple that it will be in October. Oh, but a June apple is the best apple it can be in June!

Finally, think of a newborn baby. A baby is entrusted to its mother's care. There may be a war nearby, or a storm brewing, or awful sickness nearby, but a baby is supported by the tender love and care of its parents. The higher Christian life—a life the Bible calls being "hidden in Christ"[170]—can be compared to the father-child relationship. We will be on the right track if we will only believe that "God is as good a Father as the best ideal earthly father."[171]

We can trust God with all our heart; He will direct us. As we talked earlier, regarding a woman's beauty, "our bodies are wasting away, but on the inside, we are being renewed day by day."[172] But to be renewed we must be like flowers and turn to the Son. Then we will grow, for it is natural to grow when we turn to Him.[173] He will keep us in perfect peace, but it is critical that we keep our minds focused on Him. You don't have to be transplanted somewhere else, as I once falsely thought I needed to do.

Nothing can come to us without "passing through His encircling presence" first, gaining His permission.[174] Remember that God sees and cares for the tiny sparrow. How much more does He care for you? If God puts a trial in your hand, accept it. This does not mean, however, that we must like or enjoy the trial itself, but that we must see God's will in the trial."[175]

Even in the apparently trivial but very real things, such as dealing with people who "annoy or trouble us," we need to remember to see God in everything. Having our souls in perfect peace is an attainable goal in spite of undesirable circumstances, if we keep that child-like trust in the Lord. All of our confidence must be in Him. "Our part is to trust, God's part is to work." Receive everything in your life "directly from His hands."[176] [177]

Once it was " I and not Christ." Next it was "I and Christ." Perhaps now it is even "Christ and I." But has it yet come to be Christ only, and not I at all? [178]

Oh, Lord, that my every breath would resonate Christ and Christ alone!

I was never designed to be the center of my universe. *It's not all about me, it's all about Him!*

Steve Green sings a beautiful song entitled, "God and God Alone." While the typed words here do not do justice to his magnificent tenor voice, let us read them as we commit our hearts to trust the One who is worthy of our complete trust:

> *God and God alone is fit to take the universe's throne.*
>
> *Let everything that lives reserve its truest praise for God and God alone. . .*
>
> *He will be our one desire.*
>
> *Our hearts will never tire of God and God alone.*[179]

CHAPTER NINETEEN

NINE AREAS TO FOCUS ON DURING SEPARATION AND RECONCILIATION

I HAVE SELECTED NINE PRACTICAL areas that helped me most during my time of physical separation in marriage, some of which carry over into practical help for any marriage. My hope is that you too, will find the hope and encouragement that was a life support system for me. Many of these items continue strengthening our marriage to this day. I suggest you retype the list, personalizing the word "spouse" or "husband" with your spouse's name. Keep it handy in a place where you pray, or in your Bible.

1. HAVING A SUPPORTIVE, MATURE CHRISTIAN FRIEND

I cannot tell you how much the encouragement I received from Paul and Macon Newby meant to me. They would meet with me together and guide me in God's Word. They were the first people who pointed out to me that God desired my marriage to be restored. They provided a listening ear for me to tell them when I was frustrated with Terry, yet they would not bash Terry.

They would remind me that Terry was not a Christian, but that I had the help of the Holy Spirit. When they knew I would be with Terry, they would pray for me. They would pray that I would be loving and considerate toward him. When Terry broke off our relationship, when several times he thought he no longer wanted to be married to me, Macon provided a shoulder for me to cry on. She always pointed me to Christ and reminded me of God's abiding presence in my life. Scripture says that "two heads are better than one," and having those two for a sounding board was essential to my well-being and growth in Christ. Having them beside me as fully committed, mature Christians provided the counsel and flesh and blood support that I needed.

2. PRAYING FOR MY UNBELIEVING SPOUSE

Praying for Terry was the best thing that I could do for him. Do not gossip about your husband if you are separated; instead, lift him up to the Lord. There is a peace that passes all understanding when you lay your burdens at Jesus's feet. Meeting alone with God and praying on Terry's behalf that he would come to know Him personally, somehow got my mind off insignificant things and directed me toward what really mattered in life. The Bible says to pray for your enemies, and when one spouse does not want the marriage it is as if they are the enemy! So we are called to pray for them. We don't pray for them simply to get what we want, much as we want the marriage restored. Pray without expecting anything in return for yourself. St. Augustine said that *true, pure prayer is nothing but love.* We pray for them in obedience to God, for we know that He wishes that none would perish, and that is our non-believing spouse's greatest need! You are far more likely to treat your spouse with kindness and respect if you have been praying for them. (I have included more detail on how I pray for Terry on an ongoing basis in the "How to Pray For Your Husband" section of the appendix.)

3. KNOWING THAT GOD COULD USE ME TO BRING MY HUSBAND TO HIM

The Bible tells us that if your non-believing spouse is willing to live with you, then live with him. For how do you know if you will not influence him to desire to become a Christian? Your witness of a changed and godly life lived out before him could cause him to fall in love with Jesus. Of course, you will make mistakes; we all blow it sometimes. And by all means, when he makes a mistake, don't tell him you told him so, or act like you are a know-it-all on the Bible! Don't try to go in and save him! Let grace prevail. Remember that God is merciful, and He is the one who ultimately draws each person to Himself.

In 1 Peter 3:1 we read: "be submissive to your husbands so that if any of them do not believe the word, they may be won over by the behavior of their wives." What an honor to be called to the "loving your non-believing spouse" ministry. A word of warning here: the Bible tells us it is "better to live on a corner of the roof than share a house with a quarrelsome wife."[180] (Ouch!) Conversely, that means be sweet, pleasant, and easy to live with. (Triple ouch!)

4. SURROUNDING MYSELF WITH CHRISTIAN TEACHING AND MUSIC, WHILE BEING SENSITIVE TO MY HUSBAND'S DESIRES

As you are able, listen to the wonderful Christian teaching and music that is available on the radio and Internet to encourage you in your faith. Don't listen to these programs while your husband is around if he doesn't like it. It may cause him to feel left out, or he just may not like it playing in his home. Play it when he's not around. Most non-believers are reasonable people. Would you want someone leaving tracts and books around and constantly playing Christian teaching? No! Nothing is more powerful than the witness of you putting his interests ahead of your own by respecting him, being available for him, and showing him that you love him using *his* love language.

5. WORKING ON OUR MARRIAGE IS LIKE WATERING A GARDEN

One practical thing we can do is to intentionally seek to do some active kindness each day that will please our partner. As I pray during quiet time, God often shows me a simple thing to do. Our part is to do the kind deed. We can be creative and have fun! Laughter and pleasure with our spouse helps us bring glory to God together. It can be as simple as picking up a pack of mints for his car, buying his favorite snack, folding his t-shirts, not being on the phone when he comes in, going with him to his favorite coffee place, writing him a note, putting a sticky note on his pillow, or putting a pen by his nightstand if one is always missing. We must continue to make our marriages a priority, from our appearance to our attitude! Think of how you acted when you were dating, if that helps.

Remember to thank your husband! I know I have missed many opportunities to thank my husband, and I pray that the Lord will make me an observant wife, and not unperceptive to Terry's thoughtfulness. We often thank people for a gift they give us and write thank you notes, but do we remember to thank our husbands for carrying the financial burden, for taking us to dinner, or for following through in spite of their tiredness?

It takes only a second to write a short note and put it where your husband will see it: on the steering wheel, his bathroom mirror, or where I like to leave notes—on Terry's pillow. Just a simple note that says, *"I love you,"* or *"You are such a good father!"* (Especially if a particularly hard or important thing had to be confronted or tackled in the home, and he stepped up to the plate).

In the next chapter, I've included eleven hints for refreshing your marriage. I learned these from Ray and Anne Ortlund (and a few from J.R. Miller). Ray Ortlund is formerly of Haven of Rest Radio Ministry (known today as *Haven Today*). *Haven* gave me their permission to share them with you. I've added some scriptures and practical tips of my own as I have tried to apply these helpful checkpoints. I can't say that I do all of these everyday by any stretch of the imagination, but for years I have kept this list in my prayer time to jog my memory of what is important. God has used it often to prod me to do the right thing, which I would not have done otherwise. Just reading over it helps you to keep track of it, and even just doing that can cause improvement in that area.

6. FOCUSING ON MY HUSBAND'S STRENGTHS AND WHAT WE ENJOY TOGETHER

Scripture tells us "whatever is true, whatever is noble, whatever is right, whatever is pure, whatever is lovely, whatever is admirable—if anything is excellent or praiseworthy—think about such things."[181] What positive instruction! Does your husband work and provide for you? Be thankful! Do you enjoy golf together? Play golf together! Do you enjoy walking together? Walk together! Dancing together? Go for it! What drew you to him in the first place? Think about those things.

Marriage isn't easy—even when married to another Christian. Everyone has faults. Remember Christ's words, "I have told you these things, so that in me you may have peace. In this world you will have trouble. But take heart! I have overcome the world."[182] When we find our peace in Christ, we learn what it means to be an overcomer. We can overcome our desire to be critical of our husband's imperfections. We can overcome our demanding and selfish natures. We can overcome our desire to have the last word or find satisfaction in always being right. If we look for peace in anyone else besides Christ, we will be disappointed—even if our spouse is a Christian.

So as you learn to trust Christ to meet your deepest needs, it becomes easier to enjoy your husband just as God has designed Him. Your desire to change him to meet your needs will be lessened as you learn to love him and accept him just as he is. Enjoy the husband that God has given you today, and stop withholding your heart from him until he becomes the person he is not yet. Remember that June apple I spoke of earlier: it is the best apple it can be for June! Take time daily to focus on his strengths and what you appreciate about him, rather than on what is wrong with him. Your attitude will make all the difference in your marriage.

7. ENJOYING MY HUSBAND, AND NOT IDEALIZING CHRISTIAN MARRIAGES

Before Terry was a Christian, it was easy to fall into the trap of thinking that all of life would be so much better if Terry were just a Christian. That is untrue. As I heard Jo Berry, author of *Beloved Unbeliever*, state in an interview: "If your non-Christian husband tends to burn the toast before he is a Christian, he would probably still burn the toast if he were a Christian!"[183] She goes on in her book to say, "Christian husbands come home from work tired and frustrated. They lose their tempers. They yell at the kids. They don't always pray with their wives. . . . they are just as human, and sometimes as carnal, as unbelievers are."[184] Don't allow yourself to think that if only he were a Christian, life would be a cinch.

I heard Lee Strobel, author of *Surviving A Spiritual Mismatch in Marriage*, whose wife, Leslie, became a Christian years before him, say in an interview: "It would have been easy for Leslie to say, 'If Lee would just become a Christian then he would certainly diaper the kids without complaining; and he would take out the trash without complaining; he wouldn't have a temper anymore; he'd never blow up; he'd mow the lawn without me having to bug him.' Well you know what? That's not reality, as Leslie ultimately found out!"[185] Enjoy your husband for who he is right now, and know that even in the best of Christian marriages there are still struggles!

8. READING GOD'S WORD REGULARLY

God's Word provides instruction for how to live our lives. When we don't follow God's instruction book for life, chaos and confusion result. We end up going with how we feel about it today—which may change depending upon what the weather is, what our friends are saying, or what we think seems to make sense based on our limited knowledge.

The God of the Universe, who made us, has written down His Word to guide us how to live. We do not have to guess our way through life and hope for the best! We can follow His plan as revealed in His holy Word! The result is not chaos and confusion, but a well-ordered life of peace and blessing. Go to the wellspring of life, His holy Word, for spiritual blessing and reconciliation for your family, and to nip brokenness in the bud. Take the guesswork out! Stay in God's Word! It truly is a lamp to our feet and a light for our path.[186]

9. LEARNING TO SEE GOD IN YOUR "SINGLENESS" DURING YOUR SEPARATION

(Note: All the ideas and stories in this section came to me from Elisabeth Elliot.)

Maybe you have suddenly found yourself living the life of a single person (i.e., if you are separated) as you wait on God's will for your marriage. Do you view this time period as a blessing or a curse? You should see it as a blessing.

Leave the future in God's hands and stick to the work He has given you to do. You don't have to know everything that God is up to in having you separated on any given day; just trust Him, He knows what He's doing. Living the life of a separated person is your assignment for today (which in many ways is like the life of a single person, except that you are not free to date). Many great people of faith were single, and they could not have done the work they did if they were married at the time. Single missionary Amy Carmichael dedicated herself to being the mother to 700 Indian children whom she saved from Hindu temple prostitution. Gladys Aylward, a simple, single, British parlor maid went to China as a missionary. She went on her own initiative, by the way, because she was turned down by the missions agencies as having insufficient abilities—and as being "too old" to learn such a difficult language as Chinese. (But she did learn it!) Later, to escape the invading Japanese (after years of doing mission work in China), she led the 100 orphans in her care to safety, by hiking over bandit-infested mountains. Aylward's story is told in the book *The Small Woman*, and in the movie *The Inn of the Sixth Happiness*.

Know that God is shaping you into the image of His son. Just as with Michelangelo's carving of a sculpture out of a piece of marble, it will take a lot to shape this image. The details of your life are the heavenly sandpaper that God is using to file away all those rough edges!

Read Isaiah 58:10 (ESV): "If you pour yourself out for the hungry . . . you will become like a watered garden." Proverbs 11:25 tells us that "whoever refreshes others will refresh himself." Don't sit around feeling sorry for yourself, thinking "what is wrong with me?" and that the couples are having all the fun. Reach out to help other people. When Paul and Macon asked me to serve with them as a helper in the youth program, it refreshed my soul to be able to lend a hand. Good servants are those who (such as single or separated people) are free to serve; it just takes a willing spirit.

CHAPTER TWENTY

ELEVEN CHECKPOINTS TO REFRESH YOUR MARRIAGE

THE CHECKPOINTS LISTED BELOW ARE intended to be a description of a loving wife's part in the Christian home. They are not intended to be a complete list nor a prescription for every Christian wife to follow. I keep them in my prayer folder and I read them aloud regularly in my quiet time; this has helped me to keep focused on my part as a wife.[187]

1. I WILL SAY, "I LOVE YOU" TO MY HUSBAND EVERY DAY (AT LEAST ONCE)

"Pleasant words are a honeycomb, sweet to the soul and healing to the bones."[188] Terry and I and our children say "I love you" to each other all the time. We say it before we hang up the phone. We say it before we tuck our children in bed. We write it in emails to them. I have written it on notes on refrigerators, pillows, and counters. I have typed it in Braille. I write it on the gift card on their birthday and Christmas presents. I text it to them. They text it to me. When I am apart from my husband or my children at night, we text, "Night-night. I love you." Sometimes we just hug each other for the heck of it and say, "I love you!" Say it! Write it! Text it!

2. I WILL NOT BRING UP MY HUSBAND'S PAST FAILURES TODAY

"Do not let any unwholesome talk come out of your mouths, but only what is helpful for building others up according to their needs, that it may benefit those who listen. . . . Be kind and compassionate to one another, forgiving each other, just as Christ God forgave you."[189] Forgiveness must be a habit—a way of life. Don't we want to be forgiven when we have made a mistake? We must choose to keep on forgiving. Peter asked Jesus how many times he should forgive someone. He likely thought he was being more than generous when he asked Jesus if seven was plenty. Jesus replied, "seventy-seven times."[190] I don't think Jesus meant for us to keep count to exactly seventy-seven and immediately stop forgiving for an offense on seventy-eight (for the Bible says to keep no record of wrongs[191]), but to forgive our spouses and others on an ongoing basis, as a matter of lifestyle. He was saying, "Keep on forgiving as I have forgiven you!" There used to be a commercial that said "it's the gift that keeps on giving." Forgiveness is truly the gift that keeps on forgiving!

3. I WILL PUT FROM MY MIND ANY WEAK POINTS OF MY HUSBAND, WHICH I CANNOT CHANGE, AND CONCENTRATE ON MY HUSBAND'S GOOD POINTS

"Bear with each other, and dwell on what is good and right!"[192] Simple. Concentrate on the good points of your husband!

Remember Grandmother Eve. She had everything she could possibly need or want, but she chose to focus on the one thing she shouldn't have paid any attention to, and the human race has been in a mess ever since. Look at all that God has provided in your husband, by focusing on his good points.

4. I WILL SEEK TO BRING LAUGHTER INTO MY HUSBAND'S LIFE TODAY

Have a good time together! Laugh. Have fun together. Smile. (Boy! I am talking to myself here just as much to you, if not more! I can take myself *way too seriously* and forget to smile at my husband.) As I said earlier in part one, plan or be spontaneous with a rendezvous when no one else is home! Tell your family's favorite stories; dance together if you enjoy that! Enjoy each other! "A cheerful heart is good medicine."[193] Ask yourself, "Am I fun to live with?" The Bible says the mouths of God's people are filled with laughter![194] Genuine, wholesome laughter (involving no harmful behaviors at someone else's expense) should be a characteristic of believers; laughter has God's stamp of approval! When there are multiple young children at home, it can be a stressful time in a marriage; but a freer time is ahead! It's amazing how laughter can diffuse a tense situation or a potential argument.

5. I WILL GIVE MY HUSBAND SOME LITTLE GIFT TODAY, WHETHER A TANGIBLE ONE, OR A WORD OR DEED

"A gift in secret soothes anger."[195] A note on the pillow or any thoughtful act is small in effort, but huge in effect, as we talked about in the last chapter. Remember, we were made for romance in marriage! Does your husband like candlelight?

6. I WILL NOT END THIS DAY ANGRY WITH MY HUSBAND

Before bed, say, "I'm sorry; I was wrong," so you can keep short accounts and the air cleared daily with your husband. "Don't let the sun go down on your anger."[196] Don't get into an argument late at night. The sun has already gone down! Get a good night's rest, and it may even solve itself in the morning.

7. I WILL PRACTICE LOVING PATIENCE

No matter how close you two were before you got married, much will be discovered about your spouse once you are married. As we talked about earlier, you will both be "exposed." The true self will appear, with all of its undesirable characteristics. Your husband may squeeze the toothpaste differently from you; he may have peculiar habits or tastes that you never knew of before (as he will discover about you!). Harmony takes time to develop; patience is needed. "Be completely humble and gentle; be patient, bearing with one another in love."[197]

8. I WILL PRACTICE COURTESY TOWARDS MY HUSBAND

It is so easy after the wedding is over to fall into the habit of taking your husband for granted and forgetting to extend courtesy toward him. It should not be so! Tenderness, kindness, and thoughtfulness toward your husband go a long way. Blessed is the person who is respected most by those who know him best! Make courtesy your rule, as far as it depends on you. Gifts for your husband on special days such as birthdays and anniversaries should not be empty gifts, but symbols of the courtesy you have shown him all year long. The Lord watches you everyday to see if you are faithful! Samuel Taylor Coleridge said, "The happiness of life is made up of . . . the little soon-forgotten charities of a kiss or a smile, a kind look, a heartfelt compliment." Remember: "The home that has no time for courtesy will always find time for rudeness." Don't let that happen! "Love is kind."[198]

The home conversation should be marked by loving-kindness. Home should be a place of continual retreat, nourishment, peace, and loving words. Even as I write this, I myself resolve to do better, with God's help. I will fight saying biting words that produce strife. Is that the way to speak to the one to whom I have pledged my love until death parts us?

If you, like me, have become careless, pause now and pray, and visualize your home as an oasis of warmth and gentleness. It should not be a place of petty continual arguing between husband and wife. *Lord, help me!* There should be only words of comfort and encouragement between my husband and me.

Oh, how easy it is for me to forget to even say good morning greetings and good night closings at the end of the day. These should be sweet, commonplace words as my husband comes and goes from the home, and as we wake and sleep. Lord, help me greet my husband with kindness in the morning and with goodness at night, that our home will show Christ's love instead of bitter words.

It is so easy for me to take my husband for granted and to get lazy in simply saying kind words. It takes time and energy to be either, so why not choose to be courteous? *Oh Lord, give me Your Spirit of love, and remove all bitterness from my tongue!*

9. I WILL SEEK UNITY OF INTEREST

"This explains why a man leaves his father and mother and is joined to his wife, and the two are united into one."[199] As I was writing this section, I changed my husband's name in my phone from "Terry" to "TerryJuanaOne." It is a visual reminder each time he calls me and his name pops up on my phone (or I call him), that part of me is calling. Together, we make a whole. We are a new unit that did not exist before we married.

Beware of leading separate lives! Nothing can cause a marriage to drift apart more than letting separate duties, friendships, and interests continually separate your union. Soon, your physical separation can evolve into a deep-rooted separation. This will take loving care and attention to the interests of your husband (and vice versa, but I am speaking to the women). If you continually leave your husband out of all you do and who you see, you could become callous toward him, the one you pledged to esteem higher than any other relationship. This must not be! I know the following might seem radical to some, but radical may be the necessary answer to combat the divorce rate among Christians. Listen what J.R. Miller says:

> *Every plan and hope should embrace the other. The moment a man begins to leave his wife out of any part of his life, or [if] she has plans, hopes, pleasures, friendships or experiences from which she excludes him, there is peril in the home. They should have no secrets which they keep from each other. They should have no companions or friends save those which they have in common. Thus their two lives should blend in one life,*

with no thought, no desire, no feeling, no joy or sorrow, no pleasure or pain unshared.[200]

10. I WILL MAKE SOME COMMENT TODAY WHICH POINTS TO GOD'S WONDERFUL TOMORROW

Build hope—God is in charge! He plans to give you a hope and a future![201] Encourage your spouse! Point to God's wonderful tomorrow!

11. I WILL PRAY FOR MY HUSBAND BEFORE THE DAY ENDS

I try to lift Terry up to the Lord in the mornings, including anything I know specifically about that day. (I miss some days, but I don't let that discourage me from picking it back up the next day.) Don't let your lack of prayer keep you from praying! Dom John Chapman says, "Pray as you can, not as you can't."[202] Pray for each other,[203] and together if it is possible. It is hard to be critical and angry when you are praying together!

AFTERWORD

ASSOCIATE JUSTICE PAUL NEWBY

NORTH CAROLINA SUPREME COURT

WHEN I AM ASKED HOW I encourage couples to try to reconcile, if circumstances allow the couples to do so (no harmful behaviors involved), and if the person is a Christian, then I ask, "What would God have you do?" Generally, I would have a person talk about their courtship and early marriage, focusing on the positives. I would also encourage consideration of the principles of commitment and integrity. If children were involved, I'd ask about their situations. If a person begins to desire reconciliation, I'd encourage them to ask themselves, "What can I do to be the spouse I should be?"

It is possible for couples to overcome even the most difficult separation (another woman or man involved, change of heart, etc.). First, a person needs to see a personal need for God, or a full commitment to Him. Jesus said, "If anyone would come after me, he must take up his cross daily and follow." This is a death to self— alive with Christ. Then the person must daily implement this "death to self" to serve the needs of the other person, expecting nothing in return. Finally, the person must persevere with only feedback from God—"Well done, good and faithful servant."

I absolutely have been able to use Juana's story as an example that couples really can be restored. Juana's story is such an encouragement because of how God worked in her heart to bring about a desire to know Him; then He gave her the desire to see her marriage restored; and finally, He gave her the wisdom to persevere while He worked on Terry's heart. Never say a marriage is beyond hope—look what God did with Juana and Terry.

PRAYERS YOU CAN PRAY FOR YOUR HUSBAND

NARRATIVE PRAYERS AND DAILY PRAYER FORMAT

Suggestion: Take the time to retype these, substituting your husband's name. Put on reference cards and keep for use in your quiet time.

Whether we like it or not, asking is the rule of the Kingdom.

—*C. H. Spurgeon*

NARRATIVE PRAYERS:

Elisabeth Elliot taught the first two of the following prayers to me. I heard the third prayer on an interview on *Focus on the Family* with Bill McCartney, former head football coach of the University of Colorado at Boulder and the founder of Promise Keepers; he gave an example of how he prayed for his wife. I took his prayer and changed it somewhat to apply to praying for husbands (with permission from Promise Keepers to reprint it for you here). I have given all three prayers a quick name for easy reference.

Following these prayers is a daily format for praying for your husband that I have used for over twenty years. Someone gave the daily prayer format to me, but I don't remember whom it was. I have been forever grateful for all of these prayers!

I'll Keep Him Prayer

> *"Lord, he's Your man. He's the one you've given to me—his peculiarities and his personality, You gave me. I'll take it. Help me Lord; show me ways, Lord, to make his life as pleasant and as easy as I can. Now Lord, You work in him the changes You think need to be done. Fulfill Your purposes. Help me to remember 'in acceptance lieth peace (Amy Carmichael).'"*

His Good & Unity Prayer

> *"God, help me and forgive me for being much more interested in my own good rather than Terry's good, and failing to contribute to Terry's blessing. Lord, how can I respond in such a way as to bind us together in deeper harmony and deeper unity in Jesus Christ? Lord, show me what I can do to make Terry's life as easy and as pleasant as I can."*

Power on my Husband Prayer

> *"Lord Jesus Christ, I invoke Your power and Your Spirit upon Terry. Lord, I pray righteousness and purity and holiness upon*

him. Lord, I pray that You will heal all of his scars, that You will mend up all of those things that keep him from becoming the man that he desires to be and that You call him to be. Lord God, I pray that You will breathe excitement into him and that You will bring about in Terry a hope for the future. I pray that I will have favor with him. I pray that he will see me and his heart will rejoice and his spirit will soar when I come into the room. Lord Jesus Christ, I thank You for this man. I thank You for the treasure that he is. I thank You that he loves You more than me. I pray Lord that You will minister to him and build a hedge of protection around him today. Lord Jesus, we need You. All of our hope is in You. Amen."

Prayer—secret, fervent, believing prayer—lies at the root of all personal godliness.

—William Carey

DAILY PRAYERS FORMAT:*

Sunday – For his maturity in the Lord

- That Terry would become a holy man, a man of prayer; mature in the Lord, growing in his knowledge of God (1 Thess. 5:23; Col. 4:12; Eph. 6:18; Eph. 1:18–19; Eph. 3:16–19).
- That Terry would daily seek God with all his heart, walking in the Spirit moment by moment, growing in his dependence on Him (Ps. 119:1–2; Ps. 27:4; Prov. 3:5–6; John 15:5).

Monday – For his dependence on God

- That Terry would learn to take every thought captive, to not be conformed to the world's thinking but to think scripturally (Rom. 12:2; 2 Cor. 10:5).
- That Terry would learn not to depend on his circumstances for happiness but on God alone (Hab. 3:17–19).

Tuesday – For his inward life

- That Terry's self-image would be a reflection of the Lord's thoughts toward him (Eph. 1:17–19; Rom. 12:3; Ps. 139).
- That Terry would have new strength in the midst of his busy schedule and that the Lord would infuse him with His strength (Isa. 40:31; Eph. 3:14–19).

Wednesday – For his leadership

- That Terry would become a called man, not driven, with well thought-through and prayed-through goals in life (1 Cor. 9:24–27).
- That the Lord would give Terry wisdom to lead his family physically, emotionally, mentally, financially, and spiritually (Eph. 1:17–19; James 1:5–7).

Thursday – For his stand against the enemy

- That Terry would stand firm against the schemes of the devil and resist Satan in all circumstances (Eph. 6:10–18; James 4:7).

- That Terry would not be deceived into unbelief or sin (Matt. 11:58; Gal. 6:7).

Friday – For fruit to be produced

- That the fruit of the Spirit would be exhibited more and more in Terry's life (Gal. 5:22–23).
- That Terry would learn to love as God has commanded (1 Cor.13:4–7; Rom. 12: 8–10).

Saturday – For his protection and time

- That the Lord would protect Terry, guarding his course (Prov. 2:8).
- That Terry would learn to manage his time well (Eph. 5:15).

Author unknown; I have modified the wording of these daily prayers.

PRAYING FOR YOUR HUSBAND (AS PAUL PRAYED FOR HIS FRIENDS)

Wisdom and Power – Ephesians 1:18–19

Strength in the Inner Man – Ephesians 3:16–19

Discernment – Philippians 1:9–11

Knowledge of the Will of God – Colossians 1:9

Growing Love for One Another – 1 Thessalonians 3:10–13

Worthy of Their Calling – 2 Thessalonians 1:11-12

Comforted and Established – 2 Thessalonians 2:16–17

Steadfast in Their Love for God – 2 Thessalonians 3:5

Quiet and Peaceable Life – 1 Timothy 2:1–2

Recognize All that They Have in Christ – Philemon 6

God to Work in Them That Good Will which is Pleasing Unto Him – Hebrews 13: 20–21[204]

A WORD TO CHRISTIAN WIVES MARRIED TO UNBELIEVING HUSBANDS, OR TO BELIEVING HUSBANDS NOT ACTING AS A CHRISTIAN SHOULD

Hello, dear Sister. I want to speak with just you for a moment. You have been given the gift of loving your unbelieving husband. Receive everything in your life, including your circumstances in your marriage, as directly from God's hand. As God puts a difficulty in your hand, accept it. It doesn't mean that you have to like the trial or difficulty itself, but you can learn to *see God's will in the difficulty,* as we talked about in an earlier chapter.

His will is always the will of love for you—not a will to harm you! Learn to see God in everything. Remember that nothing can come to us without first gaining His permission! If He sees the little bird, believe that He also sees every detail of your circumstances and He's on your team! Scripture tells us that He does provide for the little birds. What's more, He knows the exact number of hairs on our head! (Matthew 6:26; 10:30).

I've been where you are now standing. Since you've read this far, you know that after I accepted Christ, it was seven years before Terry came to the Lord. It was my God-given assignment during that time to love and serve my unbelieving husband, as it is yours now.

During those seven years, I prayed for Terry and focused each day on the 1 Peter 3 lifestyle, which speaks of the importance of the behavior of the Christian wife and a gentle and quiet spirit that I spoke of earlier, in the chapter entitled, "Me? A Gentle and Quiet Spirit?". The inward strength and beauty of the woman who puts her trust in the Lord became the constant song of my heart.

What was once so unnatural for us can become like breathing, when we cast ourselves utterly on Christ and trust Him to do His part perfectly. As you trust Him and stay in His Word, He will change you on the inside to know how to deal with the outside. Your behavior will be different than it would have been otherwise. Remember, we are told that your unique role during this time— who you are and how you live your life—is important to God, for His Word (1 Peter 3) tells us that it is of "great worth" in His sight.

Christ gave His life for us! Isn't living for Him with joy the least we can do? Ask Him, "What do You want me to do, Lord?" Then do it—for however long He wants you to do it.

When Jacob worked for Laban for seven years to marry his daughter Rachel, those years seemed only a few days to him, because he loved Rachel so much (see Genesis 29:20). So it is with praying for your husband to receive Christ. Praying is hard work, because we seldom get to see an immediate result. But isn't that what faith is? Praying expectantly daily, knowing that God cares and hears our prayer. But take heart and be encouraged! Your struggles will seem "light and momentary" in this lifetime compared to the reward of eternity with Christ in all His glory (see 2 Corinthians 4:17). Even on this earth, my job of being the praying wife of an unbelieving husband took seven years, until Terry received Christ—yet now it seems that I prayed and waited only a few days!

Remember, the Bible makes no distinction: a Christian wife is to act no differently toward her husband if he is not a Christian. Your role is the very same as the wife married to the Christian man. Remember that God is watching to see if you will be faithful. His eyes search the world over to find those whose hearts are fully committed to Him, and to strengthen them (see 2 Chronicles 16:9).

Pray for your husband whether he is a Christian or not, and even if you feel that you are mistreated, remember that Christ says, "If you love those who love you, what credit is that to you?" Instead, Christ says to love them without expecting to get anything back—that's how He loves us. That is love with no conditions on it. He did not say, "I will love you *if you . . .*", and you can fill in the blank with all the prerequisites we conditionally put on our love for others. (Of course, seek safety if you are in a harmful situation.)

When Jesus had only a little time left before His death on the cross, His final command to His disciples was, "As I have loved you, so you must love one another." He then said that was how all people would know that we were His followers (see John 13:34). So when you love and pray for your husband, your faith in Christ is on display. He says that our reward will be great, and that we will be sons (and daughters) of the Most High!

> *Pray for those who mistreat you. Do to others as you would have them do to you.*
>
> *If you love those who love you, what credit is that to you? Even sinners love those who love them. And if you do good to those who are good to you, what credit is that to you? Even sinners do that. . . . But love your enemies, do good to them . . . without expecting to get anything back. Then your reward will be great, and you will be children of the Most High.*
>
> – Luke 6:28, 31–33, 35

My dear friend and reader, this next part is so very important! There is one vital thought I must give you.

Learn to see Christ in your husband. When your husband comes in the door, treat him as if Jesus had just come in the door. Is there anything you wouldn't do for Christ? Does your husband want you to hold supper while he does a few things? Would you mind putting the supper on simmer for Christ? Would your husband like you to run an errand for him right when you thought you would do something else? Would you gladly divert your plans if Christ was asking you to run that errand for Him? Would your husband like a cup of coffee? Would you offer Christ a cup of coffee? As one man said, "Do we deserve to be treated like Christ?

No! But do you think your husband would be worse if you treated him as if he were Christ? I don't think so!"[205]

One day you will see Jesus face to face. He may even say to you, "Thank you for the coffee! It was just the way I like it! Thank you for simmering the supper when I had to go down the street! Thank you for washing all my dirty socks! Thank you for changing your plans and doing that errand for Me!"

You might reply to our Lord, saying, "But Lord, when did I make you your coffee just as you like it? When did I put the supper on simmer for you? When did I wash your dirty socks, Lord?"

And He just might reply to you:

"When you did it for your husband in My name, you did it unto Me. Truly I tell you, whatever you did for one of the least of these brothers and sisters of mine, you did for Me. Well done, thou good and faithful servant and godly wife! Enter into my kingdom!"

Won't it all be worth it, to hear those words?

STUDY GUIDE

Thank you for reading *Choosing Him All Over Again*! Be sure to check out the FREE *Choosing Him Companion Study Guide*.

Available for download at:
http://ambassador-international.com/books/
choosinghimalloveragain

ACKNOWLEDGMENTS

BEFORE ANYTHING ELSE, I WANT to thank Terry, for bearing the full weight of paying the bills and thus allowing me to stay home. I could not have written this book if I had had to work at a job outside our home. Terry, thank you for being such a good provider.

I am so glad that God gave me such an even-tempered, wise, decisive husband. My knee-jerk responses have needed you so many times to smooth out so many of my messes! I am blessed to have a husband who was the little boy who got upset when he got his good shoes wet after his father had just polished them. But what I appreciate the most about you is your God-given courage and strength of character to *lead*. Thank you for being such a good husband and father. Thank you for being willing to let me share our story, even though it meant that you had to go back in time and relive a painful chapter of our life together. I could not have written it without your permission. I'm so blessed by the firm commitment you have to Christ and your heart for the Gospel. Thank you that you forgave me all those years ago for leaving you, and you have never once brought it up against me. You truly are an example of Christ's forgiveness to me! I love you!

To my children—Blair, John, Alex, and Mary—thank you for just being you. I love you each so much! You know that the days you were each born were the happiest days of my life, right along with the day I married Dad! I am so proud of the young adults you are each becoming. You all are my favorite young adults in the whole world! Getting to love you, read to you, tuck you in bed, hear what your little hearts had to say, and watch you grow up has been the greatest privilege of my life.

Blair, I can picture your little face poking above the sheets, and it chokes me up even now, just thinking about it. John: oh, how my heart loves "check on me two times, Mama?" Alex, I loved how you tried to say "onion" and "spaghetti" but it came out "gunyon" and "pasgetti" for so long. Mary, I love how you "see" the inside of a person! I carry you each in my heart every single day. Oh, amazing grace, that God allowed you to know the experience of being born into a Christian home! It's all you've ever known by God's grace. You are the living, tangible, beautiful fruit of my obedience!

To my mother, Maria, known affectionately as "Chumi" to her childhood friends from Mexico, "Ya-Ya" to her grandchildren, and "Mama" to me. I thank you not only for insisting on helping me with the laundry, but also for allowing me to sit beside you and the comforting hum of your sewing machine when I was a little girl. I think it was there that my love of stories was first instilled, as you talked to me with your wonderful storytelling. Thank you for letting me write about your story, which is part of my story.

To my siblings Addie and Susanna, with whom I was raised, and to my siblings Johnny, Lollie, Juan Manuel, and Philip, who were raised in other households—I love you. While we never stood in the same country in this lifetime, my prayer is that we will all stand together for the first time in the eternal country with Jesus Christ. Perhaps that is the fateful reason our lives intersected—to come to the saving grace found in Christ alone.

To my literary agent, Blythe Daniel, who believed in the message of this book from the very beginning and had the courage to add me to her team as a first-time writer. Thank you for not giving up!

To my publishers, Tim Lowry and Sam Lowry, at Ambassador International. I cannot imagine working with finer Christian people. I appreciate the decades of publishing experience you have, and it is such an honor to be on your team to share the Gospel in written form. May we glorify Him together as the book rolls off the press!

My heartfelt appreciation goes to my editor, J.P. Brooks: your many excellent suggestions made my manuscript so much stronger!

I'm so grateful to Pamela Bunn for writing the *Choosing Him Companion Study Guide* for readers who desire to go deeper in applying the Word to their lives. Pam, you have such a heart for women to know God's heart through Bible study.

To Kelly Sokolowski, thank you that you happily checked all my scripture references, even though you are a very busy young mom!

My sincere thanks to those who gave me permission to use their stories.

My deepest admiration, respect, and appreciation for the godly mentors the Lord gave me: Paul and Macon Newby, and Elisabeth Elliot.

Bert, you were such a supportive friend during my marriage separation, and your encouragement alone would have filled up another book.

To my friend Pam Helms, who went on errands for me and brought me food so I could do my final editing.

To Barry Kirby, for being not only a soundman *extraordinaire*, but also my friend; your servant's heart blesses all who encounter you. Even though this is a written work, it goes hand in hand with my spoken work, so your commitment to operate the sound with excellence and a humble spirit inspires me. You and Ginger exemplify Christ.

To the prayer team of Capital Community Church's Morning Glory Bible study, who pray on behalf of my ministry and family, as they diligently pray every Tuesday morning for anyone who asks them to: Joan Holder, Elisabeth Hogan, Beth Burrus, Marti Sparrow, Susan King, Sarah Merriman, and Sarah Harden. To Brenda Davis, Laura Barbee, Renee Tucker, and Julia Bryan Canavan: thank you for praying for this project from your homes around North Carolina in the very beginning, before a word was typed.

To David Horner, Senior Pastor at Providence Baptist Church in Raleigh, I am so appreciative for your spiritual leadership that fed my soul as a new believer, and for reviewing the spiritual content of my manuscript.

To those friends I have met through my blog: thank you for your loyalty. I had no idea that God would one day allow me to serve women over a thing called the Internet!

Bless you, my new friend, who is reading this story. To you, my fellow sojourner in this journey heavenward, I pray that God will speak to your heart, and in the personal way that only He can do. Thank you for the awesome privilege of allowing me to share God's Word with you. May God give us the grace to live differently because of what Christ has done.

Thank you most of all to my Lord and Savior Jesus Christ,
Central personality in all human history, and
Central character in the greatest story that has been or will ever be told.
I know it is only because of You that we made it. You are more than enough.
To bring glory to Your name is my highest honor.
May You be the central focus of my heart.

"But you will receive power when the Holy Spirit comes on you; and you will be my witnesses in Jerusalem, and in all Judea and Samaria, and to the ends of the earth."

—Acts 1:8

NOTES

PREFACE

1. Hannah Whitall Smith, *A Christian's Secret to a Happy Life* (New Kensington: Whitaker House, 1983), 22.
2. Smith, general concept from page 130.

ONE
SOMETHING'S MISSING

3. 2 Cor. 10:12.
4. Ps. 111:10.
5. Mitch Temple, *The Marriage Turnaround* (Chicago: Moody, 2009), 144.

TWO
THE NOTE

6. I credit Elisabeth Elliot for the ideas in this paragraph.
7. Prov. 14:12.
8. 1 Pet. 5:7.
9. 1 Pet. 5:8.
10. C.S. Lewis, *The Screwtape Letters* © copyright CS Lewis Pte Ltd 1942.
11. My inspiration for this dialogue came after listening to Screwtape, Focus on the Family Dramatization, 2009, based on *The Screwtape Letters*, by C.S. Lewis. The demons' words are not to be taken as truth, but just as an example of how demons could connive against our growth in Christ.

THREE
A LOOK FURTHER BACK

12. Two of the people I interviewed to write this book who had experienced separation or divorce said that large geographical distance worked against their marriages. They added that they did not recommend it no matter what the monetary or educational advantages were, as the ensuing divorce and the damages it left in the wake, especially on the children, were enormous.

13. Mal. 2:16.

14. Exod. 20:5–6.

15. Phil. 3:13–14.

16. Heb. 12:1.

17. Gen. 2:24, See also Matt. 19:5, Mark 10:8, Eph. 5:31.

18. Gen. 2:18–20 (MSG).

19. Gen. 2:21–24 (MSG).

20. Elisabeth Elliot, *The Path of Loneliness* (Grand Rapids, MI: Revell, 2001), 90.

21. Heb. 4:15.

22. Trent C. Butler, Ph.D., General Editor, *Holman Bible Dictionary* (Nashville, TN: Holman, 1991), 1392.

23. Ps. 147:3.

24. 1 Pet. 3:13–14, 17.

25. 2 Tim. 2:23–24.

26. See 1 Pet. 3:8–11.

27. 1 Cor. 13:11.

28. Rom. 8:28.

29. See 2 Cor. 1:4.

FOUR
MEETING MR. RIGHT

30. Rev. 3:7b.

31. Music and Lyrics by Ron Roker, Gerry Shury, Frank McDonald, and Chris Rae, 1977.

32. Elisabeth Elliot, *Quest for Love* (Grand Rapids, MI: Revell, 1996), 64–5.

FIVE
ME? A GENTLE AND QUIET SPIRIT?

33. See 2 Cor. 4:16.
34. Smith, 22. (I've paraphrased the general concepts found in these last three sentences.)

SIX
A HOUSE BUILT ON SAND

35. Heb. 13:4.
36. 1 Cor. 7:4.
37. I am grateful to both Elisabeth Elliot and Oswald Chambers for the idea of these last two paragraphs.
38. Gen. 1:31.
39. Rom. 6:13.
40. See Song of Sol. 2:7.
41. Bible Study Fellowship meets not only all around the United States, but also around the world. A book (or books) of the Bible are studied for the year. There is a daily reading passage from the Bible with application questions, a small group for discussion, a lecture pertaining to the week's Bible passage, and take-home notes to reinforce the passage. This four-fold approach is designed for meaningful in-depth study of the Bible. BSF is an excellent organization committed to helping people of all ages and nations to study the Bible.
42. Phil. 2:4; 2:21.

SEVEN
HOUSE TORN DOWN

43. Rom. 12:2.
44. 2 Cor. 10:5b.
45. They continue to hang in our home to this very day—a visual reminder that we each bring a different perspective to our marriage.
46. Ruth Bell Graham, *Footprints of a Pilgrim* (Nashville: Word Publishing, 2001), 68.
47. 1 Pet. 3:7 (ESV).
48. 1 Pet. 3:4.
49. Matt. 23:25, 28.
50. 1 Cor. 3:18–19.

51. Prov. 28:26.
52. 1 Cor. 1:25.
53. Prov. 3:7.
54. James 1:5.

EIGHT
PROVIDENCE

55. Nancy Olson later married and became the mother of a daughter, followed by the birth of quintuplets! Kaye Crumpler married and moved to Boone, North Carolina, where her husband works for Samaritan's Purse and where they are raising their three boys.
56. Oswald Chambers, *Daily Thoughts for Disciples* (Grand Rapids, MI: Daybreak Books, published by Zondervan by special arrangement, 1976), 99.
57. In 1 Tim. 2:9, we read that Christian women are to "dress modestly, with decency and propriety."
58. Matt. 5:48.
59. For more information on locating "A Growing Marriage" seminar near you, led by Dr. Gary Chapman, or other resources by him for improving relationships, visit www.fivelovelanguages.com.

NINE
A TURNING POINT

60. Ps. 37:4–5 (ESV).
61. Prov. 3:5–6.
62. I have paraphrased the comparison of religions based on information presented in *The Case for Christ* DVD presentation by Lionsgate Home Entertainment.
63. C.S. Lewis, *Mere Christianity* (New York: Scribner, 1952), 41.

TEN
FIREWORKS

64. Elisabeth Elliot, *The Path of Loneliness* (Grand Rapids: Revell, 2001), 153.
65. Words written by John Newton, 1760s.
66. Rom. 8:21 (exclamatory punctuation mine).
67. Eph. 4:22–24 (italics mine—JM).

68.   See Gen. 25:29–34.
69.   Rom. 5:18–19.
70.   Apologetics found on pages 79–80 have been summarized from *The Case for Christ*, DVD presentation.

ELEVEN
MARRIAGE OVER

71.   Eccl. 3:1a, 3b, 4, 5b, 7b (italics mine—JM).
72.   Prov. 14:1.
73.   Rom. 8:38-39.
74.   Gal. 2:20.
75.   Smith, 47.
76.   Eph. 2:6.
77.   Ps. 18:33.
78.   Gal. 2:20.
79.   Ps. 37:4.
80.   Ps. 40:1–3, 7–8.

TWELVE
THREE WORDS AND A TRIP

81.   Johnny Evans served as punter and quarterback for the North Carolina State University football team (1974–1978). He played three years in the NFL for the Cleveland Browns, followed by three years in the CFL for the Montreal Alouettes. Today, he is the Eastern North Carolina Director for Fellowship of Christian Athletes, and since 1996 has been the radio color commentator for NCSU football. He also teaches over five hundred men and women in a weekly Bible study.
82.   1 Cor. 2:14.
83.   Matt. 26:39.
84.   Matt. 5:14–16.

THIRTEEN
NOT FREE TO DATE, IDOLS, AND EASTER

85.   2 Cor. 6:14.
86.   1 Cor. 7:12b–16.
87.   Oswald Chambers, *My Utmost For His Highest* (Grand Rapids, MI: Discovery House, Dodd, Mead & Company, Inc.,

1935), March 24.

88. See Exod. 20:5, Exod. 34:14.

89. 1 John 4:16.

90. John 3:30 (NAS).

91. Rev. 2:5.

92. John 17:4.

93. John 4:32, 34.

94. I credit F.B. Meyer and Elisabeth Elliot for the ideas in the last three sentences.

95. Phil. 4:6–7.

96. I credit Hannah Whitall Smith for the general concept of this paragraph.

97. See Matt. 4:1–11.

98. See Gen. 39:6–11.

99. 1 Cor. 10:13.

100. See 1 Tim. 6:11.

101. Smith, 101.

102. 2 Cor. 5:17.

103. Matthew Bridges, Stanza 1, "Crown Him with Many Crowns".

104. Heb. 13:20–21.

105. 2 Thess. 1:11–12; Col. 1:9.

106. 1 Thess. 3:10–13.

107. 1 Cor. 13:13.

FOURTEEN
LOVE MUST BE TOUGH

108. John 10:3.

109. Music and Lyrics by Helen H. Lemmel.

110. Ps. 27:14.

111. Ps. 130:5 (ESV).

112. Isa. 30:18d.

113. Isa. 40:31 (NAS).

114. Focus on the Family is a nonprofit organization dedicated to the preservation of the family and to the Gospel of Jesus Christ. They are best known for their daily Christian radio program, which is heard around the world on the radio and through the internet, and can be found at www.focusonthefamily.com. Their website states that Focus is "reaching more than 220 million people in 155 nations, and is dedicated to serving, strengthening and defending families worldwide. They provide practical tools for families as well as emotional support."

115. Ps. 16:5 (italics mine).

116. Mary Wilder Tileston, *Daily Strength for Daily Needs,* reproduced by BiblioBazaar, LLC (Boston: Little, Brown, & Co., 1915), 67.

117. John F. Walvoord, and Roy B. Zuck, *The Bible Knowledge Commentary* (Colorado Springs, CO: David C. Cook, 1983), 68.

118. See Matt. 21:12–13.

119. See Josh. 24:15.

120. See the book of Esther, chapters 4 and 5.

FIFTEEN
HOME

121. Prov. 14:1 (punctuation mine).

122. Eph. 3:17–19.

123. Matt. 6:14–15.

124. Prov. 10:19 (NLT).

125. Phil. 1:21.

126. Smith, 63.

127. Jer. 17:9.

128. "Dispatch: Quotables," World Magazine, April 19, 2014.

129. Rom. 5:3–4.

130. I am indebted to Elisabeth Elliot for this concept.

131. Matt. 7:13–14.

132. John 8:32.

133. Prov. 3:5–6.

134. Rom. 8:28.

135. I am thankful to J.R. Miller for the general concept in these two paragraphs, from his book *Home-Making* (San Antonio, TX: Vision Forum, 2001).

136. See Gen. 29:20.

SIXTEEN
WHAT FAITH MEANS

137. Luke 23:41b.

138. Luke 23:34.

139. John 19:30.

140. Amy Carmichael, *If* (Grand Rapids, MI: Zondervan, 1966), Part Two.

141. John 15:5.

142. Matt. 6:33.

143. Luke 9:23–24.

144. Matt. 26:39b.

145. Phil. 2:3–4.

146. Gateway to Joy broadcast, "Giving Up Your Own Way," from *Preparing for the New Year* talk series, interview with Valerie Shepard, January, 1998.

147. John 13:35.

148. I am grateful to Gregg Harris for this concept.

149. Matt. 20:26b–28.

150. Lakes' paraphrase of Phil. 2:5–11.

SEVENTEEN
REFLECTIONS ON MARRIAGE

151.   Jenny Sanford, *Staying True* (New York: Ballantine, 2010), 187.

152.   See Phil. 2:7, Heb. 2:7 (NASB).

153.   P.T. (Peter Taylor) Forsyth, as quoted in Elisabeth Elliot, *Quest for Love* (Grand Rapids, MI: Revell, 1996) 78. I am indebted to Elisabeth for all these ideas on subordination. All of P.T. Forsyth's works can be found online at http://www.luc.edu/faculty/pmoser/idolanon/Forsyth.html, accessed May 13, 2014.

154.   P.T. Forsyth, quoted by Elisabeth Elliot, Gateway to Joy broadcast, "Transforming Truths," date unknown.

155.   Mike Mason, *The Mystery of Marriage* (Colorado Springs, CO: Multnomah, 2010).

156.   J.R. Miller, *Home-Making* (San Antonio, TX: Vision Forum, 2001), 14.

157.   Prov. 27:15.

158.   Prov. 18:22.

159.   Dr. Leslie Parrott, Focus on Marriage Simulcast Conference, Focus on the Family, Powered by CCN, February 27, 2010.

160.   Miller, *Home-Making,* 179.

161.   Chambers, November 22.

162.   Richard J. Foster, *Prayer: Finding the Heart's True Home* (New York: Harper Collins, 1992), 62–63.

EIGHTEEN
YOUR STORY BEGINS HERE

163. Smith, 22.
164. Smith, 73.
165. Smith, 137.
166. Smith, 56.
167. The preceding three paragraphs have been paraphrased from Hannah Whitall Smith's classic work, " A Christian's Secret of a Happy Life," pages 22-24, 26,56, 63, 80, 137.
168. John 16:11.
169. John 16:8.
170. Col. 3:3.
171. 2 Cor. 4:16.
172. Smith, 152.
173. Smith, 164.
174. Smith, 132.
175. Smith, 137.
176. Smith, 22, 130.
177. The preceding six paragraphs have been collected and paraphrased from Hannah Whitall Smith's, "A Christian's Secret of a Happy Life," pages 25-28, 37-38, 130, 132-133, 136-137.
178. Smith, 207.
179. Words and music by Phil McHugh, *God and God Alone* (Franklin, TN: River Oaks Music, 1984).

NINETEEN
NINE AREAS TO FOCUS ON DURING
SEPARATION AND RECONCILIATION

180. Prov. 21:9, Prov. 25:24.
181. Phil. 4:8.
182. John 16:33.
183. Quoted from memory from a Focus on the Family daily broadcast, original interview date unknown.
184. Jo Berry, *Beloved Unbeliever* (Grand Rapids, MI: Zondervan, 1981), 25.
185. Focus on the Family daily broadcast, original interview aired March 30, 2009.
186. See Ps. 119:105.

TWENTY
ELEVEN CHECKPOINTS TO
REFRESH YOUR MARRIAGE

187. I am grateful for the general concepts in these points to Anne Ortlund (1–6, 10–11) and to J.R. Miller (7–9).
188. Prov. 16:24.
189. Eph. 4:29, 32.
190. See Matt. 18:22.
191. See 1 Cor. 13:5.
192. See Col. 3:13; Phil. 4:8.
193. Prov. 17:22.
194. See Ps. 126:2.
195. Prov. 21:14.
196. Eph. 4:26.
197. Eph. 4:2.
198. 1 Cor. 13:4.
199. Gen. 2:24 (NLT).
200. Miller, *Home-Making*, 25.
201. See Jer. 29:11.
202. Quoted in Richard J. Foster, *Prayer: Finding the Heart's True Home* (NY: Harper Collins, 1992), 7.
203. See James 5:16.

APPENDIX 1

204. I'm grateful to David Jeremiah for this summary of Paul's prayers.

APPENDIX 2

205. I am thankful to Elisabeth Elliot for this story.

JUANA MIKELS'S DESIRE IS TO see women's lives changed through the Gospel of Jesus Christ. Juana speaks to women's groups and churches with her story and her seminar on order, home life, and time management for the busy Christian mother. You can find her blog at www.juanamikels.com or at www.choosinghim.com. You can also find her on social media under the profile JuanaMikels.

For more Information on
Juana Mikels
and
Choosing Him All Over Again
please visit:

juanamikels.com

choosinghim.com

juana@juanamikels.com

twitter.com/juanamikels

facebook.com/juanamikels

pinterest.com/juanamikels

youtube.com/juanamikels

instagram.com/juanarmikels

google.com/+juanamikels

CONTINUED ENDORSEMENTS . . .

"Juana writes from her heart as she exposes her journey of marriage brokenness and reconciliation, giving readers hope for their future and the motivation to embrace true intimacy with God. This story is captivating because Juana details her thoughts and emotions which led her to walk away from her marriage for a time—thoughts and emotions that many wives encounter daily. Her honesty and transparency is a rare treasure, allowing others the chance to relate and not feel so alone in marital struggles. Juana's words are full of life-giving encouragement, just the kind of inspiration couples desperately need today."

—JENNIFER SMITH
Author of *The Unveiled Wife* and *Wife After God*

"Juana bares her soul as she shares her story of pain and heartache with great transparency. Not knowing where to turn due to her broken marriage, she turned to Jesus Christ, and what she found was not just hope, but redemption, grace, and love. As Juana sought to live a Christ-centered life, the Lord blessed her with a thriving, Christ-centered marriage. Juana's message will definitely encourage and equip many wives with hurting marriages."

—JOLENE ENGLE
Owner and author of JoleneEngle.com, Founder of
ChristianWifeUniversity.com, and best-selling author of *Wives of the Bible*

"Hearing Juana's story of God's grace in her life deepened my love for the gospel and gave me a sense of peace regarding God's sovereignty over all of life's struggles. I especially appreciate how Juana speaks to women from all walks of life: single, married, young, advanced in years, mothers, believers, and unbelievers. I am excited to see how the Lord will continue to use Juana and her gifts for His glory."

—RACHEL LEE BRADY

Principal, RLB Public Affairs, LLC

"God's loving pursuit of Juana and His complete restoration of her marriage display Christ's transformative power. Every woman longing for personal peace—as well as renewed hope for her marriage—can benefit from Juana's inspiring story and biblical insights."

—EMILY WICKHAM

Blogger at ProclaimingHimtoWomen.com

"God has gifted Juana and guided her fingers as she typed. He has given her a beautiful story of romance and redemption. I have laughed, cried, been convicted and helped. Some of your lessons were just what I needed as I read them."

—PAMELA BUNN

Wife of 34 years, former Teaching Leader and Area Advisor for BSF International, current Board member for BSF International

"Juana's messages always point us to Jesus, the One who knows us so personally and knows how to meet each of us right where we are. In everyday life's joys and hardships, she reminds us of His unending love and constant presence with His beloved children."

—ANNE STANCIL

Pastor's Wife, Former Women's Ministry Director, Providence Baptist Church

"Juana is a role model of Christ-like loving. She offers authenticity, transparency, and wisdom as she teaches truth and application to others. She inspires us to live our lives to glorify Christ."

—JAYNE HODGES
Marriage Mentor Ministry Coordinator,
Capital Community Church

"Juana Mikels was the keynote speaker at our women's retreat in March of 2013. Our women loved her honest sharing, her personal testimony of God's grace in her life, as well as her warm and vibrant personality. By the end of the weekend, it felt like Juana was part of our church family!"

—JENNIFER MORGAN
Retreat Director, Christ Covenant Church of Raleigh

"Juana opens your eyes to truth, bringing tears to your eyes yet joy to your heart."

—LINDA R. MORRIS
Chairman, Community Christian Fellowship

"There are certain people who stand out as guideposts in your spiritual life, pointing you in the right direction. Juana has been that for me, constantly pointing me back to truth."

—AMY TALBOTT
Blogger at AGrowingWifeandMommy.wordpress.com

"Juana's story brings light and hope into God's design for marriage. If you are less than content in your marriage, I encourage you to open the pages of this book and allow God to minister to your heart. It is my belief that those who read the words of Juana's heart will be taken on a journey that will strip you down bare—allowing God to make you whole—and in turn make your marriage all you desire it to be."

—CARLIE KERCHEVAL

Founder of ManagingYourBlessings.com

Co-Author of *Learning to Speak Life: Fruit of the Spirit*

For more information about
AMBASSADOR INTERNATIONAL
please visit:

www.ambassador-international.com
@AmbassadorIntl
www.facebook.com/AmbassadorIntl

Made in the USA
Monee, IL
01 August 2023

40231520R00213